The Transformation of
Moravian Bethlehem

The Transformation of
MORAVIAN
BETHLEHEM

From Communal Mission
to Family Economy

Beverly Prior Smaby

University of Pennsylvania Press
PHILADELPHIA

Library of Congress Cataloging-in-Publication Data
Smaby, Beverly Prior.
The transformation of Moravian Bethlehem.

Bibliography: p.
Includes index.
1. Moravians—Pennsylvania—Bethlehem—History.
2. Bethlehem (Pa.)—History   3. Bethlehem (Pa.)—
Church history.   I. Title.
F159.B5S63   1988   974.8′22   88-26128
ISBN 0-8122-8130-6

FOR MY MOTHER
AND
FOR RICH

Contents

List of Tables ix

List of Figures xi

Acknowledgments xiii

Preface xv

PART ONE

1 Historical Background 3
  The Unitas Fratrum
  The Renewed Church
  Bethlehem, the Mission Settlement
  Dissolution and Transition
  Bethlehem, the Pennsylvania Town

2 Demographic Portrait 51
  Composition
  Growth
  Migration
  Marriage
  Birth
  Death

3 The Town Setting 86
  The Construction of Communal Bethlehem
  The Town Plan of Bethlehem
  The Transformation of Bethlehem After 1762

PART TWO

4   Biographical Structures   125
The Sampling Design
Biographies as Documents
The Structure of Lives

5   Life Cycles and Values   145
Eighteenth-Century Pilgrims
Nineteenth-Century Householders

6   Secularization of Consciousness   198

Conclusion   239

Appendixes   245

Bibliography   259

Index   263

List of Tables

1-1	Daily routine in Moravian settlements	14
1-2	Weekly devotional schedule	16
1-3	Sunday schedule	17
2-1	Population composition in percentages	54
2-2	Marital status in percentages	56
2-3	Percentages of people ≥60 who were single	57
2-4	Components of population growth	62
2-5	Migration to and from Bethlehem	64
2-6	Marriage, birth, and death in Bethlehem	74
2-7	Percentages of deaths for different age groups	79
2-8	Death rates with direct standardization	80
2-9	Comparison of Bethlehem death rates with Coale and Demeny's life table models	82
3-1	Building construction sequence in Bethlehem	90
3-2	Integration of children into parents' homes after the dissolution of the General Economy	115
3-3	Characteristics of households in different types of houses in 1850	117
3-4	Distribution of family types among types of houses in 1850	118
3-5	Distribution of male and female household heads among types of houses in 1850	118
4-1	Sampling description	128
4-2	Authorship of biographies	130
4-3	Difference of means test on biography lengths	132
6-1	Partner types for females—Period I (1744–1763)	204
6-2	Partner types for males—Period I (1744–1763	205
6-3	Partner types for females—Period V (1824–1843)	210
6-4	Partner types for males—Period V (1824–1843)	212
6-5	Correlation between profession and relation to Heiland	218
6-6	Images of the Heiland—females	219

Tables

6-7	Images of the Heiland—males	220
6-8	Religious and secular relationships with kin and community—Period I	224
6-9	Religious and secular relationships with kin and community—Period V	225
6-10	Religious relationships with family members	226
6-11	Religious relationships with community members	228
6-12	Secular relationships with community members	232
6-13	Secular relationships with family members	234
I-1	List of biographies—Period I	249
I-2	List of biographies—Period V	250

List of Figures

1-1   Portrait of Sister Gertraut Graff by John Valentine Haidt   11
1-2   Portrait of Brother Martin Mack by John Valentine Haidt   12
1-3   Taxonomy of the term "Gemeine"   25
2-1   Estimated peaks of decisions to remain single in percentages   58
2-2   Population growth   60
2-3   Emigration rates by gender per thousand   67
2-4   Immigration by gender in raw numbers   68
2-5   Emigration rates by marital status per thousand   70
2-6   Marital status of immigrants in percentages   72
2-7   Crude death rates per thousand   78
3-1   View of Bethlehem in 1749   88
3-2   Example of log construction in early Bethlehem   92
3-3   Example of stone construction in early Bethlehem   93
3-4   View of Bethlehem in 1755   96
3-5   Physical organization of Bethlehem in 1760   98
3-6   Children's Lovefeast   102
3-7   Floor plan of Eastern Addition to the Single Sisters' House   104
3-8   Attic Sleeping Hall in the Addition to the Single Sisters' House   105
3-9   Map of Bethlehem in 1766   107
3-10   View of Bethlehem in 1784   108
3-11   View of Bethlehem in 1812   110
3-12   Map of Bethlehem in 1812   111
3-13   Map of Bethlehem in 1848   112
3-14   View of Bethlehem in 1852   114
3-15   Inequality in Bethlehem in 1850   119
4-1   Structure of biographies, 1744–1763   134
4-2   Structure of biographies, 1824–1843   139

Figures

6-1	Partner type as percentage of total relationships Period I: Females	206
6-2	Partner type as percentage of total relationships Period I: Males	206
6-3	Gender comparisons of relationships Period I: Heiland	207
6-4	Gender comparisons of relationships Period I: Kin	207
6-5	Gender comparisons of relationships Period I: Community	207
6-6	Partner type as percentage of total relationships Period V: Females	214
6-7	Partner type as percentage of total relationships Period V: Males	214
6-8	Period comparison of relationships: Females' relationships with Heiland	215
6-9	Period comparison of relationships: Males' relationships with Heiland	215
6-10	Period comparison of relationships: Females' relationships with kin	215
6-11	Period comparison of relationships: Males' relationships with kin	215
6-12	Period comparison of relationships: Females' relationships with community	215
6-13	Period comparison of relationships: Males' relationships with community	215
6-14	Females' images of the Heiland: Ratios of Period I and Period V percentages	222
6-15	Males' images of the Heiland: Ratios of Period I and Period V percentages	223
I-1	Biography of Anna Johanna Schmik	246
II-1	Taxonomy of Moravian relationship partners	254
II-2	Relative meanings of "Familie."	255

Acknowledgments

It is appropriate that this book about community and family was encouraged and aided by the community of scholars, friends, and family around me. Melvyn Hammarberg and Richard Dunn gave me steady support from the beginning and critiqued each of my drafts with care and interest. Philip Sagi introduced me to the world of demography, and Etienne van de Walle helped me to apply demographic principles to small populations. Ralph Schwarz generously shared his valuable insights about the development of Bethlehem as a town and contributed several of his exquisite photographs for reproduction in this book. Vernon Nelson, Archivist for the Bethlehem Moravian Archives, gave me permission to use the Archives' rich collection of manuscripts and photographs. He also gave me detailed and helpful criticisms on the entire manuscript and helped me to obtain a number of microfilms and photographs. Lothar Madeheim, Assistant Archivist, found me what I needed in the Archives and introduced me to the "Geist" of the early Moravians. Henry Williams, former director of the library at Moravian College, made it possible for me to use the library holdings, carefully read the manuscript, and offered valuable suggestions. Ruth Davis shared her home during my weekly research trips to Bethlehem, and Joseph Blasi found me "a place of my own" in which to do most of the analysis and writing. Lance Campbell spent many hours making careful enlargements for my analysis of Bethlehem's town plan. Graphics artist Charles Schaffer lent me not only his extensive graphics and typesetting skills, but his friendly counsel. Patricia Smith and Alison Anderson, my editors, put out the extra effort to keep all the publishing stages on schedule. My mother Sally Prior typed the manuscript and cheerfully helped me through many long days and nights of intensive wrapping up. My brother Russ Prior volunteered his considerable spreadsheet skills and many after-work hours to make sense of my numerous tables. My sister Joan Prior introduced me to her contacts in sociology and demography at the University of Pennsylvania and made a special trip on short notice to look up a missing reference. My children Niels and Kristin have for several years ungrudgingly helped their parents with the everyday work of keeping a family going, making it possible for me to spend more time on my studies. My husband Rich transformed my graphs from rough pencil sketches into an elegant base for the artwork and proofread the entire manuscript. Through all the years of research he has willingly shared not only mundane household responsibilities but also an interest in my work, knowing somehow when to discuss and critique it and when not to. To all of these people I give my hearty and sincere thanks. The responsibility for any errors or misjudgments in this study rests, of course, with me.

Preface

This study of the Moravian Community in Bethlehem, Pennsylvania covers the years 1741–1844. The first date marks the time when a nucleus of extraordinarily committed Moravian settlers came together on the banks of the Lehigh River to build a new society devoted to religious missions. The latter date marks the time when Bethlehem—bowing to economic pressures—allowed outsiders to own land within the town limits for the first time in Bethlehem's history. Those two dates not only bracket Bethlehem's exclusive period, they also symbolize the radical social changes which transformed Bethlehem's social, cultural, and economic structure during its first century.

Bethlehem was originally conceived as a communal enterprise. Everyone gave their labor and its fruits to the community, and the community gave them food, shelter, and clothes in return. Furthermore, even though the Moravians in early Bethlehem encouraged marriage, they lived not with members of their own families but in "Choirs" composed of people from the same age, gender, and marital status. The primary motive for this communal arrangement was religious, not social. Experience in their European communities had suggested to the Moravians that people responded well to the spiritual encouragement of others like themselves—the same age, the same gender, and the same marital status. Furthermore, it was thought that such an arrangement was more efficient, so that a large percentage of the people supported by the Bethlehem economy could act as "Pilgrims," serving the spiritual needs of people both within the Moravian fold and outside it.

In 1762, just 20 years after the founding of Bethlehem, the Unity (the governing body of the Moravian Church worldwide) legislated a thorough reorganization of Bethlehem as part of a plan to meet the financial crisis the Unity faced. Bethlehem's Communal Economy was dissolved, and families were from then on expected to support themselves independently. Husbands and wives were gradually brought together to live as conjugal units with their children in separate living spaces. The Unity's purpose was only to change Bethlehem's economics, not to reduce the religious commitment of its inhabitants. But the practice of religion in Bethlehem had been so intertwined with the communal arrangements that the two formed one system. Nearly all of the support structures for religion had been communal ones. Gradually new support structures developed, but religion was never again the central focus it had been during those first exciting years. The people of Bethlehem became a community in which each nuclear family household concentrated on the economic and social needs of its own members. At the same time, the settlement became a more integrated part of its American context. Studies by Helmut Erbe and Gillian Gollin have traced the social change in Bethlehem at an institutional level.[1] This study builds on these studies as a base and focuses on the effects of change at a more personal level.

The Moravians' early culture was unique in colonial America. Although they practiced marriage, their Choir social organization deemphasized family ties and made it possible to focus on their religious mission in a nearly monastic fashion. The Choir organization also served to separate the sexes (except as married partners) which required that women play leadership roles in Bethlehem's economic and spiritual spheres. The resulting symmetry between the responsibilities of men and women was greater than in any other colonial society, including the Quakers. In order to free the women for these roles, their children were raised in communal houses, an arrangement which socialized children equally and obscured family background to a degree unheard of elsewhere in the western world.

The great majority of colonial American studies have concerned settlers of English origin to the neglect of the many colonists from other parts of the world. This narrow focus has contributed to the modern misunderstanding of colonial history, which assumes that not only politics but culture were primarily English, whereas the colonies were in fact a fertile mixture of many cultural backgrounds.

This study of Moravians helps to expand the literature of non-English groups in colonial America. The religious and cultural roots of the Moravians were in fifteenth-century Moravia and Bohemia. In 1722 a German-speaking sub-group from Moravia sought refuge in Germany after it became impossible to practice their Protestant religion in their homeland. In Germany they revived their church and attracted new members. After they founded a settlement in Bethlehem, Pennsylvania, they continued for generations to nourish their Moravian and German culture.

The Moravians have left a particularly rich set of documents which are well preserved at the Moravian Archives in Bethlehem. Besides the

records of official governing bodies and collections of personal correspon-
dence, sermons, liturgies, hymns, and instrumental music, there are town
plans, very complete birth, marriage, and death registers, an official diary
for the congregation in Bethlehem, and diaries of the Single Brothers and
Single Sisters (the unmarried adults), which also contain information about
the Older Boys and Older Girls respectively. In addition—and most important to this project—there are hundreds of biographies, each written at
the end of a person's life for the purpose of being read at his or her funeral.
These deal in remarkable detail with the important biographical events of
men, women, children, and babies of all stations in life. The topics addressed are standardized enough to enable comparisons and generaliza-
tions, and the structure and topics in the biographies changed over the
hundred-year period, making possible a detailed study of cultural change.

The first chapter provides a brief description of changing social organizations and belief systems in Bethlehem. This story has already been
told a number of times in various histories, and appears here as an orien-
tation. The second chapter adapts tools developed by demographers to
trace the demographic history of Bethlehem during those first one hundred
years. The results correlate closely with the institutional changes, demon-
strating that the larger and seemingly impersonal institutional affairs affected events of the most personal nature such as basic health, marriage,
and the birth of children. The third chapter looks at Bethlehem from the
point of view of its material culture, describing the Moravians' use and
organization of buildings through the first one hundred years. This chapter
helps us to see how different physical settings supported different forms of
everyday life.

Having established the changes in the historical, demographic, and
physical setting in the first part of the book, I use the funeral biographies
described above to trace parallel changes on a personal level in the second
part. The fourth chapter compares the structure of people's lives at the
beginning of Bethlehem's exclusive period with that at its end. The fifth
chapter traces the life cycles which fill out these contrasting structures.
The sixth chapter uses the same biographies to study Bethlehem's changing
values. Because these biographies are idealized portraits, both positive and
negative, they cannot be treated as descriptions of actual behavior, but they
are excellent conveyors of values and norms. They tell us how Moravians
were supposed to behave and not how they actually did behave. For this
chapter I have developed a formal method of analysis based on Zellig Harris's "Discourse Analysis."[2] It allows me to compare in a consistent fashion the subtle elements of a highly religious world view with those of its

secularized transformation. The conclusion ties together the results of the other chapters and analyzes the nature of cultural change experienced by people in Bethlehem.

In general I have translated the original German sources into English, but there are a few exceptions. The most important of these are the word "Heiland" which means "Savior" and the word "Gemeine" which translates as "congregation," "church," or "community," and sometimes as all three at once. Because these two words have special connotations in Moravian culture and because these connotations change over time, I have elected to use these words in German to encourage the reader to understand the breadth and depth of their Moravian meaning from the contexts in which they are used. "Gemeine" was a dialectical word akin to the standard German word "Gemeinde." The Moravians preferred the word "Gemeine." During the early years in Bethlehem, people participated in a process of religious growth which I refer to as "awakening" and "conversion." "Awakening" corresponds to the Moravian term "Erweckung." It denotes the first experience of being awakened to one's own depravity and to one's need for a religious focus. This ego shattering event was the impetus for a long and intense search for an experience of religious stability and peace of mind. Although Moravians did not coin a specific term for such a peace-giving experience, they clearly recognized it as a concept. The experience came as a sudden insight when people first knew their human inability to overcome their human depravity. As a consequence of this insight, they were able to give themselves totally to the Heiland for his direction. I have followed the convention developed among scholars of the New England Puritans and used the word "conversion" to refer to this experience.

The financial and social system during Bethlehem's first 20 years has been translated in English as the "General Economy," the "Communal Economy," and simply as the "Economy." I have used these words interchangeably throughout. The German word "Chor" I have translated as "Choir." This matches other writings in English about the Moravians. The names for offices and governing bodies changed frequently over the one-hundred-year period, but I have elected to retain one name throughout to avoid confusion. The term "Choir Helper" is a case in point. Although Helpers were called "Caretakers" (Pfleger) during some periods, I consistently use the word "Helper" to refer to that office.

Another convention I have adopted is the use of the word "Brothers" to translate the German word "Brüder." Many members of the modern Moravian Church in Bethlehem prefer the word "Brethren," but because that was not a suitable translation in some contexts, I have settled on the more common English plural. This form has the additional advantage that its connotation more nearly resembles that of the word "Sisters."

In the early sources, the last names of women ended with an "-in" suffix. At the suggestion of the Moravian Archives I have dropped these feminine endings. This way their names will match those of their fathers and husbands. The reader should know, however, that they will not match the original records about these women.

NOTES

1. Helmut Erbe, *Bethlehem, Pa.: Eine kommunistische Herrnhuter Kolonie des 18 Jahrhunderts* (Stuttgart: Ausland und Heimat Verlags-Aktiengesellschaft, 1929; Gillian Lindt Gollin, *Moravians in Two Worlds* (New York: Columbia University Press, 1967).

2. Zellig S. Harris, "Discourse Analysis," *Language* XXVIII (1952), pp. 18–23.

PART ONE

Chapter One

Historical Background

The members of the Moravian Church have always sensed the significance of their unique history. They have nourished it in the records they kept, the books they wrote, the festivals they celebrated, and the traditions they passed from parent to child. This was as true in fifteenth-century Bohemia and Moravia as it was in eighteenth-century Pennsylvania. They were proud that their history traced a path quite distinct and different from that of the Protestants in Germany, Switzerland, and France, and they strove to maintain their uniqueness through periods of growth and repression.

THE UNITAS FRATRUM

The roots of the Moravian Church grew in the Hussite movement of fifteenth-century Bohemia and Moravia—now the western and central regions of Czechoslovakia. Jan Hus had attacked the abuses he saw among the Catholic clergy, but he tried to work his reforms within the Catholic Church. After his martyrdom in 1415, his followers formed two distinct groups: (1) the Utraquists, who argued for such changes as Communion in "both kinds" for lay people but remained similar enough to the Roman Catholics that they reached an accommodation with them in 1434 with the signing of the *Compactata*; and (2) the Taborites, who held the radical view that there was no "real presence" in Communion and who believed that reformation could never be successful within the Catholic Church and therefore did not agree to the *Compactata*. Although the Taborites were eventually suppressed as an organization, the ideas from their early period continued to live on in the writings of Petr Chelčický. Chelčický had been closely associated with the Taborites, but separated from them when they dropped their earlier commitment to non-violence. Chelčický himself never gathered a large group of followers, but when he was an old man, his example and his ideas influenced a new group which took the name "Jednota Bratrska," later "Unitas Fratrum." It was this group that represented the beginning of the Moravian Church. Their leader, a man named Gregor, had studied Chelčický's work and made it the core of the Unitas belief system.[1]

Mistrusting the sinful influences of cities, commerce, and social classes, Gregor and his followers withdrew in about 1457 to Kunwald, a village in a forested region of northeastern Bohemia known as Lititz. Here they practiced only agriculture and the necessary trades, living as simply and as equally as possible. They distinguished "essential things" (faith, love, and hope) from "merely useful things" (the sacraments and other liturgical practices). They followed Chelčický's ideas and the tenets of the Sermon on the Mount and derived from them a stance against all violence and against the swearing of oaths. Their religious commitment focused on Christ in return for his self-sacrifice, and they believed that the church and state must by nature be separate: a Christian ruler was a contradiction and office holding was unlawful. Gregor's people divided themselves into three classes: the Beginners, the Advanced, and the Perfect. Obviously reflecting a process of religious growth, these classes also represented changes in age and profession which tended to correlate with changing religious status. In 1467, the Brethren made their independence from Rome official and created a new succession of bishops by asking a representative of the Waldenses (a protestant group that had separated from Rome in the twelfth century) to consecrate one of their own members.[2]

As time passed, the Unitas Fratrum grew much larger and attracted more people from cities and from upper classes. Out of this new membership, different values developed. They began to feel more responsible to the world and less inclined to believe that cities, commerce, and social classes were in themselves evil things. As a result, in 1495 the members of the Inner Council of the Unitas Fratrum made a relaxation of Gregor's principles the basis for official church policy. The council became less strict in its rejection of office holding and the swearing of oaths and softened its absolute prohibition of violence. It also established that the Bible only was their authority, and not the ideas of Gregor and Petr of Chelčický. One group of members objected to this change and separated from the main body in protest. But the majority of members supported the relaxation of church policy. The period which followed is generally associated with the leadership of Lukáš of Prague, even though he was too young at the time to lead the church into these changes. A decade later, however, he became

4

the acknowledged leader of the Unitas Fratrum and at that time turned this official policy into a practical guide for living.[3]

Ironically, this accommodation to the culture around them made the Unitas Fratrum all the more threatening to the Catholics, and the persecution against them, which had always lurked in the background, grew more virulent, culminating in the Mandate of St. Jacob (1508) which entirely prohibited the religious practices of the Unitas Fratrum in Bohemia. During the next century the Unitas Fratrum shrank in Bohemia and expanded in Moravia, Bohemia's neighbor to the east. Although religious freedom was restored in Bohemia in 1609 with the Letter of Majesty, it was short-lived, for near the beginning of the Thirty Years War at the Battle of White Mountain (1620), the Catholics defeated the Protestants and thereby ended the public practice of the original Unitas Fratrum in both Bohemia and Moravia. A number of members emigrated to Poland where they were able to continue their protestant worship undisturbed, but over the course of the next 30 years the Unitas Fratrum was to die out almost completely in Bohemia and Moravia.[4]

They had, however, left a rich heritage of written works which spanned all but the first few decades of their existence. During the fifteenth century in Bohemia, Lukáš of Prague wrote about one hundred theological treatises, a protestant hymnal, and a catechism. In Moravia during the sixteenth century, Jan Blahoslav continued the literary tradition and translated the New Testament into the Czech language—the version which is still used today. By the end of the sixteenth century the entire Bible had been made available to the Czech-speaking population in the eloquent translation known as the Kralice Bible. During the seventeenth century, the widely respected educator, Jan Amos Comenius, a bishop of the Unitas Fratrum in exile, wrote historical and theological treatments of his church which had by that time nearly ceased to exist. All of these works constituted a record and a testimony that helped the church to survive the century of underground activity known as the "Hidden Seed" (1620–1722).[5]

But the way was not easy. During the first few decades after the Battle of White Mountain the Protestants in Bohemia and Moravia found it increasingly difficult to practice their religion. Their ministers were exiled and their books were burned. People who continued to meet for Protestant worship were arrested and tortured. They were prevented from practicing their trades, and their children were taken away for re-education in Catholic convents. They were even spied on by informers who received gold coins from the government as rewards.[6]

By the mid-1650s, the Counter Reformation was nearly complete.

The pressure had become so great that most people had simply converted to Catholicism. The only people who remained Protestants were those in the isolated mountains or those along the borders where contact with Protestants in neighboring countries was possible. These were the people of the Hidden Seed, the preservers of the old faith, who practiced Catholicism in the public eye but met secretly to read from the forbidden Bible, to sing their old hymns, and to read from the unauthorized books that they carefully hid. Usually their own lay ministers led them in worship services, but sometimes traveling protestant preachers came at great personal peril from Silesia, Saxony, and Hungary to minister to them.[7]

The Renewed Church

One such preacher was Christian David, born in Moravia of Catholic parents, but converted to the Protestant faith while working as an apprentice to a Protestant family. Concerned by the plight of these remnants of the Unitas Fratrum, he interceded for them with Count Nicholas Ludwig von Zinzendorf, who responded by offering them refuge in Berthelsdorf, his estate in Saxony.[8]

Zinzendorf was himself a deeply religious man. From early childhood he had concerned himself with religious issues. Despite his family's hopes that he would serve the Count in Saxony, he determined to devote his life to furthering the goals of Pietism. His education included exposure to a number of different versions of Christianity, including a close association with Cardinal Noailles and other Catholics during his years in France. For a number of years afterwards he continued to correspond with the cardinal. This influence gave his Pietism an unusual ecumenical bent.[9]

When a few members of the Unitas Fratrum arrived at Berthelsdorf in 1722, Zinzendorf had assumed they would simply become members of the Lutheran Church there, under the care of Johann Andreas Rothe, the Lutheran minister. He had no intention of becoming their leader nor of helping to revive their branch of Protestantism. His ecumenical views argued against it. Besides, he was a committed member of the Lutheran Church and remained so throughout his life even after his lot became inextricably combined with that of the Moravians.[10]

At first Zinzendorf all but ignored the Moravian immigrants. The first house in Herrnhut was built in his absence by Christian David, and he was astonished when he returned to find this new and unexpected building on his estate. Zinzendorf had other projects on his mind, and he wanted to keep the Moravians' Herrnhut project small. In his absence his grandmother had hired a Swiss named Johann Georg Heitz to manage Herrnhut, and Zinzendorf kept him on, hoping not to have to manage the new settlement personally. He also told Christian David that he did not wish to have more immigrants from Moravia. But David was a determined man and continued against the count's wishes.[11]

Not until major controversy developed between Rothe and the Herrnhuters did Zinzendorf begin to get involved. He intervened in 1724 with a Bible study session to help them resolve a controversy over the doctrine of predestination. Although predestination had not been a doctrine of the Unitas Fratrum, the Moravian immigrants had become persuaded of its efficacy through the efforts of Heitz, who was a Calvinist. After the study session the Moravians decided that the Bible did not support the idea of predestination.

Zinzendorf intervened again in 1727 when relations between Rothe and the Herrnhuters had seriously deteriorated. Zinzendorf obtained a leave of absence from his government post and moved to Herrnhut for a while to facilitate reconciliation. In the process he interviewed all members of the community and understood for the first time the intensity of the Moravians' wish to revive their own church, but he himself was still not ready to encourage it. On the other hand, he did recognize the need to organize and regulate life in Herrnhut. With the input of his lawyer, Rothe, and several Moravians, Zinzendorf drew up 42 statutes to that end, one of which established him as the feudal lord of the Herrnhuters. This was the first official connection between Zinzendorf and the Moravians.[12]

Later that year, Zinzendorf happened to find a copy of Comenius's *Ratio Disciplinae*. The similarity between this description and Herrnhut's new 42 statutes astounded him. He knew then that the traditions of the Unitas Fratrum had been remarkably well preserved among the Moravian immigrants, and he considered for the first time whether to help them revive their church.[13]

In 1728 when Rothe launched a campaign to make the Moravians into Lutherans, Zinzendorf supported the Moravians who wanted to keep a separate identity. But he wavered on the issue during the next few years. In 1731 he even initiated a similar attempt himself, apparently in response to growing uneasiness among the authorities in Saxony. Only when the Lot (a Moravian technique for making decisions) decided against him did he back down.[14] (The Lot will be explained in detail later in this chapter.)

Despite Zinzendorf's initial resistance, however, he gradually became the medium through which the Unitas Fratrum was revived. Zinzendorf had yearned for a worthy religious project to pour his energies into, but he had been seeking it in other places. Eventually he embraced the project that had been growing in his own garden. In 1737 Zinzendorf (who had become ordained in the Lutheran Church) was consecrated as the second bishop in the renewed Moravian Church, partly in recognition of the leading role he had already begun to play and partly so that his representation of their interests would carry more validity. (The first bishop was David Nitschmann, consecrated in 1735.) Although Zinzendorf persisted in calling himself a "Lutheran Bishop of the Moravian Brethren," [15] he was now publicly committed to the Moravians, and the next twenty-five years became a period of fulfillment for him and of revitalization for the refugees from Moravia. Together they rediscovered the ideas and practices of the Unitas Fratrum and developed them further: the Christ-centered theology of the Unitas Fratrum changed with the renewed church until Christ virtually became the whole of it; the conviction of the original Unitas Fratrum that the church should not exist only to preserve itself motivated a far-reaching missionary program to bring Christianity to the "heathen"; and the pre-1495 commitment of the Unitas Fratrum to stricter non-violence was revived.

In the new Moravian theology, God was so exalted and humans so degraded that before Christ no lines of communication existed between them. Humans had no way of raising themselves from the depths of their corruption and no hope of life after death. Because God understood the need for a mediator to bridge the huge chasm between his realm and the realm of humans, he begot Jesus who was both God and human being. As a participant of both realms, translation between the two was natural for him and even automatic, but his service extended much further. In agreeing to become human, Christ gave human beings a dignity which they had lacked before, and by sacrificing himself on the cross for their sins, he saved their souls from death. In this way he offered them a path out of their natural degraded state, and in return they owed him unending gratitude.[16]

Because of its importance to Moravians, Christ's sacrifice dominated their understanding of him. They called him the Heiland ("the Savior") and the Lämmlein ("the dear little lamb"). John Valentine Haidt, the Moravian artist, portrayed Christ on the cross and depicted his wounds in gothic detail. Hymns and liturgies focused on Christ's wounds and his death. The Moravian "Blood and Wounds Theology" symbolized the Heiland's ultimate sacrifice and served to remind people of their debt to him. In contrast to the Calvinists, Moravians believed that eternal life was a

possibility for all those who would recognize the depths of their own corruption and their absolute dependence on the Heiland.

BETHLEHEM, THE MISSION SETTLEMENT

The theology which stated that salvation was open to everyone required a
program to bring that possibility to others. Accordingly the Moravians
developed an extensive missionary system throughout the world. It was in
this context that Bethlehem was born. By 1737 the Moravians had mission
settlements in Greenland, South America, South Africa, West Africa, and
Northern Russia.[17] In 1734 Zinzendorf negotiated for a piece of land in the
newly formed American colony of Georgia and settled a small group of
Moravians there the next year under the leadership of August Gottlieb
Spangenberg, a former student at Jena in Thuringia and a new convert to
the Moravian Church. This first Moravian settlement on the North American continent fell victim within just a few years to disease and to resent-
ment against the Moravians for their pacifist stance in the face of wars with
the Spaniards.[18]

In the meantime, however, a few of the Georgia Moravians had become friendly with the evangelist George Whitefield and were hired by
him in 1740 to erect a building for the school he planned to start in Nazareth, Pennsylvania for blacks. The arrangement lasted only a few months.
An angry Whitefield ended it in November, because he could not persuade
the Moravians to embrace the doctrine of predestination. At first he asked
them to leave Nazareth immediately but later agreed to let them stay
through the winter. About this time they received instructions from Europe
to find a place for a permanent settlement in Pennsylvania, and by early
1741 they had purchased 500 acres where Monocacy Creek joins the Lehigh River. While the snow still lay on the ground, they began to build the
town of Bethlehem, destined to become the center for Moravian missionary activities in America. Late in 1741, Count Zinzendorf arrived to personally oversee the establishment of this new settlement and to develop
from here his pietistic and ecumenical cause in the New World.[19]

In addition to their missionary work, the Moravians had another
heavy responsibility: to encourage the spiritual growth of their own members as well. For them that meant to develop each person's relationship to
the Heiland. Each individual had to go through a conversion process. Even
though the result was assured and the method carefully prescribed, the
process was long, agonizing, and intense.[20] But if they persevered, Mora-

9

vians were always rewarded with salvation, joy, and peace of mind. Once converted, they had to maintain this relationship with the Heiland as their most important one, for he was now their Best Friend and Eternal Husband.

In order to encourage the conversion process and the resulting intimacy with the Heiland, the Moravians developed a unique and supportive social organization. In Herrnhut the Moravians had learned that people in similar life situations encouraged each other in spiritual growth. Several times during those early years there were examples of mass conversions among the larger living groups, which had first been established only in response to the need for group housing. After such success, the Moravians began to organize people into these communal living groups (known as "Choirs") for religious purposes as well.

Choirs were groups of people of similar age, the same gender, and the same marital status.[21] Children were raised by their parents during infancy, but when they were weaned at the age of about 18 months, their parents gave them to the care of the Nursery where they lived with other children. During the nursery years boys and girls lived together, but from the age of 4 on, the two sexes were separated, except in marriage. At that age girls joined the Little Girls' Choir and boys the Little Boys' Choir. As they grew older they graduated into other Choirs—at about 12 into the Older Girls' Choir and Older Boys' Choir, and at about 19 into the Choirs for Single Sisters and Single Brothers. Many adults lived out their lives as Single People, but a number of them married, and when they did, they became members of the Married Peoples' Choir. When one spouse died, the surviving spouse became a member of either the Widows' or the Widowers' Choir. If a widowed person married again, he or she rejoined the Married Peoples' Choir. The communal nature of the Choir system not only encouraged conversion, it also helped to maintain the relationship with the Heiland because it focused a person's attention away from family relationships and toward a close dependency on him.

Every conceivable aspect of Moravians' existence took place within their Choir. People ate together in large Choir dining rooms, they slept in large dormitories, they worked together in the fields or in industries operated by their Choir houses, and they often worshipped in the company of their Choir Brothers or Sisters. (See Figures 1-1 and 1-2 for portraits of individuals who lived in Bethlehem during the General Economy.)

This sort of existence encouraged spiritual growth in several ways. For one thing, people of the same age tended to reach similar spiritual stages at about the same time, so the Choirs functioned like support groups

FIGURE 1-1. Portrait of Sister Gertraut Graff by John Valentine Haidt

and encouraged advancement to the next stage. Secondly, Choir living de-emphasized kinship ties and thereby narrowed each person's focus onto a close relationship with the Heiland. The Choir counseling system also encouraged this direct dependence on the Heiland. Whenever people sought advice or friendship or comfort, their Choir leaders directed them to the Heiland for support. Thirdly, the almost total separation of the sexes helped to encourage a closer relationship with the Heiland. The Moravians explicitly recognized that intimate relations between people of the opposite sex could psychologically substitute for and therefore compromise a close

FIGURE 1-2. Portrait of Brother Martin Mack by John Valentine Haidt

relationship with the Heiland. This was thought to be especially true of the adolescent period, when boys and girls first become attractive to each other, because these impressionable and emotional years were also considered the most fertile ones for religious conversion. The challenge was to encourage the natural enthusiasm of adolescence in young people's religious development and at the same time to suppress it in the area of sexual growth. In order to accomplish this, Moravians very strictly enforced separation of the sexes.

The eradication of nuclear family life and the separation of the sexes in Bethlehem had an enormous effect on the lives of Moravian women. Male and female roles were much more symmetrical than in any other colonial society, including the Quakers. The primary task of the Bethlehem community was to encourage spiritual growth at home in Bethlehem and abroad in Moravian missions. Women participated freely and centrally in this task. The Choir system allowed their involvement, because it freed them from the traditional domestic labor and because the separation of sexes required their input. In order to maintain the necessary intimacy between spiritual advisors and their charges without encouraging extra-marital sexual contacts, women had to be responsible for the care of female souls and men for male souls. Single Sisters raised and nurtured girls, and Single Brothers did the same for boys. Single Sister Choir "Helpers" (spiritual leaders) took care of the souls of Single Sisters, and Single Broth-er Choir Helpers worked with the spiritual problems of Single Brothers. In addition, offices were doubly occupied by a husband-wife team. The Choir Helpers for the Married People were such a husband-wife team, each one dealing with the married people of his or her own sex. Likewise the pastor ministered to the men in the congregation and the pastor's wife to the women.

The responsibilities of women also extended to governing bodies. They were members of the Helpers Conference, the Overseers Confer-ence and the Elders Conference. As members of these governing bodies, they had a part in making the most important decisions in Bethlehem.

Underneath the symmetry of participation was an asymmetry of func-tion and symbol that later became very significant. The Choirs for Single Sisters and Widows had male caretakers who managed their financial affairs. And while both men and women could become Acolytes and Deacons, ordination as Presbyters or Bishops was reserved for men. Fur-thermore, religious imagery suggested inequality: the relation between the Heiland and human beings was explicitly compared to the male-female relationship, with the male playing the superior role and the female the inferior one.

However, during the period of the General Economy, women filled a remarkable variety of roles, and many women's biographies from the pe-riod suggest that women felt very much in the center of the important tasks in the community in Bethlehem.

Not only women, but workers of all types felt needed and important during that first twenty years. Every role was considered a significant ser-

TABLE 1-1 Daily Routine in Moravian Settlements

5:00 A.M.	Hymns sung to awaken residents
6:00 A.M.	Morning benediction and breakfast
7:00 A.M.	Work begins
9:00 A.M.	Kinderstunde ("Children's Hour")
12:00 noon	Noon meal (hymns sung before and after)
12:30 P.M.	Return to work
6:00 P.M.	Evening meal and devotional stroll
7:00 P.M.	Gemeinstunde ("Congregation Hour")
8:00 P.M.	Viertelstunde ("Quarter Hour" meeting)
9:00 P.M.	Abendstunde ("Evening Hour")
10:00 P.M.	Evening benediction
10:00 P.M. – 5:00 A.M.	Night Watch
24 hrs/day	Hourly Intercessions

vice to the Heiland. Whether a missionary in the Pilgergemeine or a cook in the Hausgemeine, a person felt a part of the religious mission in Bethlehem, because all work was considered religious. There was no such thing as secular work.[22]

The daily routine of the Moravians balanced long work hours with an intricate round of devotional services (see Table 1-1).

The daily routine has been described in illuminating detail by James David Nelson. Although Nelson's book concerns Herrnhut, much of his material about the daily life in a Moravian settlement comes from the Bethlehem records. This discussion is taken from his work.[23] People were awakened in the morning by the sound of other members singing hymns. An hour later they were expected to appear (in their night clothes or work clothes, as they wished) at the morning benediction in each of their Choir houses. This service announced the religious theme for the day in the form of a watchword ("Loosung"). Each day's watchword was chosen for a whole year and printed in advance. Moravians took these watchwords very seriously. Since they were chosen by the Lot, they represented a communication from the Heiland that had special significance for that particular day. People frequently noted connections between the watchword on a particular day and important events which took place in a member's life.[24]

Once the Daily Texts were introduced they were returned to again and again during the day—in the sermons preached, the hymns chosen, and in casual discussions between members. After a light breakfast of tea and a biscuit, the workday started at 7:00 A.M. and continued unbroken until dinnertime at 12:00 noon. The Kinderstunde ("Children's Hour") took place at 9:00 A.M. Though obviously designed for the youngest residents in the community, adults liked to attend this service whenever their duties allowed. Since childlike simplicity was a virtue to be courted among Moravians, they found the simplified explanations and the unaffected responses of the children to be inspirational and edifying.

The noon meal was the big meal of the day although it lasted only a half hour. It was blessed both beforehand and afterwards with the singing of hymns. At 12:30 P.M. people returned to their work until 6:00 P.M. at which time they ate a light supper and then took an evening stroll for personal devotions along paths prescribed for their particular Choir. At 7:00 P.M. the bell rang for the Gemeinstunde ("Congregation Hour"), the first devotional meeting of the day in which the whole Gemeine gathered together for worship. This was followed by a Viertelstunde ("Quarter Hour") service in the separate Choirs. At 9:00 P.M. the whole Gemeine met again for an Abendstunde ("Evening Hour"). And at 10:00 P.M. the Evening Benediction in each of the Choirs ended the day. If by chance some people spent a sleepless night, they were comforted by the sound of hymns sung by the night watchman every hour on the hour all through the night. In the background, and forming a protective frame to the day, were the Hourly Intercessions, covered in turn by different men and women who each took a one hour shift and prayed according to themes established in the weekly meetings of the group of intercessors.

These various daily devotional meetings were unusually short compared to the services of other Protestants. The Morning and Evening Benedictions each lasted only a few minutes. The Viertelstunde lasted just 15 minutes, as the name suggests, or even less. The Kinderstunde, Gemeinstunde, and Abendstunde rarely ran over one-half hour each. People who attended every service in the day, including the Kinderstunde, spent about two hours in devotions. Apparently, short but frequent services were considered more effective stimuli than a few longer ones. In contrast, the workdays were divided into two long sessions—the first one 5 hours long and the second 5 1/2 hours for a total of 10 1/2 hours.

The daily schedule applied to the weekdays (Monday through Saturday) and formed the framework into which the weekly devotional schedule

TABLE 1-2 Weekly Devotional Schedule

	Gemeinstunde	Abendstunde
Monday	Reading from Gemeinnachrichten	Singstunde
Tuesday	Reading from the Bible	Liturgy
Wednesday	Address from biblical text	Singstunde
Thursday	Liturgy	Singstunde
Friday	Reading from the Bible	Passion Liturgy
Saturday	?	Hourly Intercessors' Meeting

was woven. On each of these days the Gemeinstunde and the Abendstunde consisted in a different form of worship (see Table 1-2). The services were balanced to provide different religious experiences throughout the week. Bible readings took place on Tuesday and Friday. On Wednesday an address was given concerning a biblical text. On Monday selections from the *Gemeinnachrichten* were read. (The *Gemeinnachrichten* was a handwritten journal copied and distributed throughout the Moravian world. It included letters and reports from different settlements and missions and biographies about people of all ages.) On Monday, Wednesday, and Thursday evenings a Singstunde was held. Often described as a sermon in song, it was a linking of verses from different hymns to form a single idea. The leader began each verse, and the Gemeine, who knew hundreds of hymns by heart, joined in after the first few notes. The liturgies on Tuesday, Thursday, and Friday were reserved for Communicants, but all other adult services were open to any resident of the Gemeine, except the Nursery and the Little Children's Choirs.

Each day of the weekend was a special day. Friday was a weekly Good Friday, and the liturgy that day focused on the Passion. Initially the Moravians did not work on Saturday, but after the first few years they did. Even so, Saturday continued to be called the Sabbath. In some settlements this was the day on which the Hourly Intercessors held their meetings. Sunday was the Lord's day and was a weekly Easter. Since Sunday was not a workday, its schedule had more services, including the longest service of the week—the litany at 8:00 A.M., which lasted 45 minutes to an hour (see Table 1-3).

A monthly schedule of devotions lay on top of the weekly schedule. The second weekend of every month was a Gemeintag ("Congregation Day"). The children's Gemeintag (on Saturday) functioned like a Com-

TABLE 1-3 The Sunday Schedule

8 A.M.	Church Litany
10 A.M.	Preaching
2 P.M.	Kinderstunde
3 P.M.	Married People's Hour
5 P.M.	Liturgy
7 P.M.	Gemeinstunde
9 P.M.	Evening Benediction with whole Gemeine

munion day for children. It was preceded by discussions between the Children's Choir Helpers and each child individually to determine his or her spiritual condition. On the basis of these, the boys and girls who were in general allowed to prostrate themselves before the Lord were either included in or excluded from the Anbeten ("Prostration") which climaxed the day. The day began with a children's litany in the morning. In the afternoon they met for a series of children's readings (children's biographies and children's letters) from the *Gemeinnachrichten* or for a Lovefeast—a service of singing, taking a cup of coffee and a biscuit in unison, and giving each other the Kiss of Peace. The day ended in the afternoon with the Anbeten. Participants in this ceremony were considered full members of the Children's Choir.

The next day, Sunday, the adults held their Gemeintag. Readings from reports and biographies in the *Gemeinnachrichten* replaced the usual Sunday morning litany and the Sunday afternoon liturgy. The purpose of this day was to build unity with the other Moravian settlements around the world and to build commitment to the Gemeine in general. The acceptance of new members often took place on this day.

The climax in the monthly devotional cycle was reached in Communion. It was in this celebration that the sacrificial role of the Heiland was experienced each month as a personal reality by each participant. Communicants felt refreshed and newly committed to the Heiland each time they participated, and people who were not yet Communicants yearned to take part.

The celebration of Communion took place on the fourth Saturday of the month, but preparations encompassed most of a week. It began on the Tuesday before, with the formal announcement of the coming Communion—though Moravians scarcely needed to be reminded about this much-anticipated event. Wednesday through Friday was spent in intense

17

preparation for the actual Communion. Through the preparation, Communicants had the responsibility to determine their readiness for Communion. They were to look for the joy ("Freudigkeit") considered necessary for approaching the sacrament of the Eucharist—the same joy experienced at conversion upon accepting one's basic unworthiness, submitting totally to the Heiland, and receiving his grace. To facilitate this preparatory inner search, Communicants were called to their Choir Helper for a private Speaking ("Sprechen"). Since Choir members were admonished from their earliest years to be completely "offenherzig" (open with their Choir Helpers concerning the condition of their hearts), the Choir Helpers were intimately aware of the spiritual needs of each Communicant and were therefore able to guide the search in the most fruitful direction. Sometimes the Choir Helper would suggest or even require abstention from Communion if a person's condition was clearly not right, but most often people who abstained had decided independently that they were unprepared. Either way, this monthly examination was a powerful device for maintaining discipline and homogeneity in a settlement like early Bethlehem where no external laws or judicial system existed to control behavior. When people had to "stay away" from Communion they felt separated from the Heiland and isolated from the rest of the community.

The Communion service was preceded by a Communion lovefeast and by an absolution service. The lovefeast was intended to firm the bonds among Communicants and to direct their focus toward the Communion. The absolution climaxed the period of self-examination. Sometimes it was a part of the Communion service itself, but a separate service was preferable so that abstainers from Communion could still take part in absolution. Communion itself was celebrated inwardly by each participant in an effort to commune with the Heiland, but it was also celebrated in unison with the other Communicants in order to bond with fellow members of the Gemeine: all participants raised the bread to their lips at the same moment, and they passed the chalices from person to person among the congregation.

A yearly cycle of religious events was celebrated as yet another layer over the monthly, weekly, and daily cycles and included four different kinds of holidays: the usual Christian festivals, Memorial days, Choir festival days, and the two days which ended one year and began the next.

Of the commonly recognized Christian festivals, Easter was the most important, in keeping with the Moravian focus on the Heiland's self-sacrifice. It began on the Saturday before Palm Sunday and ended the Tuesday after Easter, and was commonly called Marter-Woche ("Martyrweek") or Charwoche ("Passion Week"). The framework for the first nine days of the eleven-day "week" was a collection of biblical readings recounting the "acts" of the Heiland on the days surrounding his death. So that the worshipers could experience these acts vicariously, the portion of the reading which matched each day was read on that day. Thus the Palm Sunday reading told of the Heiland's entry into Jerusalem, Monday's related his teaching in the temple and the plots of the chief priests against him, Tuesday's developed the conflicts which eventually led to the crucifixion, and so on. From Wednesday through Easter Sunday the Moravians not only heard about the acts from readings but they symbolically participated in the Heiland's actions through expressive ceremonies: on Wednesday they held a Pedilavium or Footwashing to echo the Heiland's washing the feet of his disciples, on Maundy Thursday they held the most sacred Communion of the year to mirror the Last Supper, and on Friday afternoon the Gemeine sang emotional anthems and hymn verses to recreate the mood of the most central event in their experience of the Heiland: his crucifixion and his suffering. Friday evening they met again to meditate on his burial. Saturday, the Great Sabbath, was considered the day of the Heiland's rest in the tomb, and Moravians celebrated it with a day of rest themselves. Saturday's Evening Benediction, usually a very brief service, was expanded on this day to sanctify their sleep through the Heiland's rest. The Sunday morning sunrise service was a joyous celebration of the Heiland's resurrection as is usual in any Christian service, but it had a characteristically Moravian cast. It was held in the graveyard with the worshippers surrounding the newest graves, and it celebrated the eternal life given to human beings by the Heiland's death and resurrection. Easter Monday was the occasion for a Gemeintag (Congregation Day) in which the significance of the Easter events was applied to the Gemeine. The Marter-Woche was concluded on Tuesday with a Singstunde which reviewed the events of the whole Easter story in hymn verses and set the tone for renewed commitment to the Heiland and to "His Gemeine."

Another class of yearly celebrations served to remind Moravians of their own past. The historical events celebrated each year in Bethlehem's Memorial Days are listed in the order of their historical occurrence:

1. Martyrdom of Jan Hus   1415
2. Founding of the Unitas Fratrum   1457
3. Protestant Reformation   15th & 16th centuries
4. Augsburg Confession   1530
5. Felling of first timber in Herrnhut   1722

6.	Building of first prayer house in Herrnhut	1724
7.	First Constitution of the Gemeine	1727
8.	August 13 Communion in Herrnhut	1727
9.	Founding of Hourly Intercessions	1727
10.	First mission to St. Thomas	1732
11.	First mission to Greenland	1733
12.	Naming of Heiland as Chief Elder	1741
13.	Announcement of Heiland's Chief Eldership to Gemeine	1741
14.	Founding of the Gemeine in Bethlehem	1742

This calendar of remembered events gives us a glimpse into the Bethlehem Moravians' view of themselves. They identified with the early Hussite Movement in Bohemia and with Gregor's founding of the Unitas Fratrum in Kunwald. Their ecumenical interests were reflected in their celebration of the Protestant Reformation and of the Lutheran Confession agreed to at Augsburg.[25] They placed considerable emphasis on the events which framed the renewal of the Unitas Fratrum during the 1720s in Herrnhut. They recalled the first missionary efforts to Africans, Indians, and Eskimos, using St. Thomas and Greenland as symbols. They celebrated the Gemeine's special honor of being governed by the Heiland directly. And they celebrated their own anniversary: the founding of Bethlehem. The two most important Memorial Days were the August 13th Communion (the spiritual birthday of the renewed Unitas Fratrum) and the announcement of the Heiland's Chief Eldership.

In addition to the festivals celebrated by the Gemeine as a whole, the Choirs (or sub-groups of Choirs) celebrated their own festivals separately. They focused upon events in the history of that Choir as well as events in the life of the Heiland which has particular significance for that Choir. Examples of this are the celebration of the awakening among the Single Sisters in 1730 at Herrnhut, or Christmas (the Heiland's birthday) as the teaching day for expectant mothers.

The end of one year and the beginning of the next were important days in the devotional cycle of the Moravians. New Year's Eve was an opportunity for individuals, Choirs, and the Gemeine as a whole to look back on the year which had just passed and to evaluate it in religious terms. In the year's end *Memorabilia* they recounted the contributions they had made in their efforts to promote the Heiland's cause and the blessings he had bestowed upon them. They also noted the changes in all the Choirs: new memberships, withdrawals, marriages, births, and deaths. Frequently on New Year's Eve individuals drew texts by the Lot, which were understood to have special significance for that person during the next year. In services on New Year's Day Moravians asked the Heiland for his blessing and guidance during the year ahead, and they renewed the covenant between Communicant members.

Through all this round of worship and festivals, music played an unusually significant role. Hymns had already been important in the Unitas Fratrum, as the large collection of Czech Protestant hymnals attests, but they were sung in unison only and without the accompaniment of instruments. In the renewed Unitas Fratrum under the influence of Zinzendorf, music became the most central form of worship. Hymns, according to Zinzendorf, were "a kind of answer to the Bible, an echo. . . . From the Bible one can see how God talks to human beings, and from the hymnbook, how human beings talk with God." Just as important, Zinzendorf thought the singing of hymns was "the best method for bringing God's truths into the heart and to preserve them there." [26] The biographies written for people's funerals demonstrate that he was right. People of all ages frequently answered questions about their spiritual condition with quotations from their favorite hymn verses. The biographies also demonstrate that the creation of hymns was an ongoing process in which many people took part. People often wrote hymns to celebrate important days in the lives of friends and family members or to praise the Heiland in a more personal way.

The regular practice of "Singstunde" services served not only to carry religious messages in song, they also were a way of encouraging the learning of hymns by heart. Most singing among the Moravians was done without the help of their many hymnals. It was felt not only that God's truths were better "preserved" in Moravian hearts if they knew them from memory, but that they could concentrate better on their meaning if they did not have to keep their place on the written page. Liturgies were another form of worship in song. In contrast to the Singstunde, which the leader usually improvised as the mood and the need required, liturgies were organized, written down, and repeated from time to time. [27] The Moravians sang hymns in a great variety of styles. Sometimes they sang in unison, sometimes in harmony, and they often alternated within a piece between singing together, singing separately in groups of men and women, and singing in solo voices. Outsiders were genuinely moved by the beauty of Moravian hymn singing.

Musical instruments usually accompanied the human voices. By the mid-1740s Bethlehem had an organ (built by Johann Gottfried Klemm, a

Moravian Brother), a spinet, trumpets, horns, and probably violins and flutes. The first set of trombones (soprano, alto, tenor, and bass) arrived in 1754.[28] The musicians who played these instruments were very skilled. Visitors to Bethlehem uniformly said that the quality of music in Bethlehem was better than at any other place in America and that in general Moravian music rivaled the music in the princely courts of Europe.[29]

Moravians played the religious music of the latest composers (C. P. E. Bach, for instance, and later Haydn)[30] but they also composed their own music. Both in America and in Europe a number of Moravian composers wrote anthems, cantatas, and solo songs. Although Moravians played secular music for practice and entertainment, they usually composed religious music, which centered around the human voice. For Moravians, the message of words was primary, and the instruments were there mainly to support them.[31]

Religious music was played and sung not only in worship services: musical processions accompanied workers on their way to the fields, as they began to excavate for a new building, and as members moved into a new Choir house.[32] Brass choirs played chorales from the church tower to announce Communion or to report the death of a fellow Moravian. Small groups of people planned the singing of chorales to awaken fellow Choir members on special days,[33] and individuals frequently sang hymns and liturgies by themselves as they went through their daily routines.

As we have seen, the preparations for Communion each month played a central role in the control of deviance. They were part of a larger system of deviance control which governed how people entered the concentric circles of association and how they were excluded from them. Moravians did not seek converts from among people who were already Christianized. But many people who came into contact with them desired membership. As a first step, a person requested permission "to stay" ("Erlaubnis zum Bleiben"). Once granted, the person was allowed to stay, pending good behavior.

The next step was acceptance to the circle of members ("Aufnahme"). Acceptance was not requested by the individual, but awarded by the Gemeine. After the Elders had judged the person worthy, the question was submitted to the Lot. Only if the Lot was positive could the person be accepted.

The third step was the admission to the circle of Communicants, which happened in two stages. First a person became a Candidate and was allowed to observe celebrations of Communion. Then the Candidate became a Communicant and attended Communion for the first time—an

22

event which was always mentioned and frequently described in detail in that person's biography.

The system worked to control deviance through the succession of stages: people were not promoted if they were not considered suited. To some degree, advancement from one Choir to the next worked in the same way. Some people were advanced at earlier ages than others, depending on their maturity.

Even after the person became a Communicant, the system could still control deviance, for the stages could be subtracted. As described earlier in the section on Communion, a person whose spiritual condition was not suited could abstain from Communion or, if necessary, the Elders could require abstention. If long term abstention did not work and a person acted in ways considered damaging to the Gemeine, the Elders could expel him or her from the Gemeine, which also required leaving the settlement. Although this step was not taken very frequently, the threat of being expelled was a significant part of the deviance control system.

When important decisions needed to be made, the Moravians often consulted the Lot. They wrote a statement in favor of the proposal under consideration on one piece of paper, a statement against it on another, and left a third one blank. They then inserted the pieces of paper into separate tubes, mixed the tubes up, and drew their answer from them. The result, in the Moravian view, revealed the wishes of the Heiland. A positive statement indicated that he supported the proposal, a negative one that he did not, a blank one that he was not in favor at this time but that the question could be asked again later. The first use of the Lot among the Moravians was recorded in 1727 when the first Elders were chosen. In 1728 it became the common method for deciding issues in Moravian councils. By 1733 it was the required method for approving proposed marriages.[34]

The rationale for the Lot was supported by the most sincere convictions. In the Moravian view the results of the Lot could not be by chance, but had to be signs from an all-powerful deity. Such a view was consistent with the belief commonly held in the Western world of that time: nothing happened by chance—everything was the result of divine design. Furthermore, the Moravians mistrusted majority rule because it could allow for undue influence on the part of one individual ("whoever has an extraordinary talent for speaking will bring the most votes to his side, and he can do whatever he wants") and because it placed too much trust in the hands of human beings ("the Lot represents a true recognition of our inadequacy [as human beings] and a total submission to the will of the Heiland").[35]

The Moravians admitted that the Lot was not necessarily an established part of Christian tradition: "we find no commandment in the New Testament to use the Lot, and we can't claim that the Heiland always ruled his church through the Lot, for he could also use other means, but of our own days of grace we can only say from experience that He has always let us know His will . . . through this medium and has often shown it in an extraordinary way."[36] In Synod after Synod (the church councils that set policy), they supported its continuation: "The governance of the Heiland must remain with us as long as He maintains His Brüdergemeine. He lets us know his sentiment in critical cases through the Lot and thereby keeps the course and the management of the Gemeine out of human hands."[37]

The Moravians were well aware that the Lot could be misused and were careful to prescribe how and when it could be used. Lots were not to be cast by individuals for themselves. Only Elders, acting for the Gemeine, were to cast lots. Whenever an important decision needed to be made, the Elders were to consult their own existing regulations and the Bible for a clear directive. Only if they could find nothing were they allowed to consult the Lot. (If they found nothing, they were also *required* to consult the Lot.) Neither could they consult the Lot about any proposal which went against the established principles of the Moravian Church. Before consulting the Lot, they were to discuss the proposal until they understood it thoroughly and they had to construct the wording carefully. The whole procedure was to be conducted in a reverent manner.[38] Clearly, human judgment was involved in setting up and following the framework for the Lot.

In 1741, in keeping with the concepts behind the Lot, the Moravians established the Heiland in the office of Chief Elder of their European branch. For reasons that are not clear, the American Province was excluded from the Heiland's Chief Eldership until 1748.[39]

During these years the people of Bethlehem sensed that they represented the pinnacle of development in the Moravian Church. The first decade in Herrnhut had offered freedom from the oppression they and their ancestors had suffered in Moravia, and, as we have seen, a number of meaningful religious events from the period became a remembered part of Moravian history, but the first years in Herrnhut did not approach the general level of fulfillment evident during the first years in Bethlehem. The excitement the new settlers felt as they developed their new community fairly jumps off the early pages of the Bethlehem Diary, the official account of events in Bethlehem. Many members' biographies from those years speak of the renewal they felt in their "dear Bethlehem." Zinzendorf wrote from Pennsylvania, "In all the days of my life I have never seen such a Gemeine," and Spangenberg wrote that "our dear Count Zinzendorf gives

Gemeine	Brüdergemeine (Gemeine)	Non-exclusive	Stadtgemeine	
			Landgemeine	
		Exclusive	Ortsgemeine	
			Pilgergemeine	Pilgergemeine
				Hausgemeine
	Other Christian Churches			

FIGURE 1-3. Taxonomy of the term "Gemeine"

us the commendation that we have never had a Gemeine like Bethlehem—the love, the simplicity, the religious warmth ["Herzlichkeit"], the submission to each other, the willingness and the pure sense of the Gospel: these are all things that astound everyone." [40]

The special place that Bethlehem held within the Moravian world was also reflected in the system of terms they developed to name the different kinds of settlements ("Gemeinen") (see Figure 1-3).[41] The cover term "Gemeine" referred to all of Christendom, of which the "Brüdergemeine" was just one part. Moravians rarely used the term in this sense, however, except in theoretical discussions. They preferred to use the term to refer to their own group, the Brüdergemeine. The Brüdergemeine was divided into two classes of organizations for which there were no simple terms but which were explicitly distinguished: (1) those in which the members did not live together but were gathered from the residents of a given geographical area, and (2) those in which the members lived together in a settlement and in which only Moravians were allowed to live. The first category was further divided into two categories depending on whether they were organized in rural areas ("Landgemeinen") or in urban ones ("Stadtgemeinen").[42] The second category was subdivided into "Ortsgemeine" settlements (in which families lived as separate units and were each responsible for their own livelihood) and "Pilgergemeine" settlements (in which members lived in communal Choir houses, gave their labor to the community, and received food, clothes, and shelter in return). In order to accomplish its missionary purpose, each Pilgergemeine was further divided into two parts: (1) a Pilgergemeine in the narrow sense (the mission-

25

aries who were freed from all tasks except spiritual work), and (2) a "Hausgemeine" (the providers who supported the missionaries by growing the food, making the clothes, building the buildings, and raising the children). All members of a Pilgergemeine, whether missionaries or providers, received food, shelter, and clothing in exchange for their work. No one received any wages. All property was owned by the community as a whole and not by its individual members. In short, a Pilgergemeine was designed not for the prosperity of its members but for the spiritual growth of the people they served in their missionary establishments.

Bethlehem was the first and most well-developed Pilgergemeine. It was also one of the few Pilgergemeine settlements to be established at all, because the predominant form of exclusive settlement in the Moravian world was the Ortsgemeine. The leaders of the Unity recognized that the Pilgergemeine required an extraordinary amount of commitment and that not everyone was suited to it.[43] But the special place of honor held by Bethlehem also held dangers for the future. It made Bethlehem vulnerable to attack as an exception within the Moravian world, as will become clear in Chapter 7.

More than any other man, it was August Gottlieb Spangenberg who developed Bethlehem into a vibrant and successful community. It was he who first suggested a Moravian settlement in Pennsylvania, and it was he who defined its mission—to preach the gospel to Indians and Germans and to establish schools for young people in the region. During his years as a traveling minister he had become familiar with the Indians in Pennsylvania and the lack of organized churches and schools among the German settlers there.[44] In keeping with Moravian policy at the time, their activities among the Germans were designed as a support to denominations which already existed rather than as a way to expand their own church. Traveling Moravian ministers preached to people of Lutheran and Reformed backgrounds, served them Communion, and baptized their children, but they were expressly forbidden from recruiting new members for the Moravian Church.

Bethlehem's first administrator was actually Peter Böhler, from the fall of 1742 to the fall of 1744, but for the next eighteen years, except for a three-year hiatus, Spangenberg was not only the administrator, but an inspiring leader. He was a religious man, deeply committed to the Moravian Church. He also had an unusual breadth to his abilities. He could conceive bold ideas, he knew how to make them practical, and he was able to inspire others to make them real.

In line with early Moravian practice, Spangenberg's first wife, Eva Maria, was his professional partner. From all accounts she was his equal.

Not only did she take full responsibility for the spiritual and physical well-being of the women and children in Bethlehem, but she took Spangenberg's place as administrator during his frequent travels away from Bethlehem. The biographies written during their administration spoke of her with the same respect and even reverence that they used when speaking of him. But although an unusually strong administrator and spiritual leader, she was physically quite fragile. The hard work and the strain of her job caused her to be frequently sick, and she died at the age of 55 during the Spangenbergs' three years away from Bethlehem. Spangenberg's second wife was a gentle soul who left the administrative tasks to her husband.[45]

Under Spangenberg's leadership Bethlehem grew and prospered. The population increased from 72 in 1742 to over 600 in 1759.[46] The frontier village with a few log buildings developed into an impressive town dominated by stately stone buildings, many profitable industries, and a flourishing farm. The town supported a complex network of missions and schools in Pennsylvania and other mid-Atlantic colonies. Community life focused around a daily routine of heartfelt worship and rigorous work, and members of all ages and both sexes led lives made meaningful by their extraordinary sense of purpose.

But Bethlehem was not an isolated town. It was a part of the worldwide Moravian organization which the Moravians called the "Unity." Because the ties among all Moravian settlements were close, events in one part of the system affected the rest. Early in 1743 a number of events took place which modified the Moravian Church as a whole and Bethlehem in particular for years to come. Zinzendorf and the Moravian immigrants had never come to a complete agreement about what the renewal of the old Bohemian and Moravian Church had meant. The Moravian immigrants who dominated the General Conference (the governing body at the time) wanted it to be a Church in every sense of the word: independent of other churches, recognized by other Protestants, and able to expand its membership. In short, they wanted it to be a denomination alongside others. While Zinzendorf was occupied with his missionary and ecumenical work in America, the General Conference in Europe began to develop the church as a denomination. They negotiated with rulers in several parts of Europe for recognition and established several new congregations.

Meanwhile Zinzendorf agreed that the Moravian Church should be independent and recognized, but he did not agree that it should expand its membership. This would have been inconsistent with his ecumenical efforts to unify Christian practice and to minimize the number of denominations. Instead he believed the renewed Moravian Church had the mission only to encourage its own members' religious commitment, to support Christian belief in other churches, and to make converts among the non-Christian "heathens."[47]

Zinzendorf immediately took steps to undo the expansionist work of the old Moravian group. At the Hirschberg Synod in the summer of 1743 he reduced the powers of the General Conference which had orchestrated the expansion and greatly increased his own power. He became the "advocatus et ordinarius fratrum" and took for himself the power of veto over any decisions made in conferences or synods. This represented a complete reversal of governing policy in the Moravian Church, for since the earliest days of the Unitas Fratrum it had been governed by synods and by a group of elders, but the Moravian immigrants believed it their duty to agree with the wishes of Zinzendorf since they owed him a great debt for his tireless efforts on their behalf.[48]

Even aside from this change in tradition, the autocratic rule by Zinzendorf was not good for the Moravian Church. For one thing, Zinzendorf needed the help of more sober financial managers. From the early days the finances of the Church were an integral part of the finances of the Zinzendorf family. Although he was extremely generous with his own resources he supported the extravagant building program of the next years with heavy borrowing. Secondly, in taking away the power of the General Conference, which had been dominated by the Moravian party, he strengthened the hand of the strongly pietistic faction which came to dominate the church during the next several years—the period called the "Sichtungszeit" (sifting or winnowing period).[49]

Zinzendorf encouraged this group in another way. In an effort to make the theology of the Church appeal less to the "mind" and more to the "heart," he began to create a more concrete and visual religious vocabulary. Building on the central focus in the Moravian Church—the Heiland's self-sacrifice—Zinzendorf developed the blood and wounds theology to new mystical heights. In particular he emphasized the Sidewound (the spear wound in the Heiland's side) and the healing and redemptive powers of the "juices" which flowed from it. Believers were portrayed as little bees or little worms who sucked the juices from the Sidewound. The diminutive was added to many nouns to increase their emotive quality: "Herz" (heart) became "Herzel," "Lamm" (Lamb) became "Lämmlein" and "Seitenhohl" (Sidewound) became "Seitenhölchen." Death became all-important both because it replayed the experience of the Heiland in death and because it represented the ultimate union with the Heiland. The word for death had been "Heimgang or Heimfahrt" (the journey home). It now became "Seitenhölchenfahrt" (journey into the sweet Sidewound).

Zinzendorf did not predict the effect his new mysticism would have on the Moravian Church. As he had hoped, it did increase the members' devotion to the Heiland. But he did not realize the toll this new kind of devotion would take on general discipline and on the economic well-being of the Moravian settlements. The settlements in the Wetteravian region of Western Germany were especially prone to the fervors of the Sifting Period because they were initiated and developed during this period. In Herrnhaag, Zinzendorf's young son, Christian Renatus, set the tone as a presbyter, the leader of the Single Brothers, and the manager of the whole settlement. Most members' energies were spent in devotions and costly celebrations at the expense of a stable social and economic base. Representatives of the more temperate faction (Spangenberg, for instance) tried repeatedly to warn Zinzendorf of the threat this new emphasis posed for the Church, but he ignored them until the very last moment. In 1749 when he finally realized the extremes to which his new emphasis had led, he was quick to act. He called his son to London, rebuked him, and removed him from his offices. He also wrote stern letters to the congregations which had been most involved, ordering them to cease their fanatic practices, and he sent his son-in-law, Johannes de Watteville, to make sure that they did. Late in 1749, the owner of the Herrnhaag land on which the Moravian buildings stood became disenchanted with Zinzendorf and demanded that the Herrnhaag residents renounce Zinzendorf if they wanted to stay. They elected to give up their buildings and other improvements instead. Within three years the settlements in Wetteravia were abandoned and the residents transplanted to other Moravian settlements.

Meanwhile the Sifting Period did not take hold in Bethlehem until later than in Europe. The religious language did change to some degree during the early Sifting years in Bethlehem. The focus on the Heiland's wounds became stronger, the diminutive was freely attached to nouns, and residents in Bethlehem all became "Herzel." The Spangenbergs started a Society of Little Fools—the child and the fool being symbols of the simplicity required of a converted Moravian. But religious life in Bethlehem was balanced with social and economic discipline. It was not until 1747 when Anna and Johann Friedrich Cammerhoff came to Bethlehem as assistants to the Spangenbergs that Moravians in America began to realize how much the tenor of religious life had changed in the European branch of the Moravian Church. With growing misgivings Spangenberg began to evade some of the changes he was being asked to make. But Cammerhoff had been given secret instructions to further the spirit of the Sifting in Bethlehem. In the summer of 1748, nineteen Single Brothers from Herrnhaag arrived in Bethlehem while Spangenberg was away on a trip. When he came back he was shocked at the change which had come over Bethlehem and declared himself unwilling to go any farther with the goals of the Sifting Period. Spangenberg was informed in September 1748 that henceforth he was no longer the Chief Elder of the American branch of the Moravian Church, but that Heiland's Chief Eldership would now extend to America as well.[50]

In November Johann and Juliana Nitschmann took over the leadership of Bethlehem. Unfortunately their goals extended only to developing the Sifting spirit in Bethlehem, which encouraged the same lack of attention to economic endeavors that had nearly destroyed the Moravian Church in Europe. Even the man who was then in charge of economic matters in Bethlehem (a "Brother Herrmann") concentrated on constructing buildings and not on producing goods and raising food. The result of both these leaders' policies was that Bethlehem could no longer provide for itself. In order to feed and clothe its members, Bethlehem bought food and clothes from outsiders, and since they generated little cash to pay for it, they raised the debt to staggering levels.[51]

Not only did Bethlehem suffer economically during this period, but it was wracked by dissension as well, for Bethlehem still had a strong contingent of people who disapproved of the new emphases, people who had been at the heart of the system under Spangenberg. The many new settlers from Herrnhaag and Marienborn[52] simply deepened the division. By the time Zinzendorf realized that he needed to reinstate Spangenberg, Bethlehem was near collapse.

For Spangenberg, coming back to Bethlehem in December of 1751 was like starting over. The physical plant was intact, but the system which had made such efficient use of it had been totally destroyed. It took two years of hard work on everyone's part to rebuild it. Not until September of 1753 could Spangenberg report that the residents of Bethlehem had, for the first time in several years, grown enough food that they did not need to buy any from the outside. By the end of that year he wrote that both spiritually and economically Bethlehem was again on solid ground.[53]

But during the Sifting period a seed had been planted in Bethlehem that would continue to plague the community for years to come. Hermann had blamed Bethlehem's economic woes during the Sifting Period on its communal system. A number of residents had come to agree with him, and they continued to complain after Spangenberg returned. In response Spangenberg and the leaders of the Unity decided that in order for Bethlehem to survive as a Pilgergemeine, an Ortsgemeine would have to be built nearby in order to catch the overflow of discontented people from Bethlehem. Accordingly Spangenberg began to make plans in the spring of 1753 to make an Ortsgemeine out of Nazareth. But by the time plans were fixed, the people in Bethlehem declared themselves willing to build but unwilling to move there. In order to understand their motives, Spangenberg asked everyone to write letters explaining their feelings and the reasons behind them. Although a few people were frankly afraid to be on their own economically, most made it clear that they were committed to the purpose of Bethlehem and to its communal form.[54]

Up to this point Bethlehem had never had any by-laws. Spangenberg had always believed that the spirit of cooperation and the willingness to work hard for the community purpose had to be internally motivated and not externally imposed. Now, however, Spangenberg believed that a formal agreement was necessary. The considerable mood swings that Bethlehem had endured during the last several years convinced him and so did Bethlehem's size. The town had grown larger than originally intended, and Spangenberg was persuaded that community spirit was not easily motivated within such a large group and that a way of working together had to be legislated. The result was the *Brotherly Agreement*.[55] It defined Bethlehem's purpose and described its communal system as one in which members could not own property, earn money for their work, accumulate capital, or borrow money. It also recognized that in order for the system to work, the members needed to subordinate themselves to their superiors in a willing and trusting way and to appreciate the adequate provisions made in the community for their shelter and their care (i.e., they were not to complain about what they did not have).

For several years after the Brotherly Agreement, the community of Bethlehem continued to prosper, even though it endured a severe test during the wars with Indians in 1755–56. In November 1755, Gnadenhütten, a Moravian mission to the Indians north of Bethlehem, was attacked and most of its white missionaries murdered. In the following months Bethlehem became the refuge for Indian and white Moravians and white non-Moravians from around the Pennsylvania frontier, about 600 in all. Even though many of these people were put to work, Bethlehem's economic resources were strained to their limits. In the end it was the communal system that made it possible for Bethlehem to carry the burden. Extra people could be integrated into this kind of system much more easily and productively than into a traditional system built on nuclear families.[56]

DISSOLUTION AND TRANSITION

The years after that crisis were economically successful ones, but in spite of the favorable balance sheets, the rumblings in the Unity against Bethlehem's communal system continued and gathered force. Upon Zinzendorf's death in May 1760, pressure mounted to dissolve the Communal Economy and to make an Ortsgemeine out of the old Pilgergemeine. The Unity had not yet managed to reduce significantly the debts that had grown so large during the Sifting Period. Many of the Unity's creditors had been personal friends or acquaintances of the Count. When he died, they became concerned about their loans and called them in. In a movement led by Johann Friedrich Koeber, the Unity sought to satisfy these creditors with yearly contributions to payments of interest and principal from each of the separate Gemeinen around the world. Koeber placed particular emphasis on Bethlehem, for it seemed to him that this vigorous town ought to be able to contribute substantially to reducing the debt. The European Gemeinen had already contributed considerable sums, but because so many adults in Bethlehem were missionaries or teachers supported by the adults in the Hausgemeine, Bethlehem did not have the surplus funds available. Koeber wanted to dissolve the Communal Economy and make each family responsible for its own economic support. This, he reasoned, would increase productivity and make it possible for Bethlehem to contribute its fair share.

This change would mean, of course, that Bethlehem's focus would no longer be its missionary activities, but that change in focus reflected the new emphasis in the Unity after Zinzendorf's death. The Count had been willing to sacrifice economic practicality to the religious mission of the Church. As long as he was alive, his creditors allowed for that. After his death they did not. Now, in order for the Church to survive, Koeber and his associates had to sacrifice the religious mission to economic practicality.

Spangenberg again found himself straining against the general tide. Because he had put so much effort into the initial building of Pilgergemeine Bethlehem and then rebuilding it after the Sifting, he knew it more intimately than anyone else and was at first unwilling to support such a radical change. In July 1760, two months after Zinzendorf's death, the authorities asked Spangenberg to conceive a plan for making Bethlehem an Ortsgemeine. Instead, he and his associates devised an alternate, less extreme plan. Spangenberg's motives were quite different from Koeber's. He was concerned that the spiritual commitment in Bethlehem was diminishing. His reforms were designed to address that problem and to make sure that a change did no "damage to people's souls." He was against making Bethlehem an Ortsgemeine on several grounds: (1) the town had been built as a communal settlement, so the buildings did not suit an Ortsgemeine form in which families lived separately; (2) since the intense missionary purpose for which Bethlehem was founded should continue, the communal economic system was necessary to support it; and (3) the availability of land and opportunity here in America made it much easier than in Europe for a family to become "rich and content" which diminished their religious commitment. Spangenberg had observed this pattern among the Quakers, the Mennonites, and the Schwenkfelders, and he was sure it would repeat itself among some of the members of the Gemeine in Bethlehem if families were separated into independent economic units.

For these reasons Spangenberg argued that Bethlehem should continue in much the same way it was originally conceived. According to his plan the businesses and farms would continue as communal enterprises, and members would not receive wages at the level expected by American workers at that time. Rather, in order to allow people individual choice as to the clothes they wore and the food they ate—and in order to reduce complaints—they would be given an allowance from which they could buy these necessities.

Spangenberg also suggested that Nazareth could be made into an Ortsgemeine so that members dissatisfied with the Pilgergemeine in Bethlehem could go there. He did not suggest how those people could be saved from becoming "rich and content," but he did say that such a community would make it possible for Bethlehem to decrease in size, for he still believed that Bethlehem had grown too large and that its size contributed to the waning religious and community spirit.[57]

Clearly Spangenberg's plan was not what the authorities had hoped to get. Koeber responded in April 1761 with a set of resolutions from the General Directorat in Herrnhut that all but ignored Spangenberg's suggestions and ordered that Bethlehem be transformed into an Ortsgemeine after the pattern of Herrnhut. Since this was the plan, an Ortsgemeine in Nazareth would not be necessary. Separate houses were to be built for the Married People and the children gradually integrated into their families. Only the farms and the mills were to be maintained by the Gemeine. All other professions and crafts were to be carried on independently.

Hamilton and Levering both argue that the Pilgergemeine was never intended as a permanent institution, but the evidence presented by Erbe indicates not only that it was, but that it was considered the Moravian economic and social structure which was most worthy—an example to be admired if not always emulated. Statements made by Zinzendorf, Spangenberg, de Watteville, and others between 1742 and 1762 support this view.[58] It is also true, however, that they all (including Spangenberg) eventually came to believe that it could not have lasted. They arrived at this view for different reasons. Some were persuaded by the economic concerns of Koeber. Zinzendorf, who had invented the communal raising of children, became concerned even by the late 1740s that it was having the unintended effect of "harmful equality." "According to my principles," he wrote, "all ordinary [non-missionary] parents should raise their own children so that these can experience first-hand from their earliest years the toil in life and learn to work, otherwise we get only princes or priests, only officers and no common soldiers." And in another place: "Natural caste is permanent as it is; whoever argues beyond caste and beyond the raising of children by their natural parents and wants to run everything through one comb is a fanatic." There is also evidence that he wanted Moravian settlements to become more conventional: "It must come to the point that all ordinary parents raise their children themselves just as other Christian people do."[59]

Spangenberg, on the other hand, became convinced by the waning of cooperative spirit in Bethlehem that the Pilgergemeine could not continue. He had already voiced concerns when he devised his alternate plan that "a change is necessary because [the Communal Economy] is no longer what it was in the beginning."[60] Although he was at first in disagreement with Koeber's radical solution, by May 1762, a few weeks after the change was implemented, he gave it cautious support: "The majority of families are already on their way. For some it is awkward, but it may work."[61] Seven years later, at the General Synod in 1769, he sided with those who argued that "any appearance of communal industries must be carefully . . . avoided."[62] Erbe suggests that Spangenberg changed his mind because he believed that to keep the Pilgergemeine form after the Pilgergemeine spirit had vanished would do more harm to souls than good.

The transition period was longer and more arduous than the leaders in the Unity had expected. It took until 1771 to transform Bethlehem into an Ortsgemeine. The settlement's new leaders had to redesign the buildings to house separate families. They needed to gradually reintroduce the parents to the responsibility of raising their own children. And they had to help reestablish the industries in privately held operations.

The new economy was not completely private. Some communal industries were still needed to support the religious workers and the Children's Institutes until they could be disbanded. The farms were kept entirely communal at first, as were the inns, the store, the apothecary, the tannery, the various mills, the blacksmith operation, and the pottery. Gradually, more of these operations were privatized. For one thing, the activities of the Gemeine began to decrease and not so many industries were needed to support them. The Indian Missions were de-emphasized and put under the direction of the Unity. The Children's Institutes were reduced in size until they housed only the children of missionaries. And secondly, within a few years, some of the communally run establishments began to lose money, even though they had been profitable during the Pilgergemeine years. This was especially true of the farms, but it was also true of other industries like the tannery which had always been highly profitable.[63]

Apparently it was difficult to maintain a communal spirit inside a system which was becoming privatized. Making the private economies work was the new challenge in Bethlehem. The communal workers were left out of that challenge, and the religious challenges which had motivated them during General Economy were no longer the primary focus in Bethlehem. As a result, in 1769 all the farms except one were leased to tenant farmers, and all of the industries except the mills, the store, the apothecary, and the inns were privatized.[64]

As will become clear in Chapter 3, the effects of Bethlehem's Pilgergemeine beginnings were to continue for many decades, but in 1771, the Unity declared the transition complete and set about a reorganization of Bethlehem's economy and its government in line with the agreements of the recent General Synods. These Synods marked the beginning of a major theme in the history of Bethlehem for the remainder of the eighteenth century: the control of the Unity over the details of everyday life in Bethlehem.

Following Zinzendorf's death the Moravians began to tighten their organization. While Zinzendorf was alive, their movement could be held together by his extraordinary charisma, but once he was gone, they needed to institutionalize their leadership, organize their finances, and structure their government. This step is important for any new organization, but for the Moravians it was absolutely crucial. The death of their revered leader coincided with a financial crisis that required contributions from every corner of the Moravian world if they were to survive. Because of these concerns, the primary emphasis in the Synods of 1764 and 1769 was to create a constitution, and the reorganization of the local settlements followed.[65]

In Bethlehem, the first step was a simplification and a legalization of the financial relationship between the Gemeine and the Unity. By 1771, the Unity had paid back $550,000 of its debts, but an enormous $770,000 still remained. The Unity decided that the best way to deal with the remaining debt was to make the separate settlements responsible for particular portions of it. Bethlehem's 4,000 acres of land, its buildings, and its industries had until then been considered the property of the Unity (even though they were legally held by Nathanael Seidel as Proprietor). In 1771, the "free use and disposition" of these were given to Bethlehem in the form of a perpetual lease. Their value was set at $87,000, which Bethlehem now owed to the Unity.[66] So, in effect, Bethlehem had assumed 11 percent of the Unity's debt.

In 1771, Bethlehem also acquired its first constitution—a clone of the constitutions then being established in all other Moravian settlements. The regulations concerning commercial activity and those concerning the treatment of real estate were the most important for the future of Bethlehem.

Under the new constitution, the economy was highly regulated. In order to start any sort of trade or business, a person had to obtain permission from the Gemeine. All wages and prices were to be set by the Gemeine. No monopolies were to be allowed. Furthermore, no one was allowed to buy anything outside of the Gemeine. In short, the economy may have been private in terms of ownership and responsibility, but it was not capitalistic.[67]

Real estate was also tightly controlled in the so-called lease system ("Pacht System"). People owned the buildings they lived and worked in, but the land was owned by the Gemeine and leased to the owners of the buildings. The owners could not rent or sell their buildings without the approval of the Gemeine, and if they did sell, the "limitation clause" specified that the price could not exceed the maximum amount named in the original lease.[68]

The governing system was also redesigned to be more hierarchical and therefore more centralized. Each settlement had an Elders Conference with a Gemeine Helper ("Gemeinhelfer") at its head. All the Gemeine Helpers in a Province were members of the Provincial Helpers Conference, headed by a Provincial Helper. The Provincial Helpers Conference reported to the Unity Elders Conference, the top governing body. Not only was the system hierarchical, but the members of all the Elders Conferences, including those at the local level, were appointed by the Unity Elders Conference and confirmed by the Lot.[69]

At the local level, there were other governing bodies as well: a Board of Supervisors ("Aufseher-Collegium") and a Helpers Conference, both elected by the Gemeine Council ("Gemeinrath"), which consisted of all the adult male Communicants of the Gemeine. The Board of Supervisors was in charge of all economic activity—both business and real estate—and the Helpers Conference and the local Elders Conference acted as advisors to the Gemeinhelfer, who was the head official in the local settlement. At this point women were still included in the Elders Conference as wives of ministers and as heads of the Single Sisters' and Married People's Choir organizations, but the elected officials were primarily male.[70]

Even though the local conferences had elected members, the local residents in Bethlehem had little say. Through the Gemeine Helper and the local Elders Conference the Unity had almost complete control over every conceivable aspect of life in Bethlehem: property, finance, trades, industries, education, details of community life, dress, doctrine, and missions.[71]

In the following years even the semblance of local participation vanished. In 1778, on the basis of the 1775 Synod, the Gemeine Council no longer included all male Communicant members, but only representatives from the different Choirs. It included a number of ex officio members as well as some elected members. And in 1784, the Unity did away with the office of Provincial Helper, putting the Provincial Helpers Conference directly under the control of the Unity Elders Conference. Levering suggests that the "American Provincial Government did not really exist under this arrangement. . . . What may be called the Provincial Board by courtesy was only an administrative agency of the Unity's Elders Conference, composed of appointees sent over from Europe."[72] This was the beginning of the long "close regime," as Levering has called it, a term I will continue to use through the remainder of the study. Over the years, the names of the various conferences and offices changed, but the control structure remained the same until well into the nineteenth century.

It is interesting to speculate why the Unity practiced such close supervision over the American settlements. The regulations certainly go far beyond what would have been necessary in order to organize and disperse the repayment of the debt. Spangenberg's earlier concern that people in Bethlehem might become "rich and contented" in the American economy suggests another motive as well. The controls over trade, industry, and real estate prevented the accumulation of capital through competition, monopolization, or speculation, in that way effectively separating the Moravians from the American economy. It is reasonable to assume that Spangenberg, now a leader in the Unity, encouraged these controls in order to shield American Moravians from the temptations and influences in the American economy which he felt could cause injury to their souls.

The actual effect of the supervision was quite different, because the Moravians in Bethlehem had been accustomed to independence, or to the illusion of it anyway. It is true that the Unity had ultimate control over the destiny of Bethlehem all along, as the dissolution of the Communal Economy proved. And the Unity was always closely involved in decisions like marriages and appointments of missionaries. But the opinions of Spangenberg and his advisors carried a great deal of weight with the leaders of the Unity during most of Bethlehem's years as a Pilgergemeine. Since Spangenberg understood and identified so well with the needs of Bethlehem and since he was so obviously effective as a leader, he gained the confidence of the residents of Bethlehem. During Bethlehem's Pilgergemeine years they did not feel as if their lives were being controlled by outside people who were unfamiliar with their circumstances.

A similar situation developed during the American Revolution, because the war made contacts between the Unity and the Bethlehem Moravians difficult. For three years, there were no contacts at all. So, even though the Unity intended to exercise close supervision over the activities of all Moravian settlements, the Moravians in Bethlehem were left to their own devices for a number of years. In addition, they were again blessed with a capable leader whom they trusted—Johannes Ettwein.[73] The fact that the close regime began just after this period of relative independence made it all the more difficult for the American Moravians to accept it. The contrast between that independence and the strict enforcement of the new regulations by outside appointees must have been glaring indeed.

But the effect of the Revolutionary War on the American Moravians went much deeper. It changed their attitudes in ways which the leaders of the Unity could not have predicted and did not understand.

For one thing, the Moravian Church had had a long history of pacifism, which, as we have seen, was inherited from the Unitas Fratrum. This stance was to be modified during the Revolutionary War. Actually, by the beginning of the Revolutionary War, it had already been modified to some degree. In Georgia the Moravians had refused to fight against the Spaniards, citing both their religious heritage prohibiting violence and their agreement with Oglethorpe not to have to bear arms. Later, when the

French and Indian War threatened their lives and their homes in Pennsylvania, the Moravians in Bethlehem had to reevaluate their unwillingness to bear arms, for they lived in a state governed by Quakers, who could not in good conscience bear arms to protect them as the state of Georgia had done. Consequently, they adopted a defensive stance, saying that they were not "warlike" but neither were they "quaker-like." They proceeded to build an efficient armed defense system in case of attack against their town.[74]

In 1776 the Moravians were again faced with a decision about their stance on bearing arms. By this time there was a considerable difference of opinion among the American Moravians on the issue. Some of the differences divided along generational lines. The older Moravians (especially the ministers and elders) were more inclined to be strict pacifists, whereas the younger laymen tended to feel it was their patriotic duty to bear arms. William Henry, a Moravian gunsmith in Lancaster and a Patriot, was willing to make rifles for the American troops. Even the pacifists had contrasting reasons for their stance. Johannes Ettwein was not only against personally bearing arms but against paying for substitutes as well. He felt that "resort to arms ordinarily was equivalent to murder and paying for a substitute in the militia merely hiring a murderer instead of being one." The Provincial Helpers Conference, on the other hand, supported pacifism as a matter of priorities, saying that, as missionaries, the Moravians in the exclusive settlements were already soldiers in the Heiland's army and could therefore not be allowed to fight in the Revolution since participation would distract them from their duties as missionaries. In these different opinions lay the seeds for the Pennsylvania Moravians' official abandonment of their pacifism in 1818. By the time of the Civil War, Moravians fought on both sides with no questions asked by the Church.[75]

Although Moravians differed in their opinions on non-violence during the Revolutionary War, they agreed that they must present a united front to the world, so in the end, the Moravians prohibited the members in the exclusive settlements from participation in the war and allowed it of the members of Stadtgemeinen and Landgemeinen. The exclusive settlements, however, did pledge to pay fines in lieu of appearing personally for military drills and agree to carry the public burden in other, non-military ways.[76]

The Moravians also harbored different opinions about where to place their allegiance. Some differences correlated with geographical location. The town and country congregations, being more integrated into their settings, absorbed the values around them. The congregation in New York City was decidedly Loyalist, while that in York, Pennsylvania was inclined to side with the Patriots. Since the exclusive settlements like Bethlehem were isolated, they were also more neutral, but leaned toward what has been called "passive Loyalism." They felt bound by the enduring support which they as a church had received from the British government and by the close ties they had to the Moravian community in London.[77] In line with both their pacifism and their Loyalist leanings, the Moravians in the exclusive settlements favored a diplomatic resolution to the disagreements between England and the Colonies rather than a military one.[78]

As time went on the Moravians in the exclusive settlements gradually became more pro-American, so that by the end of the war, American Moravians supported the new government.[79] In Bethlehem this growing Americanization was a response to the increased contacts with the outside world during the war. Even before the war, contacts with Bethlehem's neighbors had been increasing. This came about partly because the Moravians began to look more conventional—the dissolution of the Economy had reduced the curiosity and suspicion of outsiders. Even though the large buildings continued to look like communal dormitories, many of them were actually divided into apartments which nuclear families occupied, and individual families were responsible for their own economic well being, just as other American families were. Also, the religious practices grew more orthodox as the emphasis on the Blood and Wounds theology decreased. Furthermore, the Bethlehem Moravians' emphasis on Indian missions had always caused neighbors to distrust them. When the responsibility for Indian Missions was transferred to the Unity and the activity in that area was reduced, the neighbors' suspicions also subsided.

The Moravians themselves began to think more like their neighbors. As their missionary activity decreased, their lives grew more settled, their family life more important, and their contacts with neighbors more stable. They also became more active in the political arena—several of their men held offices in the county government.[80]

At first the war interrupted the improving relations between the people in Bethlehem and their neighbors. As the question of bearing arms arose and Bethlehem took the stance of non-participation, the old suspicions revived temporarily. Outsiders suspected that the non-violence came from a secret Loyalist stance. Bethlehem was repeatedly searched for weapons and gunpowder as a result. Furthermore, Bethlehem lay on the pathway which Pennsylvania troops traveled as they went to fight, and they resented that the Moravians were not sharing the burden.[81]

But the Moravians had promised to share the public burden in non-military ways, and soon they had their opportunity, for in December 1776, they received word that the hospital for the Continental Army was on its way. It was located in Bethlehem from December 1776 to March 1777 and again from September 1777 to April 1778. The presence of the hospital in Bethlehem caused the community considerable sacrifice. The hospital had to be located in the Single Brothers' House since that was the largest building in the town. The Single Brothers had to vacate their building, and the rest of the community had to crowd themselves to make room. Because the Single Brothers' House was not only their residence but also the location of many of their industries, their means of making a living was severely disrupted. And during the second period in the last part of 1777 and the first part of 1778, the filthy and severely overcrowded conditions in the hospital caused a typhus epidemic which spread to the Bethlehem community as well, killing many soldiers and Moravians alike. After the hospital left for good in April 1778, a bureaucratic delay prevented the return of the building to the Moravians until June. Another month was required to sanitize and repair the place. By the time the Single Brothers could reclaim their building, their lives and livelihoods had been interrupted for over one and a half years—a blow from which they never fully recovered.[82]

Through the course of the war many outsiders visited the community of Bethlehem, including a number of colonial leaders, people from the Continental Army who bought supplies from the Moravians, and the wounded soldiers who stayed in the hospital at Bethlehem. Through this intensive contact, outsiders' trust of and admiration for the Moravians greatly increased. The soldiers in the hospitals never forgot the dedication with which Johannes Ettwein ministered to the discouraged and the dying and the courage with which his nineteen-year old son helped nurse them, giving his own life to typhus in the process. And the visitors were impressed with the Moravians' piety, their educational institutions, their facilities, their industries, and their accomplishments in music and art.[83] When the war was over, many of these people took steps to develop their relationship with the people in Bethlehem further. Owners of large tracts of land tried to convince the Moravians to establish new settlements on their land, and many people encouraged them to reestablish their boarding schools so that the children of outsiders could attend. Although nothing came of the proposals to start new settlements, Bethlehem again opened a boarding school for girls, which eventually grew to well over 100 students.[84]

As their contacts with American neighbors increased, the Bethlehem Moravians also gradually began to identify with them, and as they did, they absorbed more and more of their values. The atmosphere of independence was contagious. The different American states refused to join together in a strong federation for fear of giving up local independence.

Bethlehem Moravians, too, began to argue for independence explicitly. The administrators in Bethlehem frequently complained of insubordination as the most obvious failing of their young people.[85] At the same time the exchange of people between American and European Gemeinen greatly decreased, so that European culture and values did not reinforce those of Bethlehem.[86] Thus, in the last two decades of the eighteenth century, Bethlehem was straining under opposite pressures: the strict paternal government of the Unity pushing in one direction and the "contagion" of independence in post-war America pushing in the other. Under this strain Bethlehem suffered a crisis of discipline: people attended worship services less regularly, and they used profane language which had been noticeably absent in pre-Revolutionary Bethlehem. Excessive drinking became a problem, and internal fault-finding became a fact of life in Bethlehem.[87]

These opposing forces set the stage for the problems and conflicts which characterized Bethlehem in the last part of the eighteenth century and the early part of the nineteenth. The strain affected the Single Brothers first. They were the ones who were most directly affected by the question of either bearing arms or paying the stiff fines, who were most convinced by the patriot propaganda, who had to vacate their residence to make room for the hospital, whose industries and trades were disrupted, and who were most affected by the worldly example set by the soldiers who marched through Bethlehem and stayed in the hospital. Given these experiences, the controls imposed by the Unity were hard to bear, and many young men left Bethlehem in the years following the Revolutionary War. Their numbers dwindled from 100 in 1783 to 38 in 1806. Their industries never really recovered from the disruption during the Revolution, and they began to lose money every year. They had become such a behavior problem that some among them disturbed the services in the new church across the street with their rowdiness—which also meant that they were not attending them. By 1814, their Choir house was formally disbanded.[88]

Eventually the dissatisfaction spread to other groups as well, but in contrast to the single men it was expressed not so much in behavior problems or in withdrawals from the community as in a series of conflicts.

The first of these centered on the regulations which governed the theological seminary, newly formed in 1807. The second concerned the community's reaction to the disintegration of the Single Brothers' Choir. The third involved the sale of 1,000 acres of community land which several people proposed as a way of paying Bethlehem's debts.

In all of these conflicts John Gebhard Cunow played a significant role. As the administrator of the Unity's assets in America, Cunow was a conscientious and determined man who sought to enforce the Unity's regulations to the letter, no matter what their effect in the American environment. In all the controversies he struggled against ever-growing coalitions of people advocating some action or another. It was he who nearly smothered the theological seminary with intricate regulations and who took offense when a group of men met without official sanction to discuss the situation. It was he who objected to the Gemeine's attempts to rescue the Single Brothers' Choir. And it was he who prevented the sale of Bethlehem's acreage by refusing to give his approval as administrator. It is hard to find the common thread in his stances on the different issues except that he frequently thought his opponents guilty of insubordination. He appears to have been excessively intent upon maintaining his role as an authority figure. At first he was able to convince others to join him in his position, but in the end he stood alone, abandoned even by the other members of the Provincial Board (previously the Provincial Helpers Conference).[89]

In 1817 as a response to the conflicts surfacing in Bethlehem, the Unity Elders Conference proposed a General Synod to be held in 1818. It would be the first in seventeen years. The primary concerns which the American Moravians presented to the General Synod included:

1. that the Lot not be used for marriages and that it be limited for government appointments
2. that a Gemeine be able to control its own property
3. that people be able to own the land on which their houses stood
4. that the limitation clause be eliminated
5. that members be allowed to deal with other members in civil courts of law
6. that competition among trades and businesses be permitted
7. that an individual not be allowed to hold multiple offices
8. that the Gemeine Council again consist of all adult male Communicants
9. that the Provincial Board have more authority to act on its own
10. that the Unity Elders Conference have one American member.[90]

The Synod did not agree to all these desires but enough of them were approved that the level of conflict in Bethlehem was reduced. Multiple office holding was eliminated, objectionable uses of the Lot abolished, membership in the Gemeine Council extended to all male Communicants, and the amount of commercial regulation reduced. These were immediate results of the Synod. Longer term results included the termination of Cunow as administrator and the appointment of Lewis David de Schweinitz in his place in 1822. During the next few years de Schweinitz worked with the Gemeine in Bethlehem to form a new legal arrangement between Bethlehem and the Unity. It established the Bethlehem community as actual owners of their land who could sell it as they wished.[91]

BETHLEHEM, THE PENNSYLVANIA TOWN

The Synod of 1818 and the agreements which followed it represent the end of the close regime, but the exclusive character of Bethlehem that was protected by the lease system continued a few decades longer. What would finally bring it to an end was not so much dissatisfaction from within as economic pressure from outside Bethlehem.

After the War of 1812 the American economy began to industrialize in earnest, and when the Synod relaxed control over the commercial activity of Moravian individuals, they began to participate in the general economic excitement. The area around Bethlehem was especially active. In the early 1790s a rich coal deposit had been discovered in the mountains from which the Lehigh River flowed, and in 1792 a group of men started the Lehigh Coal Company in order to mine the coal and sell it. At first the company did not grow because people could not be convinced that coal burned well. By 1820, however, people were finally learning its value, and the Lehigh Coal Company joined with the Navigation Company to form the Lehigh Coal and Navigation Company. Soon this company was transporting coal in a steady stream of barges along the Lehigh towards the Delaware River and Philadelphia.

In order to service the coal industry, better canals and railroads were built, so that by 1831 Bethlehem found itself in the middle of a complex transportation network, well connected to both Pittsburgh and Philadelphia. Bethlehem became an important stopping place along the way. Residents in Bethlehem began to participate in the general economic development both by direct investments and by establishing support industries. They built another hotel, started a retail coal and lumber operation, and expanded already existing industries.[92]

Because the economy of Bethlehem now had more ties to the regional economy, any financial crises in the region affected Bethlehem as well. Following the boom period from 1820 to 1830, a series of recessions hit Pennsylvania and the nation. People in Bethlehem who had invested heavily or expanded their businesses found themselves facing financial ruin, which in turn directly affected the finances of the Gemeine. When people no longer had the cash to buy their goods from the Gemeine, they made use of the well established credit system in Bethlehem. Many unfortunate investors also tried to bail themselves out by selling the buildings they owned, but when other Moravians could not or would not buy them, the Gemeine had to buy them instead to prevent sale to outsiders or seizure by the Sheriff. The Gemeine tried to deal with its increasing burden by selling some of its land and by selling some of the remaining industries still operated by lessees—solutions which soon reached their limit. By 1833 de Schweinitz and the Provincial Board decided that the lease system would have to be abolished as soon as the financial crisis abated. But economic panics continued through the '30s. Gradually the authorities in Bethlehem were forced to relax their restrictions on ownership, and some non-Moravians were allowed to buy property.[93]

Finally, a severe depression hit the country in 1839. It was as persistent as the Great Depression of 1929, and in Bethlehem it was made worse by a devastating flood in 1841, which destroyed many bridges (including the one across the Lehigh) and most of the industrial buildings, which had been located along the Lehigh and the Monocacy for transportation and water power. The finances of the Gemeine totally collapsed in the fall of 1842, and the authorities realized they could not wait out the situation any longer.[94]

Phillip Goepp (who had become administrator when de Schweinitz died in 1834) presided over the dismantling of the lease system. In May 1843 the Board of Supervision ("Aufseher Collegium") met to discuss a detailed committee report on the crisis. The Board unanimously accepted the proposal to abolish the lease system, and they agreed that to do so would also require the establishment of a secular government and a reorganization of the Church as well. In January of 1844 the Gemeine Council approved the decision to abolish the lease system, and immediate steps were taken to open the town of Bethlehem to non-Moravians. But because the Council could not agree on how a secular government should be organized and paid for, this step was delayed until March 1845. On Good Friday that year the residents in Bethlehem elected a burgess and other town officials to run their new government.[95]

The fact that an election and not a religious service dominated that historically most holy of days indicates the degree to which Bethlehem had changed during its first one hundred years. Bethlehem had lost its religious focus and had become a town much like many others. None were more aware of the contrast than the residents of Bethlehem themselves because ironically their appreciation for their unique past had just been rekindled in the elaborate celebration of Bethlehem's one hundredth anniversary in 1842. This awareness no doubt contributed to the crisis of identity which followed. In 1844 there were about 1,000 people in Bethlehem, and 85 percent of them were Moravians. Fifteen years later there were nearly 3,000, and only half were Moravians. Their church was just one among many in Bethlehem. And Moravians in Bethlehem knew that worldwide their church had remained small in contrast to others because the Unity had continued to limit its extension as a denomination—by 1863 there were only 20,000 Moravians in Europe and the United States and less than 100,000 worldwide. Furthermore, the residents of Bethlehem had lost their special purpose as committed communitarians supporting an extensive missionary program. In spite of their yearning for conventionality in the years before 1844, when they finally got it, they realized the extent to which they had based their understanding of themselves on their very uniqueness. For a number of years afterward the people in Bethlehem struggled with the question of who they were.[96]

During their first one hundred years the Moravians in Bethlehem had undergone many institutional changes. These, in turn, caused other changes within the tight system that Bethlehem was, altering the basic facts of life and death, the physical arrangement of the town, and the cultural norms for everyday living. Each of these other changes is described in the chapters that follow.

NOTES

1. Amedeo Molnar, "Die Böhmische Brüderunität Abriss Ihrer Geschichte," in *Unitas Fratrum: Moravian Studies,* ed. by Mari P. van Buijtenen, et al., (Utrecht: Rijksarchief, 1975) [hereafter *Unitas Fratrum*], pp. 15–17; Murray L. Wagner, *Petr Chelčický: A Radical Separatist in Hussite Bohemia* (Scottsdale, Pa.: Herald Press, 1983), pp. 29, 32, 35, 56, 150, 151.

2. Molnar, pp. 16–18, 20; Peter Brock, *The Political and Social Doctrines of the Unity of Czech Brethren in the Fifteenth and Early Sixteenth Centuries* (The Hague: Mouton & Co., 1957), pp. 46, 49, 51, 58, 59, 62, 67, 77, 79, 80, 81, 98, 101; Rudolf Říčan, *Die Böhmischen Brüder: Ihr Ursprung und Ihre Geschichte,* (Berlin: Union Verlag, 1961), p. 29; John R. Weinlick, *The Moravian Church Through the Ages* (Bethlehem, Pa.: Comenius Press), p. 35.

3. Molnar, p. 20; Brock, *Czech Brethren,* pp. 103, 121, 144, 148, 149, 160–62, 207, 241; Wagner, pp. 153, 154.

4. Molnar, p. 31; Brock, *Czech Brethren,* p. 206.

5. Molnar, pp. 20, 24, 32; Joseph Th. Müller, *Geschichte der Böhmischen Brüder,* Vol. III (Herrnhut: Verlag der Missionsbuchhandlung, 1931), pp. 292–94.

6. Adolf Vacovsky, "History of the Hidden Seed," in *Unitas Fratrum*, pp. 35, 38.

7. Vacovsky, pp. 36–38.

8. J. Taylor Hamilton and Kenneth G. Hamilton, *History of the Moravian Church* (Bethlehem, Pa.: Interprovincial Board of Christian Education, Moravian Church in America, 1967), p. 16.

9. Hamilton, *History*, pp. 17–20, 27.

10. Hamilton, *History*, pp. 29–32.

11. Hamilton, *History*, pp. 23, 24, 28.

12. Hamilton, *History*, pp. 30–31.

13. Hamilton, *History*, p. 32.

14. Hamilton, *History*, pp. 40–41.

15. Hamilton, *History*, p. 67.

16. This description was gathered from talks given by Johannes de Watteville (Zinzendorf's son-in-law) for children for their Anbeten (week 2), their Anbeten at the Ältestenfest (week 45), their Gemeintag (week 46), and their Christmas celebration (week 51). It is also based on a talk he gave for Single Sisters (week 2) and for Single Brothers (week 4) and a talk which Augustus Gottlieb Spangenberg gave for children for their Gemeintag (week 39). All the talks were given in the year 1767. (Bethlehem Moravian Archives MSS.)

17. Hamilton, *History*, pp. 52–59.

18. See Adelaid L. Fries, *The Moravians in Georgia, 1735–1740* (Raleigh, N.C.: Edwards & Broughton, 1905), for a book length description of this venture.

19. Hamilton, *History*, pp. 82–93.

20. A number of writers have held that Zinzendorf de-emphasized the painful process leading up to conversion. Hamilton says, for instance: "Zinzendorf would not concede the universal necessity of a painful struggle of repentance (*Busskampf*). Indeed he felt that no uniformity of method could be ascribed to the operations of divine grace. The *Busskampf* and *Durchbruch*, on which the Hallensians laid such stress, would be out of place in a life which, despite its sinfulness, had known the love of God as a gentle but persistent and ruling force from childhood. . . . To earnestly yearn for the mind of Christ and to covet the Christ-life was sounder evidence of conversion . . . than to be driven to a painful sifting of things lawful and unlawful." (p. 155) Other writers who make this same point include Edwin Albert Sawyer, *The Religious Experience of the Colonial Moravians, Transactions of the Moravian Historical Society,* vol. XVIII, Part I (Nazareth, Pa.: Laros Publishing Company, 1961), p. 21 and Gollin, p. 11. But whatever Zinzendorf taught, the evidence from the biographies is strong that most Bethlehem Moravians during the communal period experienced the process as painful and that the methods different people used were extremely similar. Chapter 5 describes this process in detail.

21. The material in the following pages is described more fully and documented in later chapters.

22. Erbe, p. 92.

23. James David Nelson, "Hernnhut: Friedrich Schleiermacher's Spiritual Homeland " (unpublished Ph.D. dissertation, University of Chicago, 1963), Chapters III–IX.

24. See the biographies ("Lebensläufe") written to be read at each person's funeral.

25. Gillian Gollin says the Americans did not subscribe to the Augsburg Confession, but this was a Memorial Day in Bethlehem. Gollin, p. 16; J. D. Nelson, p. 331.

26. Walter Blankenburg, "Die Musik der Brüdergemeine in Europa," in *Unitas Fratrum*, pp. 351, 360.

27. Blankenburg, p. 374.

28. Karl Kroeger, "Moravian Music in America," in *Unitas Fratrum*, p. 390.

29. Blankenburg, p. 376; Erbe, p. 94.

30. Blankenburg, p. 379.

31. Blankenburg, p. 379; Kroeger, p. 395.

32. Joseph Mortimer Levering, *A History of Bethlehem, Pennsylvania, 1741–1892, With Some Account of Its Founders and Their Early Activity* (Bethlehem, Pa.: Times Publishing Company, 1903), pp. 198, 283; Erbe, p. 93.

33. J. D. Nelson, p. 252.

34. Hamilton, *History*, pp. 39.

35. Verlass der vier Synoden der evangelischen Brüder-Unität von den Jahren 1764, 1769, 1775, und 1782, Bethlehem Moravian Archives MSS, §§575, §585.

36. Verlass, §584.

37. Verlass, §576.

38. Verlass, §585.

39. Hamilton, *History*, p. 73.

40. Erbe, pp. 19–20.

41. This taxonomy was derived from Verlass, §§61–63 and from Erbe, pp. 22–23. In later years the Pilgergemeine category was dropped, and there were only Stadtgemeine, Landgemeine, and Ortsgemeine categories.

42. Until 1748 Stadtgemeinen and Landgemeinen were not recognized in Europe. Hamilton, *History*, pp. 184–85.

43. Erbe, pp. 103, 132, 176. Gerhard Reichel, *August Gottlieb Spangenberg: Bischof der Brüderkirche* (Tübingen: Verlag von J. C. B. Mohr, 1906), pp. 140–141.

44. Hamilton, *History*, p. 88.

45. Reichel, pp. 146–50, 263–64.

46. Including nearby Nazareth and the Upper Places (Gnadenthal, Christiansbrunn and Friedensthal), the population was over 1,000. Erbe, p. 184.

47. Hamilton, *History*, pp. 94–97.

48. Hamilton, *History*, pp. 97–98.

49. Hamilton, *History*, p. 98. See Reichel, pp. 163–64 for an illuminating description of the Sifting Period.

50. Hamilton, p. 139.

51. Reichel, pp. 189–90.

52. Sawyer reports that nearly 115 people arrived from Wetteravia in 1749 and 85 more from Herrnhaag in 1751, pp. 128, 129.

53. Erbe, p. 102.

54. Erbe, pp. 104–07. Compare Jacob Sessler, *Communal Pietism Among Early American Moravians* (New York: Henry Holt and Company, 1933), p. 188. Sessler suggests that it was general prosperity which moved some people to desire less communalism, but he does not document this claim. The timing of the unrest supports Erbe's well-documented explanation.

55. See Erbe, Anlage III, for a complete copy of the agreement, pp. 166–69.

56. Erbe, pp. 115–16. Compare Sessler, p. 193, whose treatment of this period contrasts markedly with Erbe's. Sessler speculates that the war served to hold the General Economy together temporarily as the Moravians in Bethlehem joined to face the challenge of a common enemy. Erbe's solidly documented account is more convincing.

57. Erbe, pp. 128–30. It is interesting to note that the experience of other organizations supports Spangenberg's observations about the effect of size on community spirit. The Mormons have found that their wards (churches) work best when they have about 400–600 members. When they grow larger than that they routinely make two wards out of the one. The Gore Manufacturing Company has discovered the same phenomenon and keeps its plants down to that size.

58. Erbe, pp. 123, 129.

59. Verlass, §§457–58.

60. Erbe, p. 126.

61. Erbe, p. 123.

62. Erbe, p. 135.

63. Erbe, pp. 137, 147.

64. Levering, p. 413; Erbe, p. 148.

65. Levering, p. 417.

66. Erbe, p. 149; Edmund de Schweinitz, *The Financial History of the Province and Its Sustention Fund* (Bethlehem, Pa.: Moravian Publications Office, 1885), p. 19.

67. Erbe, pp. 149–50.

68. Erbe, p. 151; Levering, p. 611.

69. Levering, p. 420.

70. Levering, pp. 418–22.

71. Levering, p. 418.

72. Levering, p. 530.

73. Gollin, p. 47; See Kenneth Hamilton, *John Ettwein and the Moravian Church During the Revolutionary Period* (Bethlehem, Pa.: Times Publishing Company, 1940), for an in depth account of Ettwein's leadership of Bethlehem.

74. Otto Dreydoppel, "Rising Patriotism and Declining Pacifism," (typewritten manuscript, Moravian Archives, Bethlehem. 1975), pp. 8–9; Levering, pp. 320–30; Peter Brock, *Pacifism in the United States: From the Colonial Era to*

the First World War (Princeton, N.J.: Princeton University Press, 1968), pp. 293–96.

75. Vernon Nelson, "The Moravian Church in America," in *Unitas Fratrum,* p. 154; Dreydoppel, pp. 20–21; Brock, *Pacifism,* pp. 309, 322; Richard K. MacMaster, et al., *Conscience in Crisis: Mennonites and Other Peace Churches in America, 1739–1789, Interpretation and Documents* (Scottsdale, Pa.: Herald Press, 1979), p. 327.

76. Levering, pp. 436, 437, 441.

77. Dreydoppel, p. 17.

78. Levering, p. 434.

79. Dreydoppel, p. 23. Dreydoppel argues that the American Moravians' pacifist stance functioned as a shield behind which the American Moravians were able to sort out their allegiance.

80. Levering, pp. 427–28.

81. Levering, p. 44; Dreydoppel, p. 27.

82. Levering, pp. 451, 474–77; Dreydoppel, p. 18.

83. Levering, pp. 476, 527.

84. Levering, pp. 527–28, 534–35.

85. Levering, p. 536.

86. V. Nelson, pp. 155–57.

87. Levering, pp. 538–40, 585.

88. Erbe, pp. 153–54; Levering, p. 599.

89. Levering, pp. 586–98, 606–9.

90. Levering, pp. 611–15.

91. de Schweinitz, p. 25.

92. Levering, pp. 640–45.

93. Levering, pp. 650–52.

94. Douglass C. North, *The Economic Growth of the United States, 1790–1860* (New York: W. W. Norton & Company, 1966), pp. 200–3; Levering, pp. 672–76.

95. Levering, pp. 677–81.

96. Levering, p. 671; V. Nelson, p. 157; Ross Yates, "The Period of Questioning, Bethlehem, 1850–1876," *Transactions of the Moravian Historical Society,* XXII (1975), Part III, p. 195; *The Text-Book of the Protestant Church of the United Brethren (or Moravians) for the Year 1865* (Bethlehem, Pa.: H. Ruede, 1864), p. 146.

Chapter Two

Demographic Portrait

The Moravians invented many ways for keeping track of their membership. Each Choir made yearly catalogs of its members, giving names and ages. Births, marriages, and deaths were faithfully entered into the Church Register. The year's end "Memorabilia" reported who had transferred into or out of Bethlehem from other Moravian places during that year and who had joined the Bethlehem Congregation as converts. The Memorabilia also recorded the number of people who had left the Moravian Church, either because they were asked to go or because they wished to. Such records provide the material for a detailed demographic description which can help show the effects of institutional changes on everyday life in Bethlehem during its first century.

These records indicate that Bethlehem experienced three demographically distinct periods. The first twenty years was a period of much flux and activity. The growth rate, the net migration, and the overall level of migration were high, and marriages, births, and deaths were frequent. During this period there were more men than women,[1] and only a handful of people were over the age of 60. The early 1760s marked the beginning of a very different demographic era which lasted for half a century. Bethlehem's population abruptly stopped growing and began instead to decline. People married less frequently and later than they had before. Those who did marry gave birth to fewer children. And they experienced death at much lower rates. Migration levels both in and out declined precipitously and then stayed low. The majority of the adults were either single or widowed, and women predominated. The proportion of people over the age of 60 grew higher than in most populations. Then, beginning around 1818,[2] demographic activity increased noticeably, though it did not in general reach the levels of Bethlehem's first two decades. The rate of marriage went up, and people married at much younger ages than they had fifty years earlier, so that by the 1840s a majority of the population was married. Children were born at significantly higher rates, and people died more frequently. The growth rate and overall migration increased. The population again became slightly younger, and the proportion of men began to grow, although women were still in the majority by 1843. These three distinct demographic periods correspond closely to distinct epochs in Bethlehem's history. The active demographic period at the beginning matches the dates of the General Economy. The long period of demographic decline encompasses the period of transition to a nuclear family economy, the years of the American Revolution, and the period of the close regime (1784–1818). And the demographic quickening at the end of Bethlehem's first century corresponds quite well to the period after the Synod of 1818 when the close regime came to an end.

Measures of growth, migration, marriage, fertility, mortality, and population composition all require good estimates of population. For the crude rates, which are based on the entire population, the task is relatively easy for Bethlehem, since the Memorabilia, which report the number of people in each Choir, were produced regularly and accurately. However, the more sensitive demographic measures need population bases which are age and sex specific. These are more difficult to procure since the Choir catalogs which give the names and ages of all Choir members are missing for many of the years during Bethlehem's first century. Estimates of the age specific populations therefore require interpolations between the years for which catalogs exist.

The figures for the first years are the most difficult to manage. As a new settlement, Bethlehem needed some time to develop routines, so its census procedures were not practiced consistently until the mid-1750s. Also, the organizational boundaries of the Bethlehem community changed dramatically, so that membership lists from the early years cannot be easily compared with those of later years. At its inception, Bethlehem was a Pilgergemeine with two types of members: the Pilgrims proper, who lived away from Bethlehem for extended missionary work, and the members of the Hausgemeine, who resided in Bethlehem to support the Pilgrims. As a result many people who were intimately associated with Bethlehem rarely ever resided there. In addition Nazareth functioned as a sister settlement to Bethlehem. With its larger tract of land, Nazareth emphasized agricultural pursuits, whereas Bethlehem was the locus of craft work. The two settlements shared residential facilities for many years. Nazareth housed the Single Sisters for a few years and the Widows for a more extended time.

The Nursery was located in Nazareth for a while, and later Nazareth Hall became the main school for the boys. The Upper Places—Christiansbrunn (a settlement for Single Brothers), Gnadenthal, and Friedensthal—were adjuncts to Nazareth. At various times boarding schools were operated in Emmaus and Friedrichstown to serve all the Pennsylvania Moravian settlements. Residents from Bethlehem were moved back and forth from one of these closely associated settlements to another. Though these settlements had their own names and their distinct histories, they functioned during the first two decades as one extended community, and their residents conceived of them as parts of a whole. The early entries in the Church Register included baptisms, marriages, and deaths from all these communities, and the early census catalogs include all their residents, sometimes organized by place of residence, but more often not. By the end of the 1760s Bethlehem had become a distinct community in its own eyes, and the congregation records from then on concern Bethlehem almost exclusively.

For this study I have counted only the actual inhabitants of Bethlehem as community members, even for the early years when Bethlehem functioned as a sub-community. In this way the different demographic faces of Bethlehem through the first century of Bethlehem's existence can legitimately be compared. Bethlehem's relationship to the larger Moravian world is still reflected in the results of the demographic analysis at several points, particularly in the sections on migration and population composition.

COMPOSITION

Keeping those qualifications in mind, let us begin the demographic analysis by looking at the composition of Bethlehem's population from 1744 to 1843. Table 2-1 shows the composition of Bethlehem's population according to age, sex, and marital status. If the age composition of today's world population is any guide, Bethlehem's age distribution was imbalanced in one way or another for all of its first nine decades. During the first decade people over 60 were greatly underrepresented whereas people between the ages of 20 and 59 were considerably overrepresented. The 5–19 age group was also smaller in Bethlehem than in the world population. This age profile befits a newly constructed community like early Bethlehem. The first Moravian ships—the "Sea Congregations"—came heavily laden with young adult colonizers, many of them about to be or just married. These

53

TABLE 2-1 Population Composition in Percentages*

	1744 to 1753	1754 to 1763	1764 to 1773	1774 to 1783	1784 to 1793	1794 to 1803	1804 to 1813	1814 to 1823	1824 to 1833	1834 to 1843	World population today
AGE GROUPS											
% 0–4	14	10	6	6	7	9	8	9	12	13	14
% 5–19	25	39	30	23	21	26	28	27	28	32	32
% 20–59	60	50	57	58	51	48	47	45	45	45	47
% 60+	1	2	6	13	21	17	18	20	16	10	7
	100	101	99	100	100	100	101	101	101	100	100
SEX GROUPS (total population)											
% Female	48	53	62	58	60	63	62	62	61	58	
% Male	52	47	38	42	40	37	38	38	39	42	
	100	100	100	100	100	100	100	100	100	100	
Sex ratio	1.08	0.89	0.61	0.72	0.67	0.59	0.61	0.61	0.64	0.72	
SEX GROUPS (adults)											
% Female	44	44	57	60	64	67	65	66	62	62	
% Male	56	56	43	40	36	33	35	34	38	38	
	100	100	100	100	100	100	100	100	100	100	
Sex ratio	1.27	1.27	0.75	0.67	0.56	0.49	0.54	0.52	0.61	0.61	
MARITAL STATUS GROUPS											
% Married	48	40	37	37	37	41	46	49	55	58	
% Single	46	54	54	51	49	41	37	35	28	26	
% Widowed	5	6	9	11	14	18	17	17	16	16	
	99	100	100	99	100	100	100	101	99	100	
% Mar+Wid	54	46	46	49	51	59	63	65	72	74	
% Sng+Wid	52	60	63	63	63	59	54	51	45	42	

*The figures are based on person-years.

young people and their babies made up nearly three-quarters of Bethlehem's population during that first decade. Since such a large portion of the population was young adults, it is remarkable that they did not produce more children than they did. The reason is that even during this first decade nearly half the adults between 20 and 59 were single.

By the fifth decade (1784–93), the age distribution was exceptional in different ways. The portion of adults under 60 had begun to shrink to a more normal size, but the number of minors had shrunk also in response to the declining rates of marriage and low fertility levels mentioned earlier, so there were still many fewer children than would be expected when half the population was young adults. Adults over 60 now represented over one-fifth of the total population, about three times as much as in today's world population. Not only did the ranks of older people swell because the original large portion of colonizers had now grown old, but also because Widows often came to Bethlehem from other Moravian settlements to live out their years in the specially built Widows' House.

Bethlehem's age distribution for the tenth decade fits that of today's world population remarkably well. Since the marriage rate had increased, the portion of children matched well with that of young adults for the first time in Bethlehem's first century. Older people were still slightly overrepresented, but 38 percent of them were Widows, many of whom had lived their married lives in other Moravian settlements. If we were to exclude these extra Widows, Bethlehem's population composition figures would match that of today's world population even more closely.

Men predominated for one or two decades after Bethlehem was founded, but the population of women grew rapidly, so that by 1764 they held a large majority which they maintained throughout the rest of Bethlehem's first century. The female margin is particularly noticeable among adults. There were nearly twice as many women as men for the forty years from 1784 to 1823. Even for the ninth and tenth decades women outnumbered men by more than 3 to 2, but the male proportion was gradually increasing. The preponderance of women for most of the ten decades was a product of the men's higher tendency to leave Bethlehem and their lower tendency to move into Bethlehem for most of the long middle period.

Unusually large portions of adults in early Bethlehem were single. During the first decade, from 1744 to 1753, the proportion of Single People was already nearly equal to the proportion of Married People, but for the next forty years, staying single was the dominant way of life. Less than two-fifths of the adult population were married, whereas half the adults were single. By the early 1800s the proportion of Married People had

TABLE 2-2 Marital Status in Percentages

	1744 to 1753	1754 to 1763	1764 to 1773	1774 to 1783	1784 to 1793	1794 to 1803	1804 to 1813	1814 to 1823	1824 to 1833	1834 to 1843
MEN										
% Married	42	35	43	46	50	58	67	71	75	78
% Single	53	58	51	48	43	35	27	22	19	16
% Widowed	4	7	6	7	7	7	7	7	6	6
	99	100	100	101	100	100	101	100	100	100
% Sng+Wid	57	65	57	55	50	42	34	29	25	22
WOMEN										
% Married	56	45	33	32	28	32	35	37	44	47
% Single	38	50	57	54	50	45	42	41	33	32
% Widowed	6	5	10	14	22	24	22	22	23	22
	100	100	100	100	100	101	99	100	100	101
% Sng+Wid	44	55	67	68	72	69	64	63	56	54

begun to increase and that of Single People to decrease. This new trend continued steadily, until by the tenth decade little more than a fourth of the adults were single while nearly three-fifths were married. Interesting as those numbers are, they predict little of anyone's actual circumstance, since the marital patterns of men and women contrasted so sharply (see Table 2-2). Women were more likely to be unattached than married for all decades except the first, especially from 1764 to 1803 when more than two-thirds of the women were single or widowed. From that point on, the portion of Married Women increased, but even by 1843 it had not yet reached one-half. In contrast, from 1754 on, the portion of Married Men increased steadily, until by the sixth decade nearly three-fifths of men were married, and by 1843 almost four-fifths were. With the exception of the first two decades, women were much less likely than men to be married.

The proportion of unattached adults is of course larger than that of Single People since Widowed People are included; furthermore, the proportion of adults who were single at any one time is larger than of adults who stayed single for their entire lives. Complete and certain information about how many adults in Bethlehem never married is difficult to obtain because migration complicates the picture. However, since no one married for the first time after the age of 60, the percentage of Single People among adults over 60 can give an estimate of the proportion in the total population of people who never married.[3] Just how good an estimate depends partly

TABLE 2-3 Percentages of People ≥60 Who Were Single

	1744 to 1753	1754 to 1763	1764 to 1773	1774 to 1783	1784 to 1793	1794 to 1803	1804 to 1813	1814 to 1823	1824 to 1833	1834 to 1843
WOMEN*	0	0	3	13	16	16	32	38	28	16
			≥20	≥30	≥40	≥50	≥60			
				≥20	≥30	≥40	≥50	≥60		
					≥20	≥30	≥40	≥50	≥60	

Peak period of decision about marriage

	1744 to 1753	1754 to 1763	1764 to 1773	1774 to 1783	1784 to 1793	1794 to 1803	1804 to 1813	1814 to 1823	1824 to 1833	1834 to 1843
MEN	0	0	11	22	27	20	15	13	4	0
	≥30	≥40	≥50	≥60						
		≥30	≥40	≥50	≥60					
			≥30	≥40	≥50	≥60				

Peak period of decision about marriage

*The percentages given for women actually underrepresent the extent to which being single was a way of life for women, since Widows from other Moravian settlements came to reside in Bethlehem and inflated the number of women who married at some time in their lives.

on the way it is used. Table 2–3 shows a decided rise to a crest and a subsequent decline in the percentages of both men and women over 60 who were single. Such crests suggest that remaining single was a viable alternative to marriage for only a few decades. But which decades? Table 2-3 treats people over 60, not people at the usual age for marrying. The men represented in this chart made their decision whether or not to marry some thirty years previously and the women about forty years before.[4] So these crests are parts of waves which began much earlier. Figure 2–1 moves the waves back in time to the points when they began. It suggests that the men most frequently decided to remain single during the period of the General Economy, especially during its second decade. From that point on, remaining single was less and less attractive to men, until by the early 1800s virtually no men chose the single life. The peak for women was two decades later than for men and was more intense.[5] A number of biographies tell of Married Sisters' original reticence to marry. After 1783, according to Figure 2-1, the single life began to lose its lure for women also, but it is difficult to say if or when it vanished completely. If the decline continued, even at a much shallower slope, then women would have ceased

WOMEN

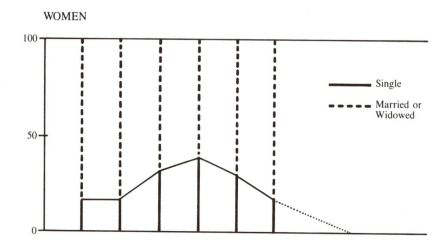

MEN

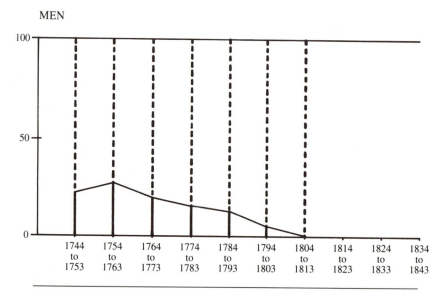

FIGURE 2-1. Estimated peaks of decisions to remain single in percentages

to choose the single life in favor of marriage by the 1840s. Purely in terms of numbers, that choice was by that time possible for most women, because the sex ratio of Single People between the ages of 20 and 35[6] had risen radically from less than .50 in about 1815 to .93 and .94 in 1825 and 1844 respectively. Evidence for the growing interest in marriage among women is the several cases of marriage between Moravian women and outsiders, enough to compensate for whatever imbalance still remained in the sex ratio. Whether or not the single life actually died out for women, it certainly did for men; for both sexes, Bethlehem had changed during the course of a century from a community in which remaining single was a viable option to one in which marriage was increasingly emphasized and singlehood rejected.

Single men and women continued to be classified in catalogs as members of the Single People's Choirs, but the function of the Choirs had changed. Initially they were institutions which offered a collective religious, social, and economic life to people who chose to stay single, but by 1843 they represented little more than a means of identifying the people who had attained adult status but who had not yet married. This was particularly true of the Single Brothers' Choir. The official record of events in that Choir, the Single Brothers' Diary, ended in the year 1817, and by the end of Bethlehem's first century, 98 percent of the Single Brothers were below the age of 29, the third quartile age at first marriage. Their average age was only 22. By 1843, the Single Sisters' Choir had not transformed quite so completely, but the process was underway. The Sisters stopped keeping their diary in 1841, and the percentage of Sisters under the third quartile marriage age increased from 26 percent in 1800 to 48 percent in 1843. Their average ages declined from 43 to 36 over the same period.

The changing patterns in the composition of Bethlehem's population quite clearly reflect the changes of policy and focus during Bethlehem's first one hundred years. The early predominance of young adults reflects the initial need for strong, energetic people to build the town of Bethlehem and to establish a network of missions. The unusually large percentage of Single People during that same period reflects the almost monastic focus of Bethlehem's first years. The gradual change from a unique Heiland-centered community to a more conventional one centered on family life is reflected in Bethlehem's shrinking single and growing married population.

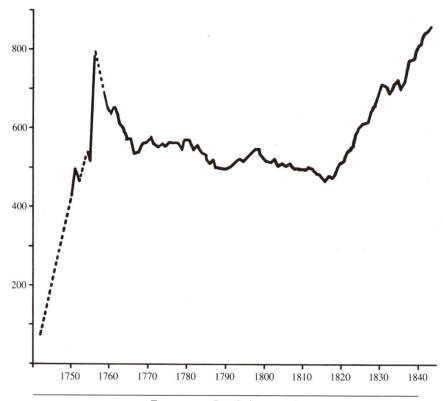

FIGURE 2-2. Population growth

GROWTH

Along with its adjunct colony Nazareth, Bethlehem was the first permanent Moravian colony in North America. As a result, Bethlehem was the primary receiver and processor of Moravian immigrants to America and experienced a remarkable growth in population during the first twenty years as a result (see Figure 2-2). The really extreme growth in 1756 was the result of the influx of refugees to Bethlehem following the Indian attack on Gnadenhütten at the beginning of the French and Indian War. During that single year the population in Bethlehem rose from just over 500 to almost 800, an increase of more than 50 percent. The Bethlehem Diary makes it clear that this sudden growth strained Bethlehem's economy almost to the breaking point and that Bethlehem played a reluctant though responsible host to all these unexpected guests. By 1760 most refugees had returned home, and the population in Bethlehem had decreased to a more manageable 630 or so. From that point the population continued to increase for just one more year, reaching 659 before beginning an insistent decline. Even if we ignore the temporary peak caused by the rush of refugees to Bethlehem during the 1750s wars with Indians, and assume instead that the population reported in 1761 represented the growth peak of the permanent population, Bethlehem had grown enormously. In less than 20 years the population had increased by 800 percent from just over 70 in 1742 to 659 in 1761.

The year 1761 marks a dramatic reversal in Bethlehem's population growth, the beginning of a long decline in population which lasted over half a century. By 1766 Bethlehem Moravians numbered only around 535—a drop of nearly 20 percent in 5 years, and for the next half century the population continued to dwindle until it was down to just over 470 inhabitants. The year 1818 again marked a watershed in the history of population growth in Bethlehem, for suddenly the decline was reversed and this little village began to grow steadily until by 1843 its local catalogers reported a population of 865.[7] Within these three decades Bethlehem had grown by 184 percent.

During its first century, then, Bethlehem's population growth is characterized by three distinct periods: 1742–1761 shows initial rapid growth, 1762–1817 insistent decline, and 1818–1844 steady growth. In order to understand the fluctuations in Bethlehem's population growth let us turn to the events which, in the demographic sense, cause fluctuations in growth—natural increase and net migration.

Table 2-4 treats these events for each decade of Bethlehem's first century. The rate of natural increase is the crude birth rate minus the crude death rate, and the rate of net migration is the rate of immigration minus the rate of emigration.[8] Both natural increase and net migration paralleled Bethlehem's population curve. During the initial twenty-year period of rapid growth and during the thirty years of steady growth at the end of Bethlehem's first century, both natural increase and net migration were comparatively high. In contrast they were relatively low during the long period when Bethlehem gradually shrank.[9]

However, net migration varied much more radically than natural increase. For this reason the course of population growth was affected more heavily by changes in net migration than by changes in natural increase for most of Bethlehem's first century. During the first two decades, net migration was high enough that natural increase added or subtracted but a small

TABLE 2-4 Components of Population Growth
(rates in numbers per thousand)

	Natural increase A	Net migration B	Growth C = A+B
1744–1753	6	106	112
1754–1763	−1	17	16
1764–1773	−3	−5	−8
1774–1783	−6	3	−3
1784–1793	−8	5	−3
1794–1803	−3	−1	−4
1804–1813	−7	4	−3
1814–1823	−5	18	13
1824–1833	1	18	19
1834–1843	8	12	20
PERIOD AVERAGES OF DECADE RATES			
1744–1763	2.4	61.9	64.0
1764–1813	−5.2	1.1	−4.2
1814–1843	1.5	15.9	17.3

increment. During the next 50 years (or the long period of gradual decline) the absolute values of net migration dropped within range of those for natural increase, so that the negative values for natural increase showed their effect on population growth. From 1814 to 1833 net migration climbed for a second time to a relatively high level, again masking any effect that natural increase had. During the final decade of this study natural increase was high enough to contribute significantly to a high growth rate, but with that exception, migration was the primary vehicle by which Bethlehem grew larger during its first century.

Population growth was clearly affected by the changing socio-economic conditions in Bethlehem. The healthy growth during the General Economy and after the end of the close regime reflect the vitality of those periods, whereas the long decline in between suggests trauma for the period in between.

MIGRATION

Net migration gives only the amount by which immigration exceeds emigration or vice versa. It tells little about the levels of migration: a migration of 1,000 into Bethlehem and 950 out would yield the same net migration as 100 in and 50 out. However, estimates are much easier to obtain for net migration than for immigration and emigration. Whereas net migration can be calculated indirectly by simple arithmetic using Bethlehem's periodic dependable population counts and registrations of birth and death, actual migration levels must be determined from records like Bethlehem's year-end Memorabilia. Although these annual reports are a rich source of migration data, they are not complete. The records for the first decade were so incomplete as to be entirely unusable. For that reason, the migration analysis which follows covers only the nine decades from 1754 to 1843. Even the second decade shows an average error of 7 percent in the reporting of migration, although much of that error stemmed from the mid-1750s, when hundreds of refugees were moving into and out of Bethlehem. Excluding years 1756–58 reduces the average error to 2 percent. After that the average error falls to 1 percent or less per decade for the rest of Bethlehem's first century.[10]

There is no obvious bias in the omissions. The Moravians were just as willing, for instance, to report that someone wanted to leave the church or that someone was asked to leave as to report that someone had joined the church. They were equally careful to mention which women came or left as which men did, and which children moved in or out as which adults. It seems safe to assume that the omissions were random. So although the migration records were not complete enough to use in the analysis of population growth they are good enough and bias-free enough to give a rough idea of the amount of migration into and out of Bethlehem, and they cast considerable light on the nature of that migration: who moved and why.

According to the Memorabilia, nearly a thousand people moved into and out of Bethlehem during each of the second and third decades. For the next three decades, migration decreased by nearly half and by 1814–23 to little more than one-third the initial levels. Migration then accelerated rapidly until the tenth decade (1834–43) when well over 500 people came or went (see Table 2-5).

Because the records are incomplete, the relationships between emigration and immigration can be indicated in only the roughest manner. For the five decades from 1764 to 1813 people moved in and out of Bethlehem

TABLE 2-5 Migration to and from Bethlehem*

	1754 to 1763	1764 to 1773	1774 to 1783	1784 to 1793	1794 to 1803	1804 to 1813	1814 to 1823	1824 to 1833	1834 to 1843
TOTAL MIGRATION	920	937	486	489	469	389	334	428	533
NET MIGRATION	111	-30	7	25	-4	18	91	120	90
IMMIGRATION/EMIGRATION									
Raw scores									
Immigration	516	454	247	257	233	204	213	274	312
Emigration	405	484	240	232	237	186	122	154	222
Percentages									
Immigration	56	48	51	53	49	52	64	64	58
Emigration	44	52	49	47	51	48	36	36	42
Rates per thousand residents in Bethlehem									
Immigration	82	83	43	49	46	40	43	44	45
Emigration	64	88	42	45	47	37	25	25	32
CONVERSION, WITHDRAWAL, AND TRANSFER									
Components of immigration									
Percent Conversion	22	5	11	1	9	6	34	23	25
Percent Transfer In	78	95	89	99	91	94	66	77	75
Components of emigration									
Percent Withdrawal	8	11	11	14	20	29	35	17	23
Percent Transfer Out	92	89	89	86	80	71	65	83	77
Total transfer migration	802	857	530	467	395	313	223	326	356
Geographical spread of transfer migration									
Percent Midstates	72	74	81	88	81	83	71	86	81
Percent South	8	6	4	1	3	5	12	4	7
Percent Elsewhere in W. Hemisphere	11	11	9	5	10	11	7	8	4
Percent Europe	8	8	7	5	7	(.3)	10	2	8

*See note 8, p. 84, and Appendix II, pp. 257–58, for an explanation of sources and computations.

in approximately equal numbers. But significantly more people moved into Bethlehem than out during the second decade (1754–63) and the eighth, ninth, and tenth decades (1814–43). The immigration/emigration ratio for those decades was 1.27, 1.75, 1.78, and 1.41, respectively.

Why did people come to Bethlehem, and why did they leave? This question can be answered to some degree by distinguishing between conversion and withdrawal on the one hand and transfer between Bethlehem and other Moravian settlements on the other. During the second decade (1754–63), converts accounted for 22 percent of all immigrants to Bethlehem, and during the last three decades (1814–43), converts ranged between 23 and 34 percent of immigrants. By contrast, for the 50 years between those two periods converts never were more than 11 percent and averaged only 6 percent of immigrants. The policy of close control by the Unity during the middle period did not encourage or attract outsiders to Bethlehem, whereas the vitality of the first and last periods did to a significant degree.

Withdrawals from the church averaged only 11 percent of total emigration for the first four decades, but then increased gradually until by 1814–23 they had reached a substantial 35 percent. Although withdrawals dropped during the ninth and tenth decades, a significant percentage of emigrants continued to leave the church. The average for the last 50 years was 25 percent.

It is important to bear in mind that for no decade after 1754 did converts constitute more than 1.4 percent of the decade population and that people who withdrew never made up more than 1 percent of the decade population. Nevertheless the percentages given in the previous paragraphs indicate that religious appeal contributed considerably to immigration at the beginning of Bethlehem's first century and at its end, and that religious disagreement or indifference accounted for a significant portion of emigration from 1794 onward.

The overwhelming majority of migrants did not join the church or leave it, but simply transferred church membership between Bethlehem and other Moravian settlements. An average of 84 percent of all immigrants and 81 percent of all emigrants were transferees. This kind of migration fluctuated greatly during the nine decades considered here. For each of the two decades from 1754–73 approximately 800 such migrants came or left. Never again during the century of this study did transfer migration approach those levels. It fell to 530 the next decade (1774–83) and dwindled to a low of 223 by 1814–23. During the ninth and tenth decades movement between Bethlehem and other Moravian settlements climbed until it reached 356.[11]

The long period of gradually decreasing migration between Bethlehem and other congregations reflects the fact that Bethlehem's role in the Moravian world had changed. Initially Bethlehem had been the psychological and physical locus of activities in North America. Missionaries identified Bethlehem as home, Bethlehem was the mother of many of the younger North American Moravian settlements, and Bethlehem was the clearing house for many Moravian immigrants from Europe who settled in other places, all activities which necessitated much coming and going. Bethlehem had originally been conceived as a center of religious service, not as a place for people simply to establish themselves. As the Unity developed different needs, however, Bethlehem ceased to play such a central religious role, with the result that residents came increasingly to identify Bethlehem as home and to focus on local needs. This change acted to diminish the opportunity or need for movement in and out of Bethlehem, a fact which was naturally echoed in the migration statistics. There is as yet no obvious explanation for the subsequent rise in the number of transfers.

On the average, near 80 percent of the transfer migration in and out of Bethlehem concerned Moravian settlements close by in Pennsylvania and in the neighboring states of New York, New Jersey, and Maryland. In contrast, movement between Bethlehem and more distant Moravian places—in North Carolina, elsewhere in the Western Hemisphere (most notably the West Indies), and in Europe—each averaged 9 percent or less for the ninety years considered here. If reliable migration data had survived for the years 1742–53, the statistics would have been more heavily dominated by Europeans, since Bethlehem and Nazareth were the first permanent Moravian settlements in North America. But by the second decade of existence, Bethlehem had ceased to depend on migration to and from Europe and had developed instead a remarkably stable migratory network, with settlements located no more than two or three days away by wagon.

Males and females contributed to migration in and out of Bethlehem in distinctive ways (see Figures 2-3 and 2-4). Males left Bethlehem for other Moravian settlements at higher rates than did females during each of the nine decades, although as the years went by the differences diminished markedly. This change was caused not by any rise in female transfer rates, but by a persistent decrease in the male rates until they approached female rates. Female transfer rates were in fact also decreasing, though less rapidly than male rates, and the two rates have a high positive Pearson corre-

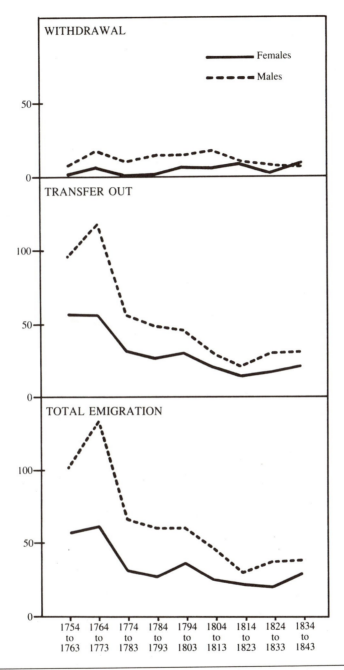

FIGURE 2-3. Emigration rates by gender per thousand

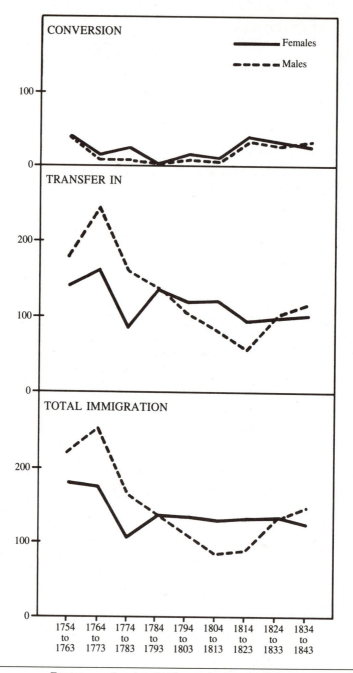

FIGURE 2-4. Immigration by gender in raw numbers

lation (.98). Apparently the tendency for Bethlehem to find an increasingly local focus affected the rates at which both men and women left Bethlehem, though the effect was greater on men than on women. (Women had always been less apt to leave Bethlehem for other Moravian settlements than men had been.)

Males also withdrew from the church at higher rates than females did. The only exception to this rule was the tenth decade, when females left the church just slightly more frequently than males, but since withdrawal in general accounts for only a small portion of emigration this small female majority was not enough to reverse male predominance in overall emigration for that decade. The result was that male emigration consistently exceeded female emigration for every decade of Bethlehem's first century.

The patterns of female and male participation in immigration were less consistent than those for emigration, but they were nonetheless distinct. Women dominated transfer immigration for three decades from 1794 to 1823, while men dominated at the beginning of the one hundred years and at its end.[12] The middle section of Figure 2-4 suggests an explanation. Women continued to transfer into Bethlehem in more stable numbers than did men throughout the century. The female range was 77, whereas the male range was 186. Women were drawn to Bethlehem by the relatively constant and unique social and economic support which Bethlehem offered to women who were alone either because they never married or because they had been widowed. Male transfer into Bethlehem varied radically and in response to Bethlehem's economic inversions. Men transferred into Bethlehem when the authorities called upon them to help realize economic transformations or when economic opportunity lured them.

For most of Bethlehem's first century, religious conversion was more likely an avenue of entry into Bethlehem for women than for men. From 1754 to 1833, 58 percent of the converts were women. From 1834 to 1843, more men converted than women, but in the absence of figures beyond this time it is not clear whether this was a temporary aberration or the beginning of a new trend.

Women and men were apparently subject to the same encouragements and limitations on conversion. The ups and downs of male and female conversion parallel each other to a marked degree, and the correlation is .89. In contrast, the withdrawal rates for the two sexes correlate almost not at all (.01). The different decision procedures for withdrawal and conversion suggest a reason for the contrast: withdrawals can result from the decisions of individuals to leave, whereas conversions require not only the consent of the individuals converting but of the organization accepting

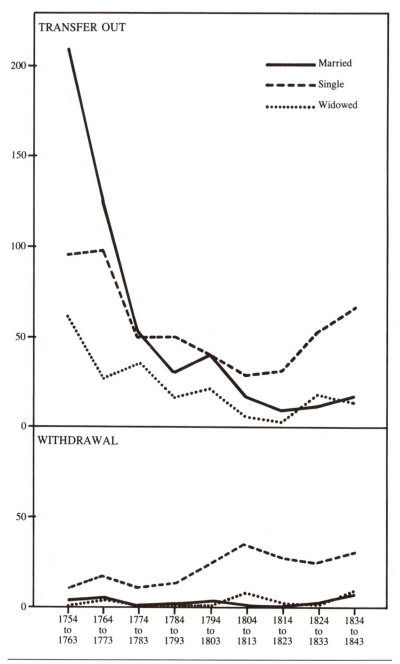

FIGURE 2-5. Emigration rates by marital status per thousand

them. Thus church policy could affect the rates of both female and male conversion and mask, to a certain degree, differences in predilection.

Marital status also affected a person's tendency to migrate in or out of Bethlehem. Initially, Married People emigrated to other Moravian settlements at much higher rates than Single or Widowed People, because of Moravian missionary policy (see Figure 2-5). During the period when Bethlehem functioned as a Pilgergemeine under the General Economy, many Bethlehem residents were called to missionary posts. Moravians required that "Pilgrims" (missionaries) be married so that husband and wife could work together and yet each minister to members of his or her own sex. Pilgrims were therefore almost always married. People who were widowed or single were more likely to remain in Bethlehem and play a supporting role as a member of the Hausgemeine, although some of them accompanied missionaries, to play that role at the missionary post. For this reason during the early period when missionary activity was Bethlehem's main function, *all* of the emigration rates were higher than they were at any subsequent point up to 1814. By the time Bethlehem's first century ended, Single People were more apt to move to other Moravian settlements than were Married People, who by then were focusing on making Bethlehem work as a community to live in rather than a missionary center to serve from. The withdrawal rates of Married People were consistently lower than those for Single People. Marriage ties increased a person's commitment to the church and made withdrawal less likely.

Of the immigrants who came to Bethlehem from other Moravian settlements a majority were either single or widowed for every decade except the ninth, when slightly less than half were single or widowed (see Figure 2-6). This may be because Bethlehem played a unique role among the Moravian settlements located in and around Pennsylvania. Built originally to accommodate the various Choirs in separate living quarters, Bethlehem found it comparatively easy to house Single and Widowed People, even after the General Economy was dissolved. Because of this, unmarried people found their way to Bethlehem from other Moravian settlements fairly consistently throughout the nine decades.

From 1754 until 1793, almost all the people who moved into Bethlehem as converts were single or widowed, but from that point on, nearly half to more than half of the converts were Married People. The growing emphasis on family life plus the economic upswing after 1818 not only encouraged Bethlehem residents to marry, but also attracted outsiders who were already married into the Moravian fold.

Although variations in net migration accounted for most of the

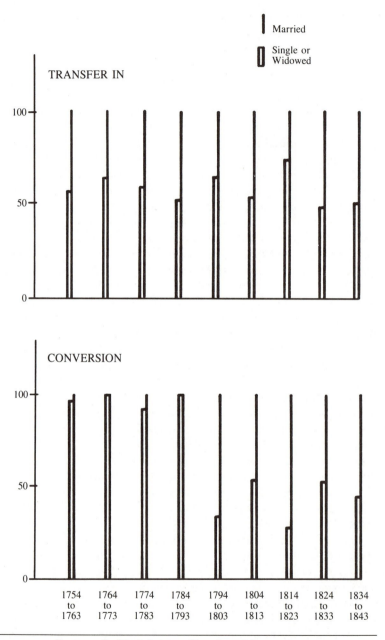

FIGURE 2-6. Marital status of immigrants in percentages

changes in Bethlehem's pattern of growth, Table 2-4 shows that natural increase also reflected the three distinct population growth periods. Let us now turn to the demographic agents of natural increase: marriage, birth, and death.

The general marriage rate in Bethlehem began at a relatively high level during the first decade, dropped precipitously into the third and fourth decades, and then climbed gradually for the remaining decades (see Table 2-6). The thorough-going adjustments that these rates imply for individual lives are apparent in the separate rates for men and women. The women who lived in Bethlehem during the first decade were eight times as likely to marry as their daughters twenty or thirty years later. The male rate dropped over the same period, but not as steeply. Bethlehem's first men were twice as likely to marry as were their sons.[13] By 1843 the female rates had more than doubled and the male rates had quadrupled from the lows of the 1770s.

One explanation for the initial peak and the subsequent drop is simply that the colonizing population was composed of a higher proportion of adults in the prime marriage ages than was the case later. But the fact that marriage rates rose steadily after the '70s (when the proportion of young adults alone could not explain the difference) reflects the increasing support for nuclear family life.

Age at marriage also fluctuated. During the same decades when the marriage rates were low, those people who did marry waited until very late in life to do it. Even during the first decade the average age at first marriage for men and women was 33 and 28 respectively—six to eight years higher than was usual during the colonial period.[14] But twenty to thirty years later people were waiting even longer to marry—the women until about 30 and the men until they were around 40. By the end of Bethlehem's first century, men and women alike married in their mid-twenties. Within three generations the average marriage age had decreased by 7 years for women and 17 years for men.

The community control over marriage is often cited as the major deterrent to marriage before 1818. However, the rate of marriage was higher and the age at marriage lower before the dissolution of the General Economy than they were afterward, even though community controls ex-

TABLE 2-6 Marriage, Birth, and Death in Bethlehem

	1744 to 1753	1754 to 1763	1764 to 1773	1774 to 1783	1784 to 1793	1794 to 1803	1804 to 1813	1814 to 1823	1824 to 1833	1834 to 1843
GENERAL MARRIAGE RATES—marriages per 1000 marriageable people aged 20–59										
Total population	76	41	23	18	29	33	33	40	56	48
Female population	207	103	37	27	39	44	44	53	77	60
Male population	119	69	59	57	114	132	130	161	203	238
AGE AT FIRST MARRIAGE										
Women	28	29	29	31	29	28	29	24	24	25
Men	33	38	41	39	34	34	31	25	24	27
BIRTH RATES										
Crude birth rates	60	21	13	13	16	21	18	22	30	37
General fertility rates—births per 1000 women aged 20–49										
All women	215	105	53	48	63	118	105	109	165	172
Married women	360	225	216	195	242	296	222	228	307	311
DEATH RATES										
Crude death rates	50	22	17	18	24	25	25	27	29	22
COMPARISON OF BIRTH AND DEATH RATES										
20 Year crude birth rates	34		13		19		20		30	
20 Year standardized death rates	35		21		18		20		23	

isted throughout. The economic troubles and the social adjustments which followed the dissolution must have made people reluctant to marry.

BIRTH

The unusually large variations in both the rates of marriage and the average ages at first marriage help to explain the fluctuations of Bethlehem's birthrate. When the marriage rate was low, the fertility rate was low, and when the marriage rate was high, so was the fertility rate (see Table 2-6). The correlation between the two variables is .95. If the average age at first marriage (especially of men) for a given decade increased, the number of fertile married years grew smaller, and the fertility rate for the next decade decreased. Correlations between average marriage age and fertility of the following decade were $-.97$ for men and $-.86$ for women. Note that the effect of increased marriage rate on fertility is almost immediate whereas the effect of increased age at marriage is not apparent until ten years or so later, when the fertility of a couple who married late in life is likely to decline. By not marrying as much and by marrying later in life, the Bethlehem Moravians were effectively limiting their birth rate during the third and fourth decades. A delay in marriage of ten years, for instance, could mean as many as 4 or 5 fewer children per family.[15]

Did the people of Bethlehem also practice more direct birth control? The evidence in Table 2-6 indicates that they probably did. When the fertility rate is computed on the basis of married women only, the fluctuating marriage rate is statistically controlled for. If there were no birth control, then approximately equal average marriage ages should have produced approximately equal married woman fertility rates, and lower average ages at marriage should have caused higher fertility rates. Neither of these conditions is met according to the figures in Table 2-6, suggesting that Bethlehem residents used some form of direct birth control. During the first, fifth, and sixth decades (1744–53, 1784–93, and 1793–1803) people married at roughly the same ages and yet the fertility rates (married women only) were 360, 242, and 296 respectively. Furthermore, people married at much younger ages during the last three decades (1814–43), but the fertility rates were lower for those decades than for the first.

DEATH

It is obvious that birth rates are apt to rise and fall with marriage rates, but it is not immediately evident that birth and death rates should correlate. For one thing, we assume that healthy, prosperous conditions produce high fertility and low mortality. We also assume that birth is more directly affected by human decision than death is. Why, then, do Bethlehem's crude birth and death rates correlate so closely (.95)? A large portion of the death rate in most societies is infant mortality, especially before the advent of pre-natal care and antibiotics. As the fertility rate goes up, so does the proportion of population in the highly susceptible first year of life. Consequently there are more deaths overall. The standardized death rate for Bethlehem (a measure which corrects for imbalances in population composition) [16] does not correlate as highly with the birth rate (.82) as the crude death rate does, a fact which supports the above hypothesis. However, even the standardized death rate shows a concave pattern over the whole century studied. Apparently other factors also contributed to the pattern. The initial high death rate is typical of immigrant populations, since people exposed to a new environment undergo a period of seasoning. As the population adjusts to the new conditions and as immigration recedes, the death rate decreases. This hypothesis can explain the extremely high initial death rates in Bethlehem and the decline after a decade or two, but what explains the rise in the 1830s and 1840s? One possibility is the increasing percentage of people over the age of 60, but the proportion of people over 60 had already grown large by 1790 when the death rate was lowest. The explanation for increasing mortality at the end of Bethlehem's first century could lie in declining health conditions, but other demographic indicators suggest an improvement in health conditions instead. Whatever the explanation, the death rate during the first decade was extremely high; during the next three it was comparatively low, and then it climbed gradually. The Bethlehem Moravians' experience of death was characterized by distinct periods just as their experience of marriage and birth was. Furthermore, the periods suggested by the rates of population growth, marriage, birth, and death match each other relatively well.

Crude death rates give only the roughest notion about the patterns of death within a population. Since death rates are important indicators of basic health in a population, it makes sense to look at mortality in some detail.

The data on mortality in early Bethlehem pose a problem. On the one hand they are detailed and accurate in the extreme. Every death which occurred in Bethlehem during the first century was duly recorded in the Church Register, including, for some periods, stillborn infants. The numbers identifying each entry correspond to numbers engraved on the tombstones. The Moravians also drew plans of their graveyard, giving the position, name, and assigned number of all deceased persons. It is clear that the statistics on death are very accurate because the plans match the Church Register entries so well.

However, accurate though the records may be, it is useless to calculate yearly mortality rates because the population of Bethlehem was so small—only about 500 people on the average or 50,000 person-years[17] over the entire century under study. Matters of chance, which for a larger population would most likely even out, greatly affected the statistics for Bethlehem. One year eight people may have died, the next year perhaps fifteen, even though the population remained stable over the two years. The figures for a given year can be entered into the demographic formulas, but the results have little meaning, for they fluctuate greatly from one year to the next. The consequence is that we cannot legitimately build a life table[18] for the Bethlehem data.

Fortunately, other less sophisticated models of mortality can identify prominent and therefore perceptible features of Moravian mortality. Though they are much less elegant than life tables, they are informative if handled carefully. (Note that in order to accumulate enough cases, the mortality data must be treated for periods of 20 years rather than 10.)

It is obvious from Figure 2-7 that mortality was extremely high during the first years in Bethlehem, that it then dropped dramatically, and that it later rose again slightly. Changing age composition caused some of this variation. During the first twenty years, 49 percent of the deaths represented children under the age of 5, an age group which in general experiences high mortality levels, and only 5 percent represented people who had reached the age of 60 or more. By the 1780s and '90s, children under 5 contributed only 13 percent and people over 60 about 56 percent to the total number of deaths (see Table 2-7).

To control for the variation in age composition, demographers use direct standardization, a procedure which establishes a standard (though arbitrary) age distribution in a hypothetical population. The overall death rate in the standard population is computed on the basis of age-specific death rates[19] equal to those in the population being studied. This procedure is usually applied to populations in different societies to compare their death rates, but it is equally useful in comparing the death rates for populations of the same society at different periods of time. The standardized

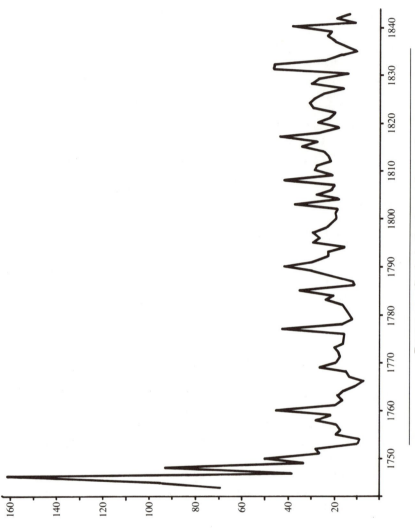

FIGURE 2-7. Crude death rates per thousand

TABLE 2-7 Percentages of Deaths for Different Age Groups

	1744 to 1763	1764 to 1783	1784 to 1803	1804 to 1823	1824 to 1843
% under 1	23	14	9	12	18
% 1–4	26	6	4	2	10
% 5–19	17	10	5	4	8
% 20–59	29	41	26	25	23
% 60+	5	29	56	57	41
% Total	100	100	100	100	100

death rates during the five twenty-year periods from 1744 to 1843 are given in Table 2-8. Considerable variation in mortality levels still remains, even though direct standardization controlled age composition. During the first twenty years in Bethlehem, Moravians of all ages endured very high mortality. For the middle sixty years, the rate settled down to a level roughly comparable to other colonies, but during the last twenty years, mortality rose slightly.

A second way of looking at mortality is to find its effect on life expectancy. For the reasons already given, it would be misleading to construct a life table for Bethlehem, but it is possible to make a rough estimate of life expectancy at birth by comparing the age-specific death rates with Coale and Demeny's Life Table Models. The labels North, South, East, and West, which Coale and Demeny use to classify their life tables, refer to areas of Europe and not to the world, since they were built from nineteenth-century mortality rates in Europe. The Northern models fit Scandinavian patterns where mortality was high in the middle-aged groups because of a great incidence of tuberculosis. Southern models describe Spain, Portugal, and Italy and are characterized by high mortality among young children. The Eastern models were drawn from mortality data in Germany, Austria, and eastern Europe, and they show high infant mortality. The Western models are conglomerates with no distinctive characteristics. Since the Moravians were predominantly German, Bethlehem's mortality statistics should best fit the Eastern models. Whether they do or not does not really matter, however, because I have used the Coale and Demeny models only as a way of estimating life expectancy. The relation between a given life table model and its associated life expectancy is purely mathematical, so if Bethlehem's age-specific death rates match a particular

TABLE 2-8 Death Rates with Direct Standardization*

	Standard popu- lation	Age-specific Death Rates by Period					Expected Deaths in Standard Population of 1,000,000				
		1744 to 1763	1764 to 1783	1784 to 1803	1804 to 1823	1824 to 1843	1744 to 1763	1764 to 1783	1784 to 1803	1804 to 1823	1824 to 1843
	A	B	C	D	E	F	A×B = G	A×C = H	A×D = I	A×E = J	A×F = K
Under 1	30	212.3	215.4	142.0	180.8	158.7	6369	6462	4260	5424	4761
1–4	112	84.1	(20.0)	(15.5)	(9.2)	33.1	9419	2240	1736	1030	3707
5–19	322	14.1	6.7	4.6	(3.6)	7.0	4540	2157	1481	1159	2254
20–59	465	15.0	12.2	12.5	13.8	13.1	6975	5673	5813	6293	6092
60+	71	(112.1)	55.3	71.4	78.6	83.1	7959	3926	5069	5581	5900
Total	1000						35262	20458	18359	19487	22714

STANDARDIZED DEATH RATES

1744–1763 = Σ G/1000 = 35.3 per thousand
1764–1783 = Σ H/1000 = 20.5 per thousand
1784–1803 = Σ I/1000 = 18.4 per thousand
1804–1823 = Σ J/1000 = 19.5 per thousand
1824–1843 = Σ K/1000 = 22.7 per thousand

*Numbers in parentheses indicate fewer than 20 deaths for the period.

Coale and Demeny model fairly closely, then the life expectancy computed from that model should predict life expectancy in Bethlehem quite well. Coale and Demeny also follow the usual demographic practice of computing separate life tables for males and females, but for the twenty-year periods we must estimate expectation of life for both sexes together, since the number of cases for each sex alone is small.

Table 2-9 juxtaposes the actual age-specific death rates in Bethlehem with those expected according to the life table models which most resemble the mortality patterns in Bethlehem. The pattern for the first period does not fit well with any Coale and Demeny life table model. Infant mortality in Bethlehem was high, suggesting an eastern pattern, but the death rate for children aged 1–4 was also high, indicating a southern pattern. Southern models fit best, and if we choose the table which matches Bethlehem's infant mortality and another one which fits Bethlehem's young child death rate, we can specify the interval within which Moravian life expectancy most likely fell. Accordingly, at birth the life expectancy for Bethlehem in the first period fell between 27.5 and 38.5, a bit closer to the lower limit than the higher one, at about 31. At age 20 a person could expect to live 36–40 more years, reaching 56 to 60. By 1764 the mortality conditions had improved markedly. For the rest of Bethlehem's first century the life expectancy at birth ranged between 45 to 52, and a 20-year old could expect to live to the age of 60 to 66.

The first period requires elaboration since age group 1–4 experienced extremely high mortality for a German population: 84.1 per thousand. During the first twenty years, the age group 1–4 represented 832 person-years and experienced 70 deaths, a good many of which were the result of severe smallpox and diphtheria epidemics. The fact that these diseases affected young children more than others was likely because children from the age of 1 1/2 to about 4 lived together in the Nursery, rather than as part of nuclear families. Once a contagious disease was contracted by any child in the Nursery, it no doubt affected many more children than would have been the case had the Moravians lived in separate family houses. In addition, these children had less contact with their older and younger siblings and their parents than would be the case in societies with nuclear family living arrangements. Infectious diseases therefore had less opportunity to spread from nursery children to other age groups than is to be expected in populations organized as nuclear families. The pattern of mortality during the period of the General Economy does not mesh with any recognized life table models because those models are based on societies with organizational structures very different from that of early Bethlehem. Soon after

TABLE 2-9 Comparison of Bethlehem Death Rates with Coale and Demeny's Life Table Models

Years	1744–1763			1764–1783		1784–1803		1804–1823		1824–1843	
Life table model	South 9 Male	Bethlm All	South 4 Female	Bethlm All	East 11 Female	Bethlm All	East 14 Female	Bethlm All	East 14 Male	Bethlm All	West 11 Female
<1 Q(x)*	190.0	187.3	245.6	189.2	179.6	130.9	131.7	159.2	158.0	145.6	146.1
<1 M(x)**	217.8	212.3	292.3	215.4	205.0	142.0	144.9	180.8	177.9	158.7	161.5
1–4	45.7	84.1	84.8	20.0	23.5	15.5	14.6	9.2	15.1	33.1	25.0
5–19	5.7	14.1	10.5	6.7	4.4	4.6	2.9	3.7	3.0	7.0	5.2
20–59	12.8	15.1	18.8	12.2	10.1	12.5	7.9	13.8	9.8	13.3	12.0
60+	78.9	112.1	91.3	55.3	73.3	69.7	68.0	78.6	73.0	87.3	71.8
Life expectancy at birth	38.5		27.5		45.0		52.5		49.0		45.0
Life expectancy at 20 years (to age 60.1)	40.1 (to age 60.1)		35.7 (to 55.7)		43.1 (to 63.1)		46.2 (to 66.2)		43.9 (to 63.9)		41.5 (to 61.5)

*Q(x) = infant mortality
**M(x) = infant death rate

the first period, Moravians began to change from communal living to family living, and from that point on their young children never again experienced such sustained high mortality. If the change in living arrangements caused mortality among young children to decline, more general changes must have contributed to the improvement of health, because mortality declined to some degree for other age groups as well. Decreasing immigration may have contributed to the improvement in health. Not only were there fewer immigrants to raise the levels of mortality as they underwent the usual seasoning, but there was less opportunity for new germs to be introduced to the already settled population.

The patterns of population composition, population growth, migration, marriage, birth, and death all reflect the distinct epochs in Bethlehem's history. In addition, there is considerable demographic evidence that the fifty-year period between the end of the Communal Economy and the General Synod of 1818 was socially stressful. The long slow decrease in the population, the increasing rates of withdrawal, the negative figures for natural increase, the drop in marriage rates, the even steeper drop in birth rates, and the astoundingly high average age at first marriage all point to extreme stress. The ages at marriage for men are particularly strong evidence of stress because they continued high even though adult male/female ratios remained near .50. In a population with two women for every man, one would expect social pressures that would lower the male age at marriage. The adjustments required by the dissolution of the Communal Economy, the burdens carried during the American Revolution, and the limitations forced by the close regime would each by themselves have been disruptive. Together, following each other so closely, they had a traumatic impact on individual lives.

The institutional changes in Bethlehem's first century altered not only the demographic context but also the town setting in which people lived these lives. The next chapter explores these changes in the use of Bethlehem's land and its buildings.

NOTES

1. During the second decade there were more females than males because most boys were being sent to the boarding school for boys in Nazareth, but among adults, men still predominated.

2. Since in general the data is processed by decades in order to even out chance yearly fluctuations which occur in such small populations, the changes which followed the Synod of 1818 show up as a change in the decade beginning in 1814.

3. This procedure was inspired by a similar one used by Robert V. Wells in his article, "Quaker Marriage Patterns in a Colonial Perspective," *William and Mary Quarterly*, July 1972, pp. 415–42.

4. These estimates are based on the knowledge that women generally married in their 20s or early 30s during the entire century and men in their 30s or early 40s during the first fifty years.

5. The actual percentages of women who decided to stay single were probably even higher than those shown in Figure 2-1 because the presence of Widows from other Moravian settlements artificially inflated the number of older women who had married at some point in their lives.

6. This age span covers at least 95 percent of the ages at first marriage for men during those two decades and 97 percent for women.

7. The lowest point was actually 1815, but the slight upswing during the next two years was consistent with the small fluctuations in previous years. In 1818 the slope increased markedly indicating the beginning of a systemic change.

8. For this study net migration was not calculated from immigration and emigration figures but from the more accurate figures on population, birth, and death, according to the formula: $(M_N = P_2 - P_1 - B + D) / Y$, where M_N = net migration, P_1 = population at the beginning of the decade, P_2 = population at the end of decade, B = number of births, D = number of deaths, and Y = number of person-years in the decade.

9. Again note that since the demographic analysis proceeds by decades, the dates in Table 2-4 do not correspond exactly to the dates of the periods defined by Figure 2-2.

10. The average error was computed according to the following formula:

$$\frac{\sum_{i=1}^{10} \overline{p_i - P_i}}{\sum_{i=1}^{10} P_i}$$

where p = the population for the ith year of the decade figured via migration records in the Memorabilia and P = the population for the ith year of the decade as given in the Memorabilia. The formula reads, "the sum of the absolute value of $p - P$ divided by the sum of P."

11. Since complete data were available for only 4 years of the last decade, the figure 356 is an estimate arrived at by averaging the extant information and expanding it for the 10 year period.

12. The male/female emigration figures are rates based on the populations at risk in Bethlehem, whereas immigration figures are raw scores. The assumption here is that males and females occur in unknown but equal numbers in the population outside Bethlehem, so that raw numbers accurately compare male and female participation.

13. The large differences between male and female rates reflect changes in the adult sex ratio from well above 1 during the first two decades to considerably below 1 afterwards.

14. A convenient tabular summary of seventeenth- and eighteenth-century marriage ages in the American colonies, in England, and in France appears in Wells, p. 429. The marriage ages of early Bethlehem Moravians are higher even than the relatively high French and English marriage ages.

15. Studies have shown that in a society which is not practicing contraception, a fertile couple typically produces a child about one year after marriage. After that, if the mother nurses her children for one year and if the infants being nursed live that long, the spacing between children is likely to be about two years until waning fertility begins to lengthen the spacing. See John Demos, *A Little Commonwealth*, who cites Robert G. Potter et al., "Application of Field Studies to Research on the Physiology of Human Reproduction," *Jrnl. of Chronic Diseases*, 1965, 1125–40.

16. A more detailed account of the standardized death rate is discussed later in the chapter.

17. A "person-year" is an abstraction used by demographers. To say "50,000 person-years" means that an unidentified number of persons lived a total of 50,000 years. For example, it can mean that 50,000 people lived a total of 1 year each, or that 500 people lived 100 years each, or any other combination of numbers which multiplies to 50,000.

18. The life table is a demographic model of mortality. It represents the pattern of death for a hypothetical population of 100,000 or 10,000 or 1,000 people all born the same year. The death rates for each year of life are based on the age-specific mortality rates for 1 year of an actual population. Various columns in the life table give such information as the number of people in the cohort who died during a given year of life, the number in the cohort left at the end of each year, the age-specific mortality rate for each year of life, and life expectancy (or average number of years left) at each year of life.

19. Age-specific death rates are the crude death rates computed for the population in a particular age group. By choosing age ranges large enough so that at least 20 deaths occurred over a twenty-year period, relatively reliable mortality rates result which also reveal some of the variation over time. It should be noted that in spite of the large age ranges and time spans, for some groups during some periods, there were still not 20 deaths. The rates based on such cases have been placed in parentheses.

Chapter Three

The Town Setting

THE CONSTRUCTION OF COMMUNAL BETHLEHEM

When Moravian pioneers first set foot on the site of future Bethlehem in February of 1741, they found fertile soil, a forest of trees, and good water. By 1761 they had turned those raw materials into an imposing little town with over 50 sturdy buildings[1] and just under 50 industries[2] centered on about 2500 acres of cleared fields, mature orchards, gardens, and meadows.[3] Visitors were always impressed with the idyllic and durable appearance of Bethlehem, and they marveled at the quantity and quality of goods produced there. As early as 1751, one visitor remarked in amazement that even in the largest cities one could not find a greater variety of industries or ones carried on with more skill than in the village of Bethlehem. (See Figure 3-1 for a drawing of Bethlehem in 1749.) Others praised the quality of Bethlehem's grain crops, saying they were the best in all of Pennsylvania.[4] But the Moravians in Bethlehem accomplished even more than this. Their efforts extended beyond the borders of Bethlehem to daughter colonies in Nazareth, Christiansbrunn, Gnadenthal, and Friedensthal. There they built another 50 buildings and intensively developed another 5,000 acres of land. In addition to all this physical development, the Bethlehem Moravians supported a vigorous missionary program in North America among other European settlers and among Indians, and in the West Indies among slaves. When we learn that all the settlements in the Bethlehem-Nazareth complex never housed more than 1,300 people, including 400 children,[5] we can wonder how they managed to do so much in the space of just twenty years. A look at the construction process makes it clear that the pioneers developed Bethlehem not only by working very hard, but by carefully planning which buildings to build first and which second, by using those buildings in flexible ways, and by balancing their goals against each other.

The construction of communal Bethlehem was carefully sequenced from the beginning (see Table 3-1). The little band of Moravians who arrived on Bethlehem soil that bitter cold February of 1741 desperately needed shelter. They were no longer welcome in Nazareth where they had been building a school for the evangelist George Whitefield. Because of their disagreement with him over the doctrine of predestination, he had requested in November 1740 that they leave as soon as they could find a place to stay. On such short notice they could not construct a proper building right away. Instead they had to quickly put together a small, temporary First House with green lumber and no stone foundation. Before they could ready a larger building, sixteen people had come to live in these limited quarters, and they had to share it with their cows and horses.

But in spite of their obvious need for more space, the pioneers wasted no time constructing other temporary buildings. Instead they immediately began to plan for a permanent Bethlehem. Even before they built the First House, in fact, they had cut logs in order to season them for a more substantial communal residence. And while waiting for the logs to dry out, they opened a quarry to provide stone for its foundation. By the end of September, hewn logs, cut stones, and an excavated cellar lay ready, and the Moravians in Bethlehem began to build the communal building known as the Gemeinhaus—again according to a carefully devised sequence. We must infer from the arrangement of doors, windows, and stairs that the Moravians conceived the Gemeinhaus as a unit. However, instead of constructing the whole building starting from the foundation and proceeding to its walls and roof, they built it in three separate sections because of limitations on timber size. This method had the added advantage that they could use each section as it was ready.[6] Construction of the west section proceeded rapidly. Enough of it was complete by December of 1741 that with some scurrying about they were able to finish two rooms and to host Count Zinzendorf in a manner which more nearly suited his high station than did the cramped and primitive First House. The central section was walled in by June 1742, just in time to shelter the 56 colonists in the First Sea Congregation, although the carpenters and masons in the group had to finish windows, partitions, floors, and chimneys after everyone moved in. The eastern section took much longer. Though they began to build it in August of that same year, they did not complete it until over a year later.[7]

One reason for the delay was, again, careful planning. As soon as the pressure for living space was somewhat relieved, the Bethlehem pioneers shifted their efforts and focused on the construction of buildings to house a series of industries. Between 1742 and 1745 the Moravians built in quick

FIGURE 3-1. View of Bethlehem in 1749 (mistakenly labeled 1750)

succession not only a millwork and a sawmill, which obviously helped with the construction of other buildings, but a blacksmith shop, a tannery, a grist mill, a pottery, and a linseed oil mill.[8] Although the Moravians established them to meet their own needs, these industries almost immediately provided income, as their non-Moravian neighbors came to buy pottery and oil, and to have their flour ground, their horses shod, and their wagons repaired.[9]

To help provide food the pioneers also raised a barn and several grain storage buildings during those first years, and they actively bought land surrounding Bethlehem, until in 1761 the original 500 acres had grown to 4,991 acres, consisting of 24 separate purchases.[10] Just as energetically as the Moravians bought land, they cleared it, supplying themselves at the same time with lumber and cordwood. Already by 1748 they had surrounded the small cluster of buildings at Bethlehem with 675 acres of fields, meadows, gardens, and orchards. By 1759 they had cleared 2,454 acres of land around Bethlehem.[11]

During the late 1740s the Moravians suspended construction of industrial buildings for a time and concentrated again on residential structures. This change in emphasis was no doubt a response to the growing population in Bethlehem. Beginning in 1743 the European Moravians fed Bethlehem a steady stream of colonists until, by 1750, well over 400 people lived there on an everyday basis. In order to house all these new people, the Moravians built the first Single Brothers' House in 1744 followed by the Married Men's House and the Bell House in 1746, the second Single Brothers' House in 1748, the East and West Bell House Extensions in 1748 and 1749, and a private dwelling in 1749 for the Horsefield family who kept their own separate economy. Apparently Bethlehem had also begun to attract a number of visitors, because in 1745 the Moravians built the Crown Inn to lodge them a controlled distance away on the other side of the Lehigh River.[12]

Sequencing was also evident in the choice of construction materials. Until 1744 the buildings in Bethlehem were almost entirely log structures with stone foundations. (See Figure 3-2 for an example.) The pressure of starting a settlement from scratch forced the pioneers to use rapid construction techniques, but by 1744 the emergency was apparently past, because in that year the residents of Bethlehem finished the first of the stone buildings that would eventually dominate Bethlehem. That building was the first Single Brethren's House (later the Single Sisters' House) mentioned above. During the next two decades nine out of every ten buildings were made of stone. Most residences built between 1744 and 1749 were stone structures,

Table 3-1 Construction Sequence in Communal Bethlehem*

Date	Dwellings		Industrial Buildings		Other Buildings	
	Mat'l	Building	Mat'l	Building	Mat'l	Building
1741	Log	First House				
1742			Log	Millwork Bldg	Log	Men's Infirmary
					Wood	Large Barn
1742–3	Log	Gemeinhaus				
1743			Log	Blacksmith Shop		
1743			Wood	Tannery		
1743			Log	Grist Mill		
1744	Stone	1st Single Brothers' House (Later Single Sisters' House)	Wood	Sawmill		
ca. 44			Log	Pottery		
1745			Log	Oil Mill	Log	Crown Inn
						Farm Buildings
1746	Log	Married Men's House				
1746	Stone	Bell House				
1747						Two Barns
						Several Stables
1748	Stone	2nd Single Brothers' House				
1748	Stone	Eastern Extension Bell House				

Year	Material	Civic & Residential	Material	Industrial	Material	Commercial & Other
1749	Stone	Western Extension Bell House				
1749	Stone	Horsefield House				
1750			Stone	Pottery; Blacksmith, Locksmith, Nailsmith	Stone	Barn; Stables
1751	Stone	Old Chapel (Dining Room for Married Choir)	Stone	Grist Mill; Fulling Mill	Stone	Old Chapel
1752	Stone	North Extension Single Sisters' House		Flax Breaking House	Stone	Apothecary; Indian Hotel
1753					Stone	1st Store (Addition to Horsefield House)
1754	Stone	Married Men's House			Stone	Waterworks
1756			Log	Sawmill	Log	Indian Chapel
1759			Stone	Rebuilt Fulling Mill		
1759			Stone	Dyeworks and Clothiers		
1760					Stone	Sun Inn
1761			Stone	Tannery	Stone	Waterworks
1761				Blacksmith Bldg. Extension		
1762	Stone	Eastern Annex to Single Brothers' House			Stone	2nd Store

*The purpose of this table is to depict the focus of construction at various points during the General Economy. There was no attempt to include every building. The information comes from Levering's book, Murtagh's book, and Ralph Schwarz' unpublished research.

FIGURE 3-2. Example of log construction in early Bethlehem. This building was built in 1746 on Sisters' Lane on the site where Central Church has stood since 1803.

and in 1749, when they began to construct more industrial buildings, the residents of Bethlehem chose to make them of stone as well. (See Figure 3-3 for an example.) By 1768, nearly 70 percent of all the buildings in Bethlehem were stone, including not only most residences and industrial buildings, but the Apothecary, the Store, the Waterworks, the Indian Hotel, and the Sun Inn.

Throughout the formative period, the Moravians remained flexible about how they used their buildings. The Bell House was originally built in 1746 as a residence for the Married People, but just three years later it became the headquarters of the Girls' Seminary. The old log pottery was turned into the residence for Widowers when the Stone Pottery was built in 1749. The Single Sisters took over the first Single Brothers' House as soon as the second Single Brothers' House was completed in 1748. A large stone house built in 1754 had many guises. Originally intended as a House for Married Men, it almost immediately became a school for boys, and then, in turn, a home for younger children, an apartment house for families, and, sometime after the General Economy was dissolved, a house for

FIGURE 3-3. Example of stone construction in early Bethlehem. This is the Single Sisters' House Complex, 1744–1773. Note the characteristic brick arches above the windows.

the older people who had lived under the General Economy and therefore had no private means of support in their old age. A building, once constructed, was always used, even if the original need had changed.

Bethlehem Moravians showed the same flexibility in their use of buildings in other Moravian settlements. The Older Girls and the Single Sisters moved to the Whitefield House in Nazareth in 1745 and remained there for over three years until a house was available in Bethlehem. The Widows occupied a log building in Nazareth from 1755 to 1768 when the Widows' House in Bethlehem was completed. And buildings in the towns of Oley, Maguntsche, Germantown, the Great Swamp, Friedrichstown, and Nazareth served as schools for the children of Bethlehem at one time or another.[13]

The Moravians in Bethlehem boasted only a few personal belongings. Although modest living was dictated by their values, it also facilitated all these moves. When the Married Men vacated their newly built house in February 1755, so that the Boys' Institute could move in there, the sick women and nursing mothers with their infants took over the building that the boys had occupied, and the men moved into the building which the women had used. Within just one day, the Moravians had moved 165 people and all their personal belongings.[14]

Such economy clearly had practical advantages, but it was motivated by the Moravians' religious commitment as well. Zinzendorf conceived Bethlehem as a Pilgergemeine and not as a place to settle down comfortably.[15] His followers must have wholeheartedly supported the idea, for even from the first months and without even modest material comfort, Moravians from Bethlehem traveled among German settlers and among Indians, filling spiritual needs or attempting to create them. Such insistence on balancing their various goals was important. The years ahead required that the Moravians build not only Bethlehem, but scores of daughter colonies in other places. If the Moravians had first provided for their own basic physical comfort and waited for the luxury of leisure, they would likely never have begun their religious mission in the outside world. Moravians in Bethlehem had to learn to manage both their spiritual purpose and their physical needs at the same time.

It was not always easy to maintain this balance. When Zinzendorf came to America late in 1741, he stimulated religious work to such a degree that Father Nitschmann, who had been left in charge of developing Bethlehem with a mere handful of assistants, had to send an urgent request for help in April 1742. The First Sea Congregation was expected in less than three months and not only was the central section of the Gemeinhaus far from complete, but time for spring planting had arrived. Zinzendorf's answer at that time was that religious work was more important,[16] but he apparently also understood that religious work required a solid economic base, because in June of that same year he divided the Pilgergemeine at Bethlehem into its two parts in order to institutionalize a balance between the spiritual and the physical. The Pilgergemeine,[17] in the narrow sense, ministered spiritually both to members in Bethlehem and to people outside the Moravian Church. The Hausgemeine (the domestic or local community) provided food, shelter, and clothing for all members of the Gemeine,[18] including the "pilgrims." Since people could themselves choose which group to join or could leave the decision in the Savior's hands (i.e.

the Lot), they were more likely to support their own group enthusiastically. And since the division of labor made it clearer how both the religious and secular work would get done, people were able to concentrate on their assigned tasks and relax about the responsibilities given to others. In this way, the never-ending need for physical development and domestic support could not overwhelm Bethlehem's spiritual focus, but neither would that focus die from lack of practical support.

THE TOWN PLAN OF BETHLEHEM

The buildings of a carefully planned community like Bethlehem reflect the goals and values of its builders. If the original builders of a community understand how to implement its values in the physical setting they create, then its structure will help to maintain them. Even if they do not, once it is built, the physical community will limit the kind of life that can be led within its boundaries. Either way, the relationships between buildings and the arrangements and functions of their rooms can tell us a good deal about how their inhabitants lived.

By 1761 the main outlines of early Bethlehem had been drawn. What did Bethlehem look like, and what does that tell us about life there?[19] One of the most impressive characteristics of Bethlehem was its large buildings, constructed to house members in a communal fashion. (See Figure 3–4 for an etching of Bethlehem in 1755.) New members could deposit any money they had with the community treasury and get it back if they left. But while they remained in Bethlehem they each lived simple lives inside those large buildings on an equal footing with everyone else. They all slept in the dormitories of their Choir houses and shared a small living room with several other people. They ate together in large dining halls which were served by communal kitchens. They had little in the way of personal articles—just equal allotments of simple clothes and the tools they needed in their trades. They owned no real estate—it was held by a proprietor in trust for the Gemeine —but they all had an equal share in its use. It is true that Zinzendorf was housed more comfortably during his stay in Bethlehem, that Timothy Horsefield lived with his family in a one-family house, and that James Burnside lived with his family on their farm along the road to Nain. But with these exceptions the people of Bethlehem lived in a culture that supported equality of condition to a degree unheard of elsewhere in colonial America.

FIGURE 3-4. View of Bethlehem in 1755

Striking in the physical organization of communal Bethlehem is the element of separation—separation of residence from industry, of Moravians from non-Moravians, and of Whites from Indians (see Figure 3-5).

The communal residences were centered primarily on Sisters' Lane (present-day Church Street) with the graveyard a short walk behind. Various farm buildings lined up at right angles to Sisters' Lane along what later became Main Street. Down the hill in two directions and somewhat separated from the central residential buildings were two industrial sections, a major one to the west on Monocacy Creek and a minor one to the southeast near where the Monocacy emptied into the Lehigh River. One mile west of Bethlehem stood the buildings of the village Nain where Indian converts had lived since 1758. Two inns served visitors and travelers from outside the Moravian fold, the Crown Inn to the south across the Lehigh River and the Sun Inn on Bethlehem's rim to the north. Kitchen and herb gardens lay near the residential buildings but grain fields stretched for hundreds of acres in all directions from the central area and on both sides of the river.

The spatial relationship between residence and industry is actually more subtle than the map of Bethlehem shows. Some industries (such as spinning, weaving, glovemaking, and shoemaking) were not separated at all, but carried on in portions of residential buildings, especially in the Single Sisters' and Single Brothers' Houses. Also, a few apartments were attached to industrial buildings like the pottery and the millwork shop. It may even be the case that the Moravians did not *intend* to separate residence from industry. As if to unify the industrial and residential quarters, they built the industrial buildings out of the same solid limestone with the same red brick arches over windows and the same attention to proportion and aesthetic detail as the residences along Sisters' Lane.[20] The map of Bethlehem suggests that proximity to water may have determined where the Moravians put their industries. Most of the industries located along the Monocacy needed its water either as power (like the oil mill and the gristmill) or as an ingredient in the industrial process (the wash house or the bleach house, for instance). Some industries, like the tannery, used water *both* as power and as an ingredient. Since various industries have traditionally used running water for waste removal, it is likely that the tannery also used Monocacy Creek for the removal of its industrial wastes.

The separation of non-Moravians from Moravians during the communal period was also more subtle than the town plan by itself suggests. As early as September, 1742, the residents of Bethlehem became concerned about the effect of too much contact with outsiders. They arranged

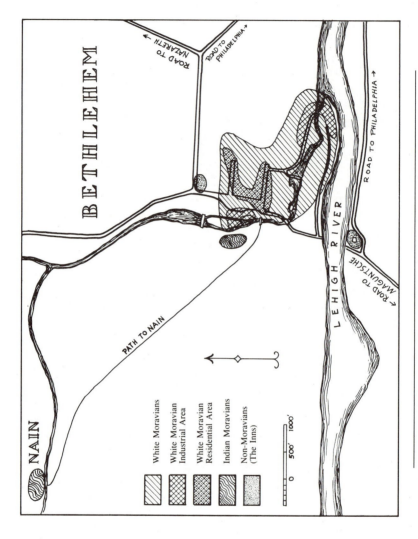

FIGURE 3-5. Physical organization of Bethlehem in 1760

for a lovefeast with nearby non-Moravians to inform them that they did not want to be "as neighbors" with them, and they began to discuss the necessity of a "house for strangers" where the latter could stay under the supervision of a Brother or Sister. As a stopgap, they constructed a small log house for strangers in 1742, but in 1745 they completed the more substantial Crown Inn on the south side of the Lehigh River. By 1760 the Sun Inn was ready to house guests a little distance to the north of settled Bethlehem. But in spite of these strictures, outsiders were not confined to the inns at Bethlehem's outer edges. They were allowed to visit the various Choir houses and schools, attend worship services, inspect the industries, and walk the grounds. They were even sometimes entertained with concerts by Moravian musicians. But when they toured Bethlehem, they came in by invitation and under escort.[21] This practice suggests that the Moravians built their inns on the margins of their town not to thwart all contact between residents and outsiders, but to regularize that contact and to keep it from interfering with community life and the routine of work in Bethlehem. By offering their guests comfortable lodging and good food at some distance from the community center and inviting them in when it was convenient, the Moravians preserved their reputation as good hosts and yet maintained necessary control over the visits of outsiders.

Moravians likewise did not avoid contact with Indians. Their well-developed North American missionary program attests to that. In Bethlehem itself several young Indian Sisters lived with the Single Sisters, and Indian Moravians who died in Bethlehem were buried in the community graveyard among white Moravians of their age and sex.[22] But whenever a large group of Indian Moravians lived in Bethlehem, the white Moravians regarded the situation as temporary. This was already the case during the mid-1740s when Moravian Indians lived in the section of Bethlehem called Friedenshütten, located near the Monocacy to the southeast of Bethlehem. During 1746 most of them were transferred to Gnadenhütten 30 to 40 miles up the Lehigh from Bethlehem, but in 1752 the Indian Hotel was built to house Indian guests at the western edge of Bethlehem just across the Monocacy. After Gnadenhütten was attacked by other Indians in 1755, Moravian Indians there fled back to Bethlehem for protection from both whites and Indians. At that time a chapel was built near the Indian Hotel so that the Indians could have separate worship services, but again the white Moravians considered the Indian village in Bethlehem a temporary one.[23]

The Indians helped to maintain themselves by making baskets, by fishing in the Lehigh, and by guarding harvesters from possible Indian attack.[24] But the whites in Bethlehem perceived the Indians as a foreign element and built a separate village (Nain) for them a mile away from Bethlehem in 1758. The Indians moved there and for a time planted their Indian corn on the fifty acres which the whites had cleared for them. A few years later they were moved even further to the newly constructed Indian village called Wechequetank some 20 miles from Bethlehem, partly in response to agitation from neighbors, partly to provide more hunting grounds,[25] and partly to reduce Bethlehem's responsibility for Indian missions after the dissolution of the General Economy.

It is clear in all this that Indians quite naturally did not abandon their traditional cultures when they converted to Moravianism. It is also clear that the Moravians in Bethlehem did not expect them to, but neither did they require of themselves an attempt to live in one community with groups of Indians who practiced cultures quite different from their own. To do so would be to create cultural conflict. Living in an integrated fashion with Indian individuals was another matter. While groups of Indians would support each other in maintaining their traditional ways, individual Indians who sometimes lived in Bethlehem's Choir houses could be expected to and did accommodate themselves to Moravian cultural practice. Although Bethlehem Moravians in general chose not to live with their Indian converts, they provided good land for them to live from separately, recognizing that Indians, by converting, had divorced themselves from established Indian groups and required help in reestablishing themselves on a land base if they were to regain economic independence.

Separation was also a key element of the organization within the residential section of Bethlehem. The two sexes were separated from each other by the way buildings were arranged as well as by the ways the buildings were used. Most conspicuously separated were the unmarried adults, housed at opposite ends of the residential area. The Single Brothers' House was at the western end of Sisters' Lane near the main industrial section whereas the Single Sisters' House was on the easternmost border of the residential area. Widowers lived near the Single Brothers in the old pottery right in the industrial section. In 1761 the Widows lived in Nazareth, but plans were being made to erect a building for them in Bethlehem directly across Sisters' Lane from the Sisters' House—again at the eastern edge of the residences and a decorous distance from the unattached men.

The separation of the sexes began at a very early age. Boys and girls were raised apart from each other beginning at the age of about 5 when they were promoted from the Nursery into their respective Choirs. They lived from that age on in or near the houses of the single adults of their own sex, whose job it was to raise them.

Even married men and women lived for the most part with Choir siblings of the same sex rather than with their marriage partners. Levering suggests that this arrangement was an economic necessity and gives as evidence the fact that a few married couples did have couple apartments by 1761.[26] Erbe, on the other hand reports a change in Unity policy. There was no plan to build separate apartments for married couples until the Unity decided to end Bethlehem's focus on missionary work. Furthermore, once married people began to live together, they continued to do so in spite of community balance sheets which looked a good deal bleaker after the General Economy than they had during it.[27] This new commitment suggests that changing values were responsible for the difference, not changing fortunes. Whatever the intention, the fact is that as of 1761, fifty couples or about five-sixths of the married men and women lived with people of their own sex.[28]

In their Synod minutes, the Moravians explained quite explicitly why they so conscientiously separated males from females. "We must remain steadfast concerning the careful separation of the sexes. . . . This is not based on any reputation for a particular saintliness; rather it comes from the awareness of human wretchedness and sinfulness, and [we practice it] in order to prevent opportunities for sin and seduction which can result from unnecessary associations between the sexes." There followed a series of rules governing any necessary encounters between two people of opposite sexes, stating among other things that a third person with official status had to be present, even if the two people were biological siblings and even if they were high in the church hierarchy.[29] The message was clear. Since human beings were, in their view, by nature weak and corrupt, they needed every possible support from their community to control behavior they deemed undesirable—in this case, sexuality between people not married to each other. And no matter what their positions or relationship, they required the aid of external regulation.

Accordingly, the physical separation of males from females extended beyond the location of residential buildings to other aspects of the town plan. The industries which most intensely occupied women—flax-breaking, bleaching, and laundering—were located in the southeastern industrial section not far from their Choir house whereas the male dominated industries were concentrated in the western industrial area. Separate male and female footpaths for recreation and meditation were care-

FIGURE 3-6. Children's Lovefeast. The girls and women gathered on one side of the room and the men on the other. The room, in this case, was in Herrnhut, but the practice was the same in all Moravian churches.

fully engineered to prevent casual contact between men and women not married to each other. The paths avoided each other and shunned any buildings or places where a member of the opposite sex was likely to appear.[30]

The arrangements within buildings also contributed to the scrupulous separation of the sexes. The large hall in the Gemeinhaus used for community meetings and worship services had separate entrances for each sex. These two entrances were on opposite sides of the room. Men and boys seated themselves in the benches adjacent to their entrance, and the women and girls in the ones next to theirs. An aisle separated the two sections. (See Figure 3-6, which depicts such a room in Herrnhut.)

Even the separated residences of unmarried people were arranged in ways which discouraged contact between the sexes. Figure 3-7 shows a floor plan of an addition to the Single Sisters' House. Although this extension was built in 1773—more than a decade after the communal period—it is one of the best plans to show typical room use in communal residences. The attic of a Choir house was typically an open dormitory, large enough to sleep all residents of the house (see Figure 3-8). For daytime activities each person was assigned to one of several small living rooms ("Stuben") along with half a dozen other people. One of them was designated Room Supervisor, whose job it was to oversee the activities of the others assigned to that room and to report findings to the Choir Helper, the leader of the entire Choir. One large room was set aside for Choir worship services. Another was a dining room for meals which were taken in common.[31] Such an organization of activities emphasizes community to the total exclusion of privacy. Individuals lived every moment in spaces which included other individuals of the same sex, making intimate contact between unmarried members of the opposite sex nearly impossible, and the lack of any illegitimate births in Bethlehem attests to the effectiveness of the arrangement.

Although most Married People also shared rooms and slept in dormitories with married people of their own sex, they met as a Choir with both men and women for eating and worshipping. And judging from the birth rate during the period of the General Economy, husbands and wives had frequent opportunity for intimate contact alone. But the emphasis for Married People as for Single People was on public living. A 1758 inventory of goods and furniture in Bethlehem lists thirty-five beds in the Married Men's House, and thirty single beds and two double beds in the Married Women's dormitory. Even the intimate meetings of husband and

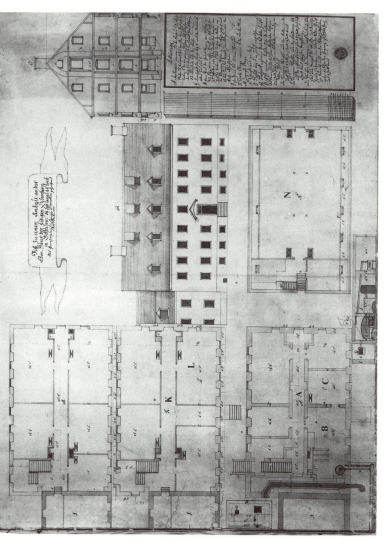

FIGURE 3-7. Floor plan of the Eastern Addition to the Single Sisters' House. The addition measures 44 feet by 69 feet. The kitchen (B) and its sideroom (C) are in the basement (A); the weaving room (L) is on the first floor (K). Other rooms on the first and second floors are unlabeled, but they must also be workrooms, given their large size. A sleeping hall (N) comprises the attic.

FIGURE 3-8. Attic Sleeping Hall in the Eastern Addition to the Single Sisters'
House

wife must have been public in the sense that they had to take turns with
other married couples in occupying a room with a double bed.[32]

Regulation of sexuality was not the only reason behind the separation
of the sexes in Bethlehem, since even Married People lived apart from
their spouses in Choirs of their own sex. This arrangement must also have
supported the Communal Economy which governed Bethlehem until 1762.
During that time people labored not for themselves or for their families,
but for the whole economy. They received no money, just their share of
food, shelter, and clothing. The physical arrangements in Bethlehem
clearly supported such an economy. Because people lived less intimately
with members of their own family than with other members of the Gemeine, their loyalties to the Gemeine naturally grew while their commitment to their family as a separate entity waned.

THE TRANSFORMATION OF BETHLEHEM AFTER 1762

The year 1762 marked the beginning of a new phase in the construction
and use of buildings in Bethlehem.[33] In response to events following the
death of Zinzendorf two years before, Moravians began in 1762 to dissolve

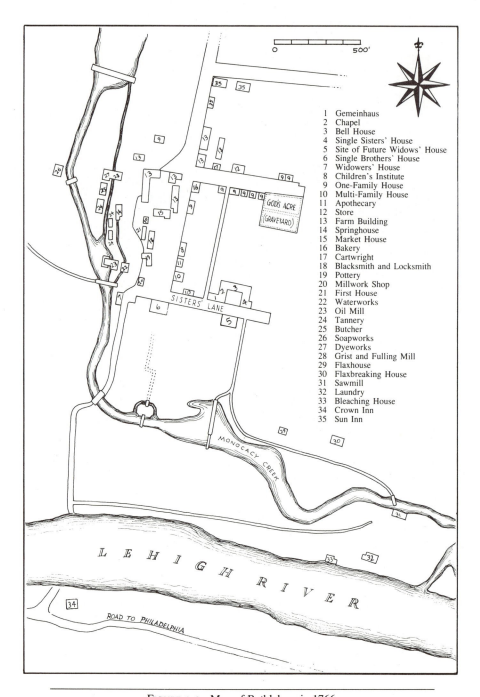

1 Gemeinhaus
2 Chapel
3 Bell House
4 Single Sisters' House
5 Site of Future Widows' House
6 Single Brothers' House
7 Widowers' House
8 Children's Institute
9 One-Family House
10 Multi-Family House
11 Apothecary
12 Store
13 Farm Building
14 Springhouse
15 Market House
16 Bakery
17 Cartwright
18 Blacksmith and Locksmith
19 Pottery
20 Millwork Shop
21 First House
22 Waterworks
23 Oil Mill
24 Tannery
25 Butcher
26 Soapworks
27 Dyeworks
28 Grist and Fulling Mill
29 Flaxhouse
30 Flaxbreaking House
31 Sawmill
32 Laundry
33 Bleaching House
34 Crown Inn
35 Sun Inn

GOD'S ACRE
(GRAVEYARD)

SISTERS' LANE

MONOCACY CREEK

LEHIGH RIVER

ROAD TO PHILADELPHIA

FIGURE 3-9. Map of Bethlehem in 1766

Bethlehem's Communal Economy and to develop an economic system based on nuclear families (see Chapter 1). Physical arrangements in Bethlehem soon reflected this new emphasis, but the large buildings along Sisters' Lane (Church Street) continued to recall Bethlehem's communal beginnings.

Since the communal focus in Bethlehem had until 1762 de-emphasized family life, the designers of the economic transformation assumed that they needed to encourage a nuclear family life style in order to support the new economic system. The earliest plans for transition stated that the primary need was to provide separate living quarters for each of the couples in the Married Peoples' Choir and that parents would gradually integrate their children into their separate households as they could afford to maintain them. Single adults were to continue living in their Choir houses. The only change for them was that after 1762 they received wages for their work and paid for their keep out of their earnings.[34]

Initially then, the authorities in Bethlehem needed only to provide separate quarters for the fifty couples who had been living in Choirs. This they accomplished in a flurry of construction during the early 1760s. They built new houses designed for families along what became Main and Market Streets. They divided larger buildings into apartments, and they expanded the apartments already attached to the inns, the mills, and the craft houses. The greatest remodeling problem was how to provide a separate kitchen for each family. Before 1762, there were perhaps six or seven kitchens in all of Bethlehem—each one associated with a Choir house or a school. Just as the designers of Pilgergemeine Bethlehem supported their communal economy by building only a few large kitchens, the architects of Ortsgemeine Bethlehem apparently understood that separate family kitchens provided many daily opportunities to help people identify with their own immediate families.[35]

The construction of residences required that the farm buildings be moved further north into the next block of Main Street. By 1774, this transfer was complete. With this shift Bethlehem began to shed its rural and communal organization and become more obviously an urban collection of family houses lined up neatly along Main and Market Streets. A map of Bethlehem in 1766 (Figure 3-9) shows Bethlehem at the brink of this transition, with the appearance of new single family dwellings but also with the original barnyard still mostly intact. A view of Bethlehem in 1784 shows the emerging town of nuclear families as smaller residences already began to encroach on the barnyard in its new place on Main Street (see

FIGURE 3-10. View of Bethlehem in 1784

Figure 3-10). However, the large buildings along Sisters' Lane still remained an impressive part of the Bethlehem landscape and still reminded the viewer of Bethlehem's communal beginnings.

Another period of intense construction began in the 1790s (inspired in part by Bethlehem's fiftieth-year anniversary in 1792) and extended into the nineteenth century. Johannes Ettwein and other leaders in Bethlehem had hoped to build a large church in time for the celebration, but construction did not begin until 1803 and was not complete until 1806. After this point, Bethlehem's appearance was greatly altered. Not only did this large building become the dominant focal point, but it introduced a style of architecture new to Bethlehem. This building, constructed with the help of designers and builders from Easton and Philadelphia, featured majestic windows and fine decorative detailing. It was more similar to the Federal style mansions of Philadelphia than to the elegantly simple stone buildings which had dominated Bethlehem until then. (See Figure 3-11 for a view of Bethlehem in 1812).

Other development at this time began to change the basic scheme of the town. In 1789 Ettwein drew up a new plan for Bethlehem which increased the number of house lots. In 1790 a large building for the Girls' Seminary was constructed behind the Gemeinhaus. In 1794, a bridge was built across the Lehigh River. In 1812, the farm was moved from Main Street to a point several blocks to the East. A map of Bethlehem at the end of 1812 (Figure 3-12) demonstrates how, for the first time in Bethlehem's history, the Bethlehem Farm was quite separate from the residential area. Bethlehem also operated four other farms north of the town and another on the south side of the Lehigh River on property that was formerly the Crown Inn.

Later changes made Bethlehem even more urban. The two story Third Store (built originally in 1794) was transformed into the Eagle Hotel in 1823 through a remodeling which included an additional floor. Other buildings like the Sun Inn also gained a story, and in 1846, the buildings along the east side of Main Street became taller when the hill underneath them was shaved away, making a new first story out of their basements. Now that Main Street was more level, it and Church Street (formerly Sisters' Lane) became the axis on which Bethlehem's street grid was established and expanded. Bethlehem also grew more connected to the outside world when the canal from the Delaware reached it in 1829 and when the railroad from Philadelphia reached it mid-century. A map of 1848 shows the extensive development along Broad, Market, and New Streets

FIGURE 3-11. View of Bethlehem in 1812

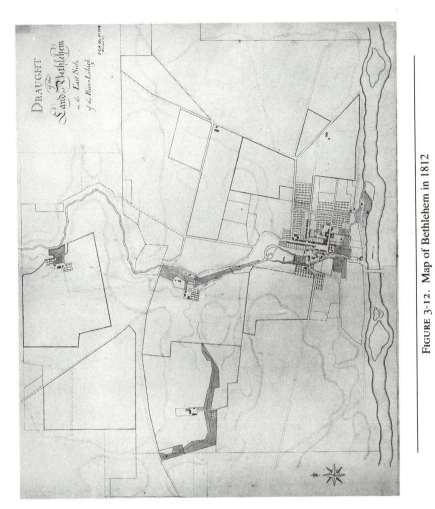

FIGURE 3-12. Map of Bethlehem in 1812

FIGURE 3-13. Map of Bethlehem in 1848

(see Figure 3-13). It also shows the canal and considerable development on a road which parallels it. Figure 3-14 depicts Bethlehem in 1852. In little more than a century, the little mission settlement had become an impressive little city.

As extensive as the change eventually was, it did not come easily at first. Bethlehem's early builders had so successfully built a town which reflected Bethlehem's Pilgergemeine structure that the buildings themselves limited the ease with which Bethlehem could become anything else but a Pilgergemeine. It was not enough simply to build new family houses, for that would have left the large and expensive communal buildings without any function. These buildings had to be reorganized into separate

112

apartments. The result was that even by 1850 Bethlehem had only two houses for every three households, whereas virtually all the other towns in Northampton County had a house for every household. The only exceptions to this were Nazareth (also a Moravian settlement) with about three houses per four households, and Easton, the county seat, with six houses per seven households.[36] Conditions in Bethlehem were probably not any more crowded than elsewhere, because the multi-family buildings were large, but more than in other towns, the arrangements in Bethlehem required contact and cooperation between neighbors as they lived in and maintained a building they shared. It was no doubt this contrast which inspired the Duke of Weimar to remark when he visited Bethlehem in 1825 and 1826 that "the residents of Bethlehem live in great harmony, constitute only one single family and because of similar educations and constant association seem to have absorbed very similar habits."[37]

Among the first to foresee that Bethlehem's physical structure would complicate the transition was Spangenberg, the man who more than anyone else had brought life to the Pilgergemeine idea in Bethlehem. In 1760 when he heard the suggestion to change Bethlehem into an Ortsgemeine, his first reaction was, "There stand the buildings which aren't at all suitable."[38] Since Spangenberg was so closely associated with the formation of early Bethlehem, his objectivity concerning a radical change in Bethlehem might be suspect, but even Friedrich Marschall, the person in charge of the transition, eventually had to agree with Spangenberg. After struggling for four years and the task still far from complete, he remarked wearily, "Although the circumstances of the people who live privately have improved in many ways, nevertheless the whole place was never set up for family life."[39] But in the end Marschall and his successors managed to overcome the physical constraints. By 1850, Bethlehem had in fact become a town of nuclear families.

As the original plans had suggested, the first step was to relocate married couples in private spaces and the second was to integrate children into the homes of their parents. The records do not indicate how the Moravians enlarged the apartments of married couples to make room for their children, but it is clear that they found solutions because gradually more and more children came to live with their parents. In 1764, two years after the dissolution of the General Economy, only 24 percent of the children in Bethlehem under the age of 12 lived with their parents. Slowly that percentage increased until by 1769, 35 percent of the children in that age group lived with their parents. Then the transition proceeded more rapidly. By 1770, 49 percent of those children lived with their parents, and by

FIGURE 3-14. View of Bethlehem in 1852

1771, 57 percent did (see Table 3-2). After that point, the style of keeping records changed and they are imperfect, so it is difficult to tell exactly when the transition was completed. In 1774 the year's end Memorabilia report that some children still lived in dormitories, but since they no longer distinguished the younger children from the older ones, the percentages cannot be compared with those of the previous years.[40] However, it is safe to assume that by the late 1770s virtually all parents who resided in Bethlehem had their children living with them at home. From 1780 until 1785 (when the school was reorganized to include outsiders) only half a dozen girls lived in the dormitories of the Female Seminary. These were the daughters of missionaries whose care was still assumed by the church.[41]

The records give some hints about how the parents managed this change. Infants had always lived with their mothers until they were weaned and ready at about 18 months to move into the nursery. After 1762, instead of putting them in the Nursery, we can assume that parents began to keep their toddlers at home, because the Nursery was ended within a few years.[42] If this assumption is correct, parents cared for all their infants and 75 percent of their nursery-aged children by 1764, and from 1765 on, parents had at home with them all their infants, all their nursery-aged chil-

TABLE 3-2 Integration of Children into Parents' Homes after the Dissolution of the General Economy*

	Catalog of Children				Location of Children		Children 5 or Over with Parents	
	Infants 0–1	Nursery 1–4	Older 5+	Total	Percent in Institutes	Percent with parents	Number	Percent of all children with parents
1764	5	36	92	133	76	24	—	—
1765	5	32	85	122	69	31	1	3
1766	7	28	81	116	68	32	2	5
1767	4	26	82	112	68	32	6	17
1768	8	22	75	105	68	32	4	12
1769	5	25	68	98	65	35	4	12
1770	5	22	65	92	51	49	18	40
1771	9	21	65	95	43	57	24	44

*See Appendix, II, p. 258 for an explanation of sources.

dren, and some of their older children as well. By 1767, 17 percent of the children living with their parents were 5 years or older, and by 1771, 44 percent were. Thus parents were able to take on the care of their children in a way that was gradual and that grew naturally from their accustomed practice of caring for their infants.

Complicating the transition was the continuing concern that boys and girls be kept separate as they grew up. The Synod Minutes suggest that there are times "when children of both sexes cannot properly be kept together and when the age or the personal circumstances of the children themselves make living with parents unadvisable."[43] Bethlehem must have taken these instructions seriously. In 1768, 27 families included children. Of these families 14 had only male children and 12 had only female children. Just one family had a male child and a female infant. This restriction must have retarded the assimilation of children during the first years after the dissolution.

Unfortunately I found no records between 1771 and 1850 that indicated where each family member lived. The latter year, however, marked the first year in which a census located households in buildings, and it showed that Bethlehem had by that time become a place which was strongly oriented toward family. Virtually all the families lived in separate apartments with all of their dependent children, and nearly half had houses to themselves. The bonds between parents and children and between brothers and sisters were apparently as strong in Bethlehem as in other places because extended family households were as common there as in towns which had always been organized around family life. In 16 out of 313 households, extra adults could be identified as probable siblings or parents of either the husband or wife because they shared the family name, and/or they were the appropriate age.[44] The number of extended family households was probably at least double that amount (i.e. at least 32) since sisters, nieces and nephews of both husband and wife and brothers of the wife could not be identified by shared surnames. We can therefore estimate that at least 10 percent of Bethlehem households in 1850 included people who were extended family relatives of either the husband or the wife. Furthermore, in any community the percentage of families who at one point in time have extended family members living with them is smaller than the percentage of families who at some time in their life cycle have relatives living with them.

Another measure of the importance of extended families is the frequency with which brothers and sisters or parents and children lived as close neighbors. Again, from the census records alone, it is possible only to locate clusters of families who share last names. In Bethlehem 18 pairs or 36 families with the same name lived within three houses of each other. In addition, some married daughters must have lived near parents and some married sisters must have lived near brothers or sisters, so it is likely that at least twice that many or over 20 percent of the families lived as close neighbors with extended family members.

Even though families in Bethlehem, more than in other Northampton County towns, shared duplexes and apartment houses, the 1850 census shows that Bethlehem's real estate was used and divided in ways that supported individual family life. Of the households in Bethlehem 49 percent lived in one family buildings, 34 percent in two to four family buildings, and 17 percent in buildings which housed seven or more families. If we look at the characteristics of the households in those three categories we can begin to understand how the different house types functioned. Tables 3-3, 3-4, and 3-5 together suggest that families progressed through the house types as they matured. Households in two to four family houses were generally small nuclear families of modest means, headed by young male adults. Households in one family houses were larger nuclear families or families with apprentices, servants, and/or extended family relatives. They were generally well-off and they were usually headed by middle-aged males. Households in the larger apartment buildings were usually older, female solitaries who owned no real estate at all. This pattern suggests that families started out in the relatively modest two to four family houses. As they grew in size, maturity, and wealth they moved into the one-family houses. When the children had grown up and married and the husband had died, the surviving widow moved into a small apartment.

Not everyone participated in this progression. Some families were

TABLE 3-3 Characteristics of Households
in Different Types of Houses in 1850

	House Type		
	One family house	*Two to four family house*	*Seven or more family house*
Median age of household head	43	34	51
Average household size	5.5	3.5	1.7
Average value of real estate holdings	$2200	$390	$0

117

TABLE 3-4 Distribution of Family Types
Among Types of Houses in 1850

	House Type			
Family type	One family house	Two to four family house	Seven or more family house	
NUCLEAR				
Raw score	70	76	13	
Percent	44	48	8	100%
FAMILY + OTHERS				
Raw score	80	20	3	
Percent	78	19	3	100%
SOLITARY + OTHERS				
Raw score	1	7	3	
Percent	9	64	27	100%
SOLITARY				
Raw score	6	9	35	
Percent	12	18	70	100%

TABLE 3-5 Distribution of Male and
Female Household Heads Among Types of Houses in 1850

	House Type			
Gender	One family house	Two to four family house	Seven or more family house	
MALE				
Raw score	144	92	7	
Percent	59	38	3	100%
FEMALE				
Raw score	13	20	47	
Percent	16	25	59	100%

still living in the two to four family houses during mature middle age even
when they had grown quite large. The heads of these families were often
unskilled laborers, and they had little or no real estate. They apparently
could not afford the next step. Others were well enough off to begin marriage in the one family houses, and widows from a few of these fortunate

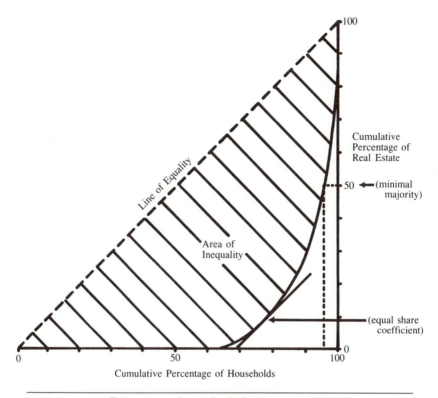

FIGURE 3-15. Inequality in Bethlehem in 1850

families continued to live in the family home as solitaries. These exceptions suggest that by the middle of the nineteenth century the residents of Bethlehem shared Bethlehem's buildings unequally. Figure 3-15, a Lorenz curve, represents the degree of inequality in real estate holdings in Bethlehem according to the records in the 1850 census.[45] Less than 5 percent of the households controlled 50 percent of the private (i.e. non-church) real estate (see minimal majority), and 78 percent of the households owned less than an equal share of the real estate (see equal share coefficient).

This high degree of inequality is symbolic of the dramatic change in the use of Bethlehem's land and buildings during its first century. Bethlehem had begun existence as a communal settlement. A proprietor held all the real estate in trust for the Gemeine but individual residents in Bethlehem shared equally in the use of the land and buildings. At the time of the transition the church authorities sought to maintain Bethlehem as an exclusively Moravian settlement by preserving its control of Bethlehem's real estate, which a proprietor continued to hold in trust. Residents rented what they needed for their homes and businesses. The result was that for over fifty years after the transition Bethlehem residents were unable to increase their wealth through investment in real estate. But as the land around Bethlehem began to increase in value and as economic ties between Bethlehem and outsiders grew stronger, Bethlehem residents identified more and more with the land and the buildings they used. So whenever the church decided to sell some of its holdings to relieve its financial woes, it found ready buyers. But because some people had accumulated more money in the course of running their trades and professions, the available real estate was distributed in an unequal fashion. The unequal ownership of Bethlehem's buildings and the land beneath them indicates just how thoroughly individual and family enterprise had managed within just ninety years to eclipse Bethlehem's communal beginnings.

NOTES

1. Map of Bethlehem in 1758 in Levering, p. 391; William John Murtagh, *Moravian Architecture and Town Planning; Bethlehem, Pennsylvania and Other Eighteenth-Century American Settlements* (Chapel Hill: University of North Carolina Press, 1967), pp. 23–93; Erbe, pp. 78–79.

2. Erbe, pp. 65–66, 179–80.

3. Plan of Bethlehem Lands, December 1761, Levering, p. 352; Erbe, p. 58.

4. Levering, pp. 255, 430; Erbe, p. 62.

5. Erbe, p. 183.

6. According to Murtagh, the developers of Bethlehem quite frequently used this technique. The whole complex which included the Gemeinhaus, the Chapel, the Bell House, and the Single Sisters' House was apparently designed as a unit but built piecemeal, and within that the Bell House and the Single Sisters' House were each built in three stages, Murtagh pp. 36–46, 51. However, Murtagh's work is being questioned by more recent researchers.

7. Levering, pp. 77, 144; Murtagh, p. 26.

8. Murtagh, pp. 30–32, 48, 90–93; Levering, p. 145.

9. Erbe, pp. 65–75, Levering, p. 161.

10. Levering, p. 352.

11. Erbe, p. 58. Compare also the drawings of Bethlehem in 1750, 1755, and 1757 reproduced in Levering on pages 290 and 358.

12. Murtagh, pp. 36, 46, 51–62, 69.

13. The first half of Levering's history of Bethlehem is filled with accounts of all these comings and goings.

14. Levering, p. 285.

15. Levering, p. 128.

16. Levering, p. 144.

17. See Figure 1-3 in Chapter 1 for a taxonomy and complete explanation of these terms.

18. Levering, p. 129.

19. See Delores Hayden, *Seven American Utopias: The Architecture of Communitarian Socialism, 1790–1795* (Cambridge, Mass.: MIT Press, 1976) for an interesting study of the relationship between architecture and cultural values in other communitarian settlements.

20. Levering, pp. 388–89; Murtagh, pp. 30–32.

21. Bethlehem Diary, August 27/September 7, 1742. Bethlehem Moravian Archives, MSS. Levering, pp. 372–74, 388.

22. See the Diary kept by the Single Sisters for lists of roommates including young Indian women. See the Church Register and maps of the cemetery for details of burials.

23. Levering, pp. 193, 352.

24. Levering, pp. 346–47.

25. Levering, pp. 352, 368–69.

26. Levering, p. 283.

27. Erbe, pp. 131, 140, 145–46.

28. Levering, p. 382.

29. *Verlass der vier Synoden . . . von den Jahren 1764, 1769, 1775, 1782,* §§78f.

30. Bethlehem Diary, June 20/July 1, 1742

31. See Murtagh, pp. 24, 43, 61, 83 and Levering, pp. 284–85, for plans and uses of rooms in various Bethlehem buildings.

32. Inventarium derer Mobilien in Bethlehem 1758, Bethlehem Moravian Archives, MSS.

33. I am indebted to Ralph Schwarz for his considerable help in the following description of Bethlehem's development. His extensive and careful research into the architectural development of Bethlehem has not been published.

34. Erbe, pp. 140–141, 176.

35. Erbe, p. 140.

36. U.S. Census, Northampton County, Pennsylvania, 1850.

37. Charles Bernhard, Duke of Sachse-Weimar-Eisenach, *Travels Through North America During the Years 1825 and 1826 by His Highness Bernhard, Duke of Sachse-Weimar-Eisenach* (Philadelphia: Carey, 1828), p. 155.

38. Quoted in Erbe, p. 128.

39. Quoted in Erbe, p. 145.

40. Memorabilia, 1764–1780. Bethlehem Moravian Archives, MSS.

41. Census catalogs for Little Girls, 1780, 1781, 1782, 1800. See also Levering p. 534 and Spangenberg's Comments quoted by Erbe, in a note on p. 139n.

42. Erbe, p. 140; Levering, p. 383.

43. Verlass, §157; Memorabilia, 1768.

44. U. S. Census, Northampton County, 1850. In a few cases when a woman

had a surname different from the family she lived with and was old enough, I counted her as the mother of the wife. Two characteristics of the data justify this procedure: 1. Single or widowed women were easily able to live as separate house-holders in the converted Choir houses and the majority did, so that the exceptions are likely to be related to the husband or wife. 2. Very few women over 25 and under 50 lived with other families, so it seems safe to assume that women did not continue as servants beyond the age of 25 or so.

45. In a Lorenz curve the horizontal axis is the cumulative percentage of households, and the vertical axis the cumulative percentage of real estate. If every-thing were shared equally, 1 percent of the households would own 1 percent of the real estate, 10 percent of the households would own 10 percent of the real estate, and so on. In the case of perfect equality, the Lorenz curve coincides with the line of equality. Any Lorenz curve below that line defines an area of inequality. One man, P. H. Goepp, was the proprietor of all the Moravian Church holdings in the entire Northern Province of the Church, and his personal holdings were not sepa-rated from his proprietary holdings. Altogether his holdings totaled $250,000 or 40 percent of all the holdings listed in all of Bethlehem. Obviously his proprietary holdings could not be included or the Lorenz curve would have been very inaccu-rate. Since he was probably well-off (most church authorities were), his personal holdings were estimated at $30,000 along with the next highest holder of real estate.

PART TWO

Chapter Four

Biographical Structures

The Moravians experienced sweeping social changes during their first one hundred years in Bethlehem in response to the radical alteration in their economic system. In 1742, the first settlers had committed themselves to the total sharing of the products of their labor in a communal economy. In turn, the community was responsible for their shelter, their food, and their clothing. A scant twenty years later, Moravian authorities began to require that families provide their own livelihoods in separate household economies.

As a corollary to the economic change the patterns of residence shifted. During the communal period, community members had lived in dormitories housing "Choirs" of people whose age, sex, and marital status were the same. After the economic change, Bethlehem Moravians were forced to live more and more as nuclear families in separate houses or apartments.

Even the demographic rhythms responded to the basic economic change. During the twenty years of communal living, people in Bethlehem married in high numbers, they gave birth to many children, and they experienced catastrophic death rates. Settlers and missionaries to other Germans and to Indians bustled in and out of Bethlehem. Then suddenly, with the economic change, the level of demographic activity plummeted. For a time, as people adjusted to the changes, they married much less frequently and had fewer children. After the first heavy exchange of personnel, they moved less often. The population began to decline. Only by the 1820s did the marriage and birth rates rise and the population start to grow.

These changes were accompanied by parallel changes in the behavior the community expected of its members. Such expectations are reflected in the biographies which Moravians wrote about members who had just died. The biographies served in the first place to evaluate the life just completed, but the Moravians also took every possible advantage of these biographies as a way to teach individuals about the Moravian way of life. They read them aloud not only at the funerals of their respective subjects, but on Choir festival days, during daily prayer meetings, or in fact at any gathering of two or more people. Individuals also read the biographies from *Die Gemeinnachrichten* when they meditated by themselves. This early Moravian journal published a sample of the most "edifying" biographies from Moravian settlements around the world. If the biographies could help teach young Moravians how Moravians were expected to behave, they can do the same for us. With this theory in mind, I have chosen to examine the biographies in considerable detail here and in the following chapters.

THE SAMPLING DESIGN

In order to analyze this set of biographies with the necessary sensitivity, I designed a sample of them that reflects crucial elements in Bethlehem's history and culture. Because biographies were written to be read at funerals, the sample had to be based on the population of people who died in Bethlehem, rather than on Bethlehem's total population. From 1742 to 1844, 1,375 people died in Bethlehem. These people represented a great variety of ethnic groups including Germans, English, Scandinavians, French, Irish, American Indians, and Blacks. But since 1,011 (or nearly three-fourths) of them were either born in Germany or of German parentage, we can assume that cultural attitudes in Bethlehem were predominately German. For this reason I have sampled only from the German population, for which there were 710 biographies.

Another limitation was made in terms of time. Each of the chapters in Part I identified two contrasting but stable periods of about twenty years each, with a long transition period in between. For this analysis of biographies I have chosen to focus on the two more stable periods because stability is more likely than transition to generate a complete system of behavioral expectations, and the effects of cultural change will be more obvious. In order to remind the reader that these twenty-year periods are not contiguous but spaced sixty years apart, I call them "Period I" and "Period V." They are the first and fifth twenty-year periods in Bethlehem's first century, and they match fairly well with the period of the General Economy and the period after the end of the close regime, respectively. During Period I, there were 189 German biographies and during Period V, there were 269.

Using these first and fifth period biographies I took a random sample from each of eight sub-groups, defined primarily on the basis of the Moravian distinctions of sex, age, and marital status, but modified as required in order to include enough cases within each category. Moravians divided childhood into four periods: infancy ($0-1\frac{1}{2}$ years), nursery period ($1\frac{1}{2}-4$), younger childhood ($5-11$), and older childhood ($12-18$). To simply accept the Moravian classification as the basis for the sample would leave some classes without any cases of death or without biographies. Before the age of 4, for instance, the percentage of childhood deaths for which there were biographies was small, so that one category, $0-4$ years, was defined to cover the first two Moravian classes. From the age of 5 until the late teens, the mortality rate dropped radically, so that it was necessary to combine younger and older childhood into one category. The upper boundary was set at 19, since marriage rarely occurred before the age of 20; in this way the next age category, active adulthood, was defined more suitably for comparisons between Married People and Single People.[1] The upper age limit on active adulthood was set at 59 for a variety of reasons. For people who had attained adulthood, the average age of death was around 60. Also, people who died before this age were often described as dying young. And until the age of 60 or so, adults were commonly still active in the affairs of religion, economy, and government. Dividing the age categories further by sex and marital status as the Moravians did produced sixteen different sub-groups for each of the twenty-year time periods (see Table 4-1). While sixteen sub-groups may seem too many, they are necessary to the analysis, because Moravians themselves made these distinctions or ones close to them, and because we wish to know if these distinctions correlated with their different expectations for these sub-groups.

Four biographies were chosen randomly from each sub-group whenever there were four or more biographies to choose from.[2] Though the number of cases in each cell is small, to have chosen more cases for each sub-group would have made the total sample unmanageably large. It should also be clear that we can analyze the biographies using only one or two parameters rather than all of them simultaneously. We can compare the sexes, or the age groups, or the time periods, or marital status groups,

TABLE 4-1 Sampling Description

	1744–1763			1824–1843		
	Male	*Female*	*Total*	*Male*	*Female*	*Total*
0–4						
Deaths	51	49	100	51	33	84
Biographies	3	3	6	14	7	21
Sample	3	3	6	4	4	8
5–19						
Deaths	7	19	26	10	10	20
Biographies	4	14	18	7	6	13
Sample	4	4	8	4	4	8
20–59 SINGLE						
Deaths	21	7	28	10	6	16
Biographies	19	6	25	6	5	11
Sample	4	4	8	4	4	8
20–59 MARRIED						
Deaths	10	17	27	25	13	38
Biographies	9	14	23	23	10	33
Sample	4	4	8	4	4	8
20–59 WIDOWED						
Deaths	2	0	2	0	1	1
Biographies	2	0	2	0	1	1
Sample	1*	0	2	0	1	1
60+ SINGLE						
Deaths	1	0	1	3	20	23
Biographies	1	0	1	2	17	19
Sample	0*	0	1	2	4	6
60+ MARRIED						
Deaths	2	1	3	21	7	28
Biographies	2	1	3	21	6	27
Sample	2	1	3	4	4	8
60+ WIDOWED						
Deaths	2	0	3	14	45	59
Biographies	2	0	3	12	42	54
Sample	2	0	3	3*	4	8
TOTALS						
Deaths	96	93	189	134	135	269
Biographies	42	39	80	85	94	179
Sample	20	16	36	25	29	54

*The original sample in these cells each included one biography that was incomplete, so it was left out of the final analysis in each case.

or any combination of these parameters, so that most comparisons will be made using many more than four cases. If fewer than four biographies existed for any sub-group, as was the case for thirteen sub-groups, whatever biographies did exist became part of the sample unless they were incomplete. For eight of these thirteen sub-groups, all of the people who died left biographies (for example, Married People over 60 from Period I), so for those groups there was no problem of under-representation. For the remainder of the thirteen sub-groups it was assumed that the biographies survived or were produced on a random basis. In point of fact no strong biases within any age group were discovered which would give greater representation to some kinds of people than to others (i.e. the kinds of people classified by sex, wealth, occupation, social class, etc.) Table 4-1 shows, however, that relatively few biographies exist for the number of children who died between the ages of 0–4. The conclusions about these young people will be the least reliable unless the existing biographies are extremely homogeneous.

If each cell had been filled with four sample cases, there would have been 128 biographies in the sample. The actual sample has 90 cases, 45 of which are male and 45 female. The first period is represented by 36 cases and the fifth period by 54.

BIOGRAPHIES AS DOCUMENTS

Before analyzing the content of the biographies, it is first necessary to describe them as documents to see if their purpose, their authorship, their relative lengths, or their structure affect the analysis in any way. Their original purpose has already been mentioned: they were intended as evaluations of the lives of people who had just died as well as devices for teaching Moravians by example how they should behave. Both of these purposes suggest that the biographies idealized the lives of their subjects and cannot be depended upon to reflect actual behavior. But since this study focuses not on actual behavior but upon behavioral rules or norms, idealized biographies are the perfect source. The idealizations are not all positive. Although most of the lives described were apparently ideals to be emulated, a few were negative examples to be avoided. These negative portraits are as informative as the positive ones are.

Since I intend to analyze the contents of these biographies, their authorship is an important issue. Perhaps a minister or a Choir leader would emphasize the religious life of the subject, whereas a family member might focus on the subject's family life. If the biographies for the first period were written by one kind of author and those for the last period by another kind of author, then it would seem that we must assume that any differences are due to the change in authors rather than a change in behavioral rules.

It is somewhat difficult to determine authorship directly since most biographies do not explicitly state who wrote them. A few biographies were obviously autobiographies, since they were written in the first person, but the description of the final illness and death was of course written by another person. Other biographies were obviously written by husbands—they used the words "we" and "my wife." But for most biographies all we can do is use the contents to judge who might have known such information about the subject.

The results of the analysis are surprising (see Table 4-2). Since Moravians in Bethlehem had changed from a communal settlement to one based on nuclear families, I expected the role of family members as authors to increase across the time periods. It did, but not to the degree I expected. During the first period the content of 12 percent of the biographies was supplied totally or partly by family members, whereas by the fifth period 33 percent of the biographies had at least some input by family members.

The most striking change was the decrease in the number of biographies for which the subjects themselves must have supplied the informa-

TABLE 4-2 Authorship of Biographies

	Self plus Gemeine	Gemeine	Family plus Gemeine	Family
PERIOD I				
Percentages	34%	56%	6%	6%
		96%		
Combination percentages			12%	
PERIOD V				
Percentages	6%	63%	23%	10%
		91%		
Combination percentages			33%	

tion. During the first period 34 percent of the subjects contributed significantly to their own biographies, whereas during the fifth period only 6 percent did.

But the most unexpected finding was that a majority of the biographies was written by an official in the Gemeine during both periods. In fact, the percentage rose from 56 percent to 63 percent. And for both periods more than 90 percent of the biographies showed evidence of input by the Gemeine.

Even though there was increased input from family members, it is clear that the Gemeine played a steady and significant role in the production of biographies during both periods. It is therefore safe to assume that differences in content reflected changes in cultural norms and not just changes in authorship. If a particular biography emphasized family, it did so not only because a particular author chose to do so, but because it was culturally accepted to emphasize family.

The biographies vary greatly in length. Some are one-page sketches; others are full of detail and go on for many pages. We need to know whether these differences in length are systematic. If we know the age of the biographical subjects or the sex or the marital status or the period of time during which they lived, does this knowledge help us to predict the length of the biographies?

The first step is to devise a dependable measure of length. The number of pages does not qualify because the size of handwriting varies too much. Neither does the number of sentences, since some writers combine many thoughts to make one sentence, while others write more simply. We are really interested in counting the number of thoughts or statements made in each biography. Since the linguistic reformulations described in Chapter 6 convert each biography into a series of simple statements, we can count the number of such statements in each biography and obtain a dependable measure of its length.

Table 4-3 shows the weighted averages of the various sub-groups in the sample. The difference of means test on this sample shows that the biographies of females are virtually the same length as those of males. Likewise, the biographies written during the first period are nearly the same length as those of the last period. The average lengths of the different marital status groups *do* vary (the difference between Married and Widowed People is particularly large), but since the variance for Married People is large and the sample size of Widowed People is small, the difference of means is insignificant. The only contrast for which the difference of

TABLE 4-3 Difference of Means Test on Biography Lengths

	Sample N	Weighted average	Weighted variance	Student's t	Significance level
TIME PERIOD					
Per I	36	131	976	0.13	Insig.
Per V	54	127	2368		
MARITAL STATUS					
A. Sing	22	137	1729	0.48	Insig.
Marr	26	177	6795		
B. Marr	26	177	6795	0.80	Insig.
Wid	12	110	429		
C. Wid	12	110	429	0.63	Insig.
Sing	22	137	1729		
SEX					
Females	45	128	2229	0.02	Insig.
Males	45	127	1389		
AGE					
Minors	30	96	1635	1.29	.10*
Adults	60	155	2062		

*A significance of .10 is based on a one-tailed test since I predicted that adults' biographies would be longer than minors'.

means test approaches significance is that which compares adults with children. On the average, the adults' biographies are more than 60 percent longer than the children's biographies and the significance level is .10. Because the children's lives were cut short, it is to be expected that their biographies will be shorter than those of adults; therefore the differences in length should cause no problem for the analysis of content.

THE STRUCTURE OF LIVES

Since the structure of the biographies is relatively standardized for each period, it can be conveniently described using flowcharts with two types of boxes: *rectangles,* each of which describes a topic in the biography, and *diamonds,* each of which represents a decision to be made before the next appropriate topic can be identified: is the person male or female, for instance, or is the person married or single? The topic boxes reflect important expected events in the lives of different classes of individuals, whereas the decision boxes reveal the significant distinctions used to separate people into classes.[3]

Figure 4-1 shows the standard paths for the biographies from the first period (1744–1763). It suggests that the paths expected for people of all ages, of both sexes, and of different marital status groups, were remarkably similar. Of the 24 topic boxes, 11 are shared by every class of people and 18 are shared by all adults. To guide the paths through the 24 topic boxes, only 6 decision boxes are required.

Let us first look at the 11 boxes shared by all sub-groups of Moravians, including children 0 to 4 years old. These, we might call "core" boxes. They can tell us what was expected of virtually every individual who lived in Bethlehem during that first twenty years.

Biographies began appropriately enough with birth. Usually the date and place of birth sufficed, but in the case of one-year-old Anton Peter Böhler, the event of birth was drawn out with great detail and emphasis, beginning with the many miles he traveled with his mother before birth as she and his father carried out their missionary responsibilities and ending with the near-miracle of his blooming recovery after a difficult birth.

Following the topic of birth, the biography identified the person by family membership naming at least the father and often the mother. If the person was connected with the early history of the Moravian Church, especially during the period of the Hidden Seed in Moravia, the story of that early connection became a part of his or her identity. Through these accounts of great suffering and wondrous escapes during the early history of the church, later readers gained a sense of their own identity as Moravians.

The next topic shared by the biographies of all classes of Moravians during the first period was a character description. For the infants this function was usually fulfilled by a few adjectives like "lively," "cheerful," or "quiet." Older children and adults were often described with elaborate examples: conversations with other children and adult leaders or stories about habits or peculiarities.

After the character description came an evaluation of the person's religious state. This took the form of determining if the person had developed the proper humble relationship with the Heiland. Even the infants were subjected to this scrutiny by seeking some sign that they thought about the Heiland. One infant was reported to look pleased whenever he heard something about the Heiland. Another pointed to her hand, which indicated that she was thinking about the Heiland's wounds. Children of only 5 or 6 began, ideally, to engage the Heiland directly and to grapple

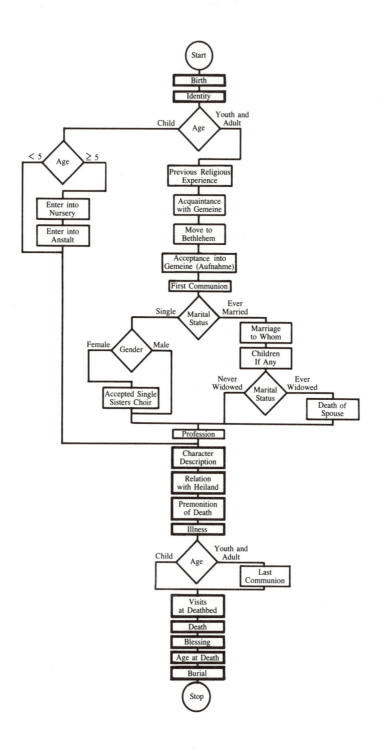

with their own state of corruption. Young adults were expected to have accepted their own abject condition and their complete dependence on the Heiland.

The next topic addressed was premonition of death. With few exceptions the subjects of the biographies were reported to have sensed that they would soon die even before there were any signs of serious illness. Babies were thought to show this by being especially affectionate with their parents the day before they died. Older children and adults predicted that they would die during a specific period: before the year was out, for instance, or before their next birthday.

After the premonition of death, the biography reported the beginning and course of the final illness and told of visits and significant conversations between others and the dying person. It reported the date and time of death and reported that the dying person was blessed by his or her Choir and the Gemeine during the moment of death. The age of death was given in years, months, and days. Lastly, the burial was reported and sometimes described in detail.

In addition to the topics shared by everyone, there were a number which applied to only some of the cohort groups. People who reached the age of 5 or more experienced various rites of passage. (See the middle section of Figure 4-1.) Children of 5 or more graduated to the Institute ("Anstalt").[4] Adults traced the religious path which culminated in Acceptance into the Gemeine ("Aufnahme") and First Communion. After that, single women joined the Single Sisters' Choir, and the date of marriage was given for Married Brothers and Sisters.

In spite of these differences, the structure of these biographies from the first period suggests that there was supposed to be one major focus in the lives of all Moravians and that this focus was religious. Even children under one year of age were supposed to be aware of the Heiland and to sense when they were about to "go home" to the Heiland in death. Of the 11 core topic boxes, 6 of them have religious content: relation with the Heiland, premonition of death, visits at the deathbed, death, blessing, and burial. Of the 6 additional topics expected for all classes of adults, at least 4 also have religious content: previous religious experience, acquaintance with the Gemeine, acceptance into the Gemeine, and First Communion. Even the other 2, the move to Bethlehem and profession, were treated in religious terms. The ways in which each of these topics contributed to the

FIGURE 4-1. Structure of biographies, Period I, 1744–1763

development of the religious focus in first period Bethlehem will be discussed in detail in the next chapter.

Up to this point I have dwelt on the remarkable uniformity in the biographies of the different kinds of Moravian individuals during the first period, and in doing so I have briefly discussed the information represented by the topic boxes. But as James Spradley suggests in a different type of analysis,[5] the dimensions of contrast used by a society can give us evidence about that society's world view which is at least as important as the evidence drawn from similarities. Therefore let us now turn to the information in the decision boxes of Figure 4-1.

We know that the Moravians distinguished among their members by contrasts in age, gender, and marital status. These were the attributes used to divide people into different Choirs. Chapter 3 indicates that gender distinctions were uppermost in the minds of the original designers of Bethlehem, for the two sexes were carefully kept apart by the town plan and by the use of spaces within buildings. In contrast, people of different ages—as long as they were of the same sex—had frequent contact with each other. This would suggest that expectations should contrast more for men and women than for the different age groups within each gender group.

The decision boxes of Figure 4-1 indicate just the opposite case.[6] For a society which practiced the scrupulous separation of the sexes, even to the point of housing married women and married men in different buildings, the expected path of life was surprisingly uniform. The only difference in the paths usually reported for men and women was that for single women it was important to name the date at which they became a Single Sister, whereas for single men the act of joining the Choir of Single Brothers was not specifically mentioned. Though life within the Single Brothers' Choir was often described, it was in the context of the Brother's work life or his religious progress and never as a topic of notice by itself. A way of measuring the overall homogeneity between the expected lives of men and women is to say that only 1 decision box in Figure 4-1 asks the gender of the person, and that it governs only 1 out of the total 24 first period topic boxes.

Of the 6 decision boxes, 2 ask about marital status in order to determine whether the path should go through the boxes for "marriage" and "children," and later whether it should address the death of a spouse. The most interesting distinction here occurs between single and married women. Although most married women were Single Sisters before they married, the biographies of married women rarely mentioned the date they became a Single Sister. The one exception in this sample was a woman who died only one month after her marriage. Her experience as a Single Sister still loomed large, and it was important to emphasize. For the other married women, their entry into the Single Sisters' Choir was shadowed (as for all men) by subsequent events in their lives. But the expected path for all adults, regardless of marital status, is amazingly homogeneous: the 2 decision boxes concerning marital status govern only 4 topic boxes out of the 22 possible for adults.

The remaining 3 decision boxes concern the question of age. Children did not have previous religious experiences, since they had not lived long enough. They were born into the Gemeine and most of them were born in Bethlehem, so they did not have to become acquainted with the Gemeine and then move to Bethlehem. They had not yet reached the age for acceptance into the Gemeine or for the First Communion. And later, during the final illness, they did not have a Last Communion, because they had not yet had their first. Children were further divided at the age of 5. Those 5 or older had lived in the Nursery and had graduated into the Anstalt. The 3 decision boxes which ask about age govern 12 topic boxes or half the total.

The decision boxes of Figure 4-1 suggest that during the first period, age determined the expectations for individuals a great deal more than gender did. During this time, females and males were supposed to live separate but quite similar lives.

The structure of the biographies for the period from 1824 to 1843 contrasts sharply with that of the first period biographies. As Figure 4-2 demonstrates, the structure for the later period is much less homogeneous and a good deal more complex than for the first period. There are 34 different topics shown in the fifth period flowchart, only 5 (15 percent) of which are shared by all classes of people. They represent the barest frame of a person's life: birth, final illness, suffering in the final illness, death, and age at death. They are the most concrete, the most physical of the 34 fifth period topics.

The only other topics shared by very many classes of biographies are those representing religious rituals. In addition to the above 5 topics, minors shared baptism and adults shared acceptance into the Gemeine, First Communion, and final blessing. Though most adults presumably were baptized, only the biographies of women ever mentioned it.

In addition to these, 2 more topics occurred in the biographies of all classes of men and women, but they occurred in different contexts so that their meanings changed. For women the topic of religious status usually followed their character description, and it preceded the onset of the final illness, suggesting that women were expected to emphasize religion during their daily lives. For men, it came after the onset of illness, as if religion was expected to play a major role only when their daily lives were about to be cut off. The biographies of all classes of adults also included descriptions of character, but married women and men were evaluated in their roles as spouses and parents, whereas single women and all men were evaluated in terms of their roles as workers.

These different uses of similar topics contribute to the overall conclusion that the fifth period biographies, in contrast to those from the first, indicate sharp differences in the expectations for people of different age, sex, and marital status groups.

By the 1830s and 1840s the biographies of infants had become brief and depersonalized. In addition to the scanty framework consisting of the date of birth, baptism, final illness, the date of death, and age at death, the biographies of infants from the last period depended on readymade poems to express sentiments of grief and religious consolation. These later biographies no longer described the character of infants, or reported the beginning of a relationship with the Heiland, or told of visits at their deathbeds. They suggested that the Moravians of the mid-nineteenth century placed few expectations on their children until the age of 3. When children reached that age, their parents began to judge their character and to hope that they would live to become contributing members of their society, and these concerns found their way into their children's biographies. Age also determined whether or not school, or apprenticeship to a trade, or medical treatment for illness, or hope for recovery was mentioned. The total result is that 17 decision boxes from the fifth period flowchart ask the question of age, and these 17 boxes in turn govern 29 topic boxes out of the total 34.

Likewise the biographies of males and females contrasted with each other a great deal more during the last period than they did during the first. The biographies of all men described the learning of a profession; those of married women did not, even if they had professional lives as teachers or midwives. The biographies of single women told of acceptance to the Older Girls' Choir and the Single Sisters' Choir; those of single men said nothing of graduations from one Choir to the next. Single and widowed men were cared for by relatives, whereas solitary women were usually not. Widows' biographies usually described their grief upon the death of a spouse, whereas widowers' biographies usually did not. In female biogra-

FIGURE 4-2. Structure of biographies, Period V, 1824–1843

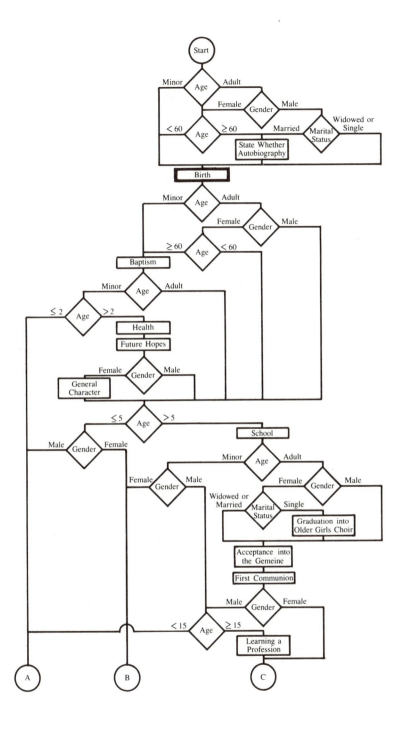

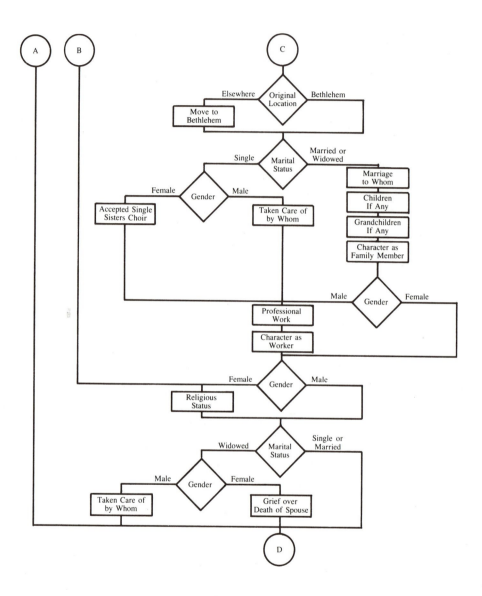

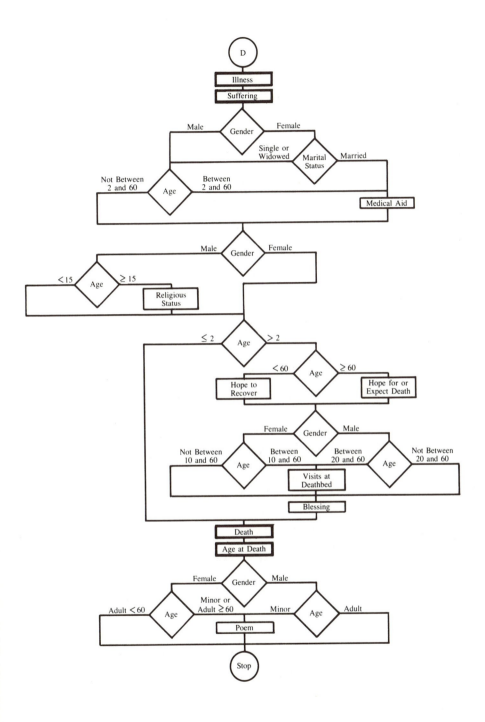

phies the discussion of religious status was a part of the general character description whereas male biographies included it with the account of the final illness. The biographies of older women frequently ended with a religious poem, whereas those of older men rarely did.

Whereas the flowchart for the first period biographies requires only 1 decision box to distinguish between the biographies of males and females, and that box governs only 1 of 24 possible topic boxes, the flowchart that represents the biographies from the last period requires 15 gender decision boxes. These 15 decision boxes in turn govern 17, or half of the 34 possible topic boxes.

Marital status also made a bigger difference in the biographies of different people during the last period than it did during the first. The 2 marital status decision boxes from the first period govern only 4 topic boxes out of 22 possible for adults. In contrast, the 5 decision boxes asking for marital status in the fifth period flowchart govern 13 topic boxes out of a possible 31 for adults.

Of the three important distinguishing factors, age was clearly the most significant, and it had become even more important than it was for the first period. Whereas the age decision boxes control 50 percent of the topic boxes from the flowchart for the earlier biographies, they control 85 percent of the topic boxes in the flowchart from the later period.

Gender distinctions, though less important than age, had also become more important for the later biographies than for the earlier ones. Gender distinctions govern only 4 percent of the topic boxes on the earlier flowchart and 50 percent of those on the later one.

Furthermore, marital status had also grown more prominent for the biographies of the mid-nineteenth century than it was for those from a century before. Marital status controls 18 percent of the topic boxes on the first flowchart and 42 percent of those on the second.

All three of these factors combine to make a complex set of different expectations for the different age, sex, and marital status groups of the later period. By 1840 the picture of 1760 had turned upside down: the earlier Moravians carefully segregated their people according to those groups, but expected much the same kind of living from everyone. The later Moravians had successfully integrated all these groups into nuclear and extended families, but they expected the members of each group to live lives quite different from one another. In the analysis of content that follows in the next chapters I will use the factors of age, sex, and marital status to organize the discussion since they played an increasingly important role in the definitions of expected behavior among the Moravians as time went on.

The next two chapters fill in the outlines sketched in this one. The first of these treats the biographies from the perspective of typical life cycles, using traditional narrative techniques. The second one uses the biographies to learn about secularization in Bethlehem as it molded expectations and goals for individual lives. It uses discourse analysis and other formal methods to find and measure religious and secular emphases and to trace changes over time.

NOTES

1. The exact age at which a child entered an older category varied from case to case, so that the boundaries given here are approximate. For instance, some people joined the Single Sisters or Brothers, and thereby became adults, at the age of 17, while others were not recognized as adults until the age of 21.

2. The random sample I drew was disproportionate across the cohort groups. That is, each cohort is represented in the sample by 4 biographies, no matter what its proportion of the underlying population (as long as there were at least four biographies to choose from). This was necessary because the number of biographies available from each group varies greatly, depending largely on the death rate for that group. By including 4 biographies from each group, I could insure that it was represented by enough biographies to make the analysis valid.

3. I built the flowcharts from detailed outlines which I made of all the individual biographies in the sample. I first included the most commonly occurring topics in the order they usually occur; then by adding decision boxes, I was able to refine the flowchart to fit the cases of different individuals. The resulting flowcharts do not describe every individual biography perfectly, but they describe most of them quite well. If a certain topic appeared in the biographies of the majority of people in a certain age, sex, and marital status group, I included it. If it did not, I left it out. Thus, when I say that the biographies of women included trait X while those of men did not, I mean that *most* women's biographies included it and *most* men's did not.

4. The Anstalt provided an education as well as a place to live for children from the ages of 5 to about 12. Boys and girls were separated when they joined the Anstalt, into the Knäbgen Anstalt and Mädgen Anstalt respectively.

5. See Chapter 10 in James Spradley, *The Ethnographic Interview* (New York: Holt, Rinehart & Winston, 1979).

6. There are many ways in which decision boxes can correctly guide paths through flowcharts. For instance, one could put all the decision boxes at the beginning of the flowchart so that the paths for each subgroup of the population will be entirely separate from each other. Another alternative requires that only 1 topic box of each type may occur in the flowchart so that decision boxes are necessary throughout the flowchart if there are differences within the population (see attached

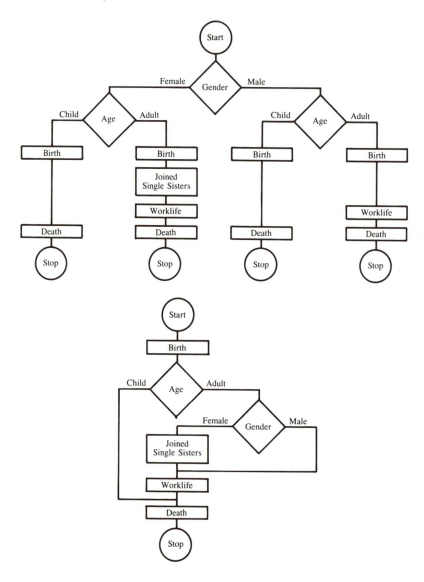

charts). In order to show where the expected path converges for different groups, I have followed the latter approach with the exception that in the flowchart for the fifth period the *Religious Status* and *Taken Care of by Whom* topic boxes occur more than once. To combine them makes the flowchart so complex that it is nearly unintelligible.

Chapter Five

Life Cycles and Values

The standardized structure of the biographies developed in Chapter 4 forms the warp into which typical life cycles were woven. Let us now look at the biographies in more detail to determine the ideals which guided these life cycles and the stages which served as ladders to the ideals. It should be noted that during the periods under consideration, no one moved through all these stages. Neither the period of the General Economy nor the period after the end of the close regime lasted for much more than twenty years. Children born at the end of each period just barely reached adulthood when it ended. Therefore our understanding of the Moravian view of life cycles is built not from examples of complete life cycles from birth to old age, but from snapshots of Moravian life as it was lived by people of various ages and marital statuses. It is, in short, a reconstruction of the abstract plan for life as the Moravians of each period conceived it.

Eighteenth-Century Pilgrims

In Pilgergemeine Bethlehem, Moravians were trained to serve the Heiland as they progressed from one Choir to the next. Each of these steps marked the beginnings and ends of different stages in life. During the first stage, from birth until they were weaned, children lived with their parents, or more precisely, with their mothers.[1] At anywhere from 15 to 20 months they were brought to live in the Nursery with the other toddlers under the care of a few Single Sisters, whose profession it was to raise them. At the age of 4 or 5, they graduated from the Nursery, where girls and boys were together, to the Little Girls' and Little Boys' Choirs, where boys and girls were kept quite separate, even from their own siblings of the opposite sex. From this point on they were raised by single people of their own sex.

Children graduated from there into the Choirs for Older Girls and Older Boys at the age of 12 or so, and at the age of about 19, young people joined the Single Sisters' or Single Brothers' Choirs. While many adults stayed single for the rest of their lives, others took marriage vows, and thereby joined the Married People's Choir. When one spouse died, the other joined either the Widows' or Widowers' Choir. I discovered no names for these stages. It was not the stages which were named but the people who lived them. A person is a Grosses Mädgen (Older Girl), for example, or a Lediger Bruder (Single Brother), or a Witwe (Widow).

Graduation from one Choir to the next was celebrated with a religious ceremony in which sermons were read outlining the life style expected during the next stage. These stages were modeled on appropriate segments of the life of the Heiland, and in the case of the Single Sisters, upon the role of the Virgin Mary as well. The ceremonies for the girls and women included the tying on of bonnet ribbons in colors which differed, depending on their Choir: Little Girls and Older Girls wore red; Single Sisters, pink; Married Sisters, blue; and Widows, white. These ribbons, which they wore during all waking hours, signaled their Choir membership and advertised their marital status at a glance. Boys and men had no similar external sign, for reasons that are not clear.

The first period of a child's life was spent with the child's parents. The length of time varied greatly from one child to the next and was apparently determined by how long the mother breast fed her child: infants still living with their mothers were usually called Säuglinge or "Sucklings" and the ages at which they were put into the Nursery were between 12 and 24 months, the period when infants are most easily weaned.[2] Further evidence is found in letters from Maria Spangenberg. She writes about a special class within the Married People's Choir of Stillende (nursing mothers) and also about mothers who wished to put their children into the Nursery as soon as they were weaned.[3]

The period with the mother actually began before birth, for the Moravians believed that the actions of the mother influenced the child in her womb. Little Anton Böhler, for instance, traveled with his mother at least 1,000 miles before he was born while she went about her duties as a missionary. As a result he was thought to be "by nature a Pilgrim."[4] The birth itself was a joyful event, attended by great thanksgiving towards the Heiland who was responsible for giving the newborn child to the parents and to the Gemeine. Judging from Anton's experience, the birthing room was crowded, for "everyone" anxiously watched him struggle to breathe. When he finally gained control and even became quite lively, "all of those surrounding him" were deeply moved. Anton's father and (obviously) his mother were included, but who the others were is not stated.

Moravian infants continued to be surrounded by interested and doting adults. During Anton's first day of life, he was introduced to the community of Sisters and Brothers during the evening quarter-hour service. Taken to each one in turn he was greeted by everyone with a welcoming kiss, as they sang a hymn to him and "their hearts melted like wax." Ordinarily he would also have been baptized at this gathering, but his father had already baptized him immediately after his birth, since no one thought that he would live.

As infants grew, unrelated adults continued their interest and took an active part in their upbringing. Anton's biography names 10 adults besides his parents who played with him, sang to him, gave him medicine for an eye infection, reprimanded him, wrote songs for him on his 1st birthday, and prayed for him both before and during his final illness. Another infant, nine-month-old Johanna Ettwein, was visited by some of the Sisters and they discussed her later among themselves. Her biography implies that these Sisters came as much to visit her as to see her mother.

We know from censuses and inventories that mothers and fathers usually lived in separate buildings and that infants resided with their mothers. However, they apparently also had close contact with their fathers. Anton's father was absent for three weeks when Anton was 9 months old, and when he returned, Anton "recognized his father at first glance and was so happy that he didn't know whether to cry or what. He hugged his father, fixed his eyes upon him, and scarcely wanted to leave him for several days afterward." Close ties between infants and their fathers must have been considered important since the biographer emphasizes this reunion to such a degree.

Judging from Anton's biography, mothers were expected to include their infants in nearly every venture. If the mother of an infant traveled from Bethlehem, the child went with her; before Anton was a year old he had made five trips back and forth between Bethlehem and Philadelphia. In those days, such trips required two days each way, and some of Anton's trips took place in cold and windy winter weather, in sweltering summer heat, or heavy rain. Since Anton's parents were especially active missionaries, he probably traveled more than infants of the people who were associated with the Hausgemeine and who therefore stayed in Bethlehem, but the census records indicate that babes in arms were always with their mothers, in Bethlehem or on the road. Perhaps the extent of traveling is more surprising with respect to the mothers than with respect to their children.

Nursing mothers obviously had to keep their infants close by. What is significant is that nursing mothers apparently continued to lead the same outwardly directed lives focused on the needs of the Gemeine that they had led before their children were born.

During this period with parents, children were already expected to begin relating to the Heiland. Anton "greatly loved the Lamb, whose image was undeniably stamped deeply into his heart. If someone spoke to him in a simple way about such things, then he would look delighted, and often, when he was in the company of Brothers and Sisters who were discussing amongst themselves such important matters, he would gaze at them quite solemnly, just as if he understood what they were saying." Johanna Ettwein "often pointed with her tiny finger into the palm of her little hand, which made us see that she was thinking how the Lamb had his wounds there." Johann Schlegel, just 16 months old when he died, was "a child who, in his short life, showed that he had much joy from and was greatly impressed by the wounds of Jesus." Whether infants actually had the beginnings of a relation with the Heiland is less important than the fact that such a relationship was ascribed to them.

After being weaned and placed in the Nursery they had little contact with their parents, for the Moravians were motivated to keep children and parents apart. Since both parents worked for the Gemeine, the Moravians sought to free them from the everyday responsibility for their children. But more than that, the Moravians wished to educate children without the influence of parents. Zinzendorf's design in Bethlehem was to raise a new kind of person, devoted to the life of a pilgrim, and he looked not to the parents, but to the Anstalten to accomplish this goal. Also, practical experience had demonstrated, in the words of Spangenberg, that "the [children] not raised in the Gemeine make for mere rubbish in the Anstalten." In an attempt to deal with such children, the Moravians began a reform school a protected distance away from Bethlehem on the other side of the Lehigh.[5]

Parents played almost no role in the biographies of children older than 18 months, which suggests a rather complete separation between parents and children. The biography of 5-year-old Johannes Sehner identifies him as the son of Peter and Maria Sehner(t), but with that exception, they were not mentioned in his biography, not even in the scenes around his deathbed. (We know from Maria's biography that she and her husband were living and working in Bethlehem at the time.) A similar pattern is repeated for most of the seven other children, aged 5–19, whose biographies are included in the sample. Though the parents of six of them lived in Bethlehem or in nearby Pennsylvania towns, only one parent was reported to have visited her child during the child's final illness. Although we should probably assume that in actuality these parents did visit their dying children, the point is that the writers of the biographies chose not to mention such visits. Instead these biographies tell in detail how these children discussed death and other serious matters with their Overseers and with their Choir Brothers or Sisters.

Even during young adulthood, separation from parents was apparently considered necessary, especially if the parents were not members of the Gemeine. Johanette Salterbach writes in her autobiography about her struggle to separate herself from the influence of her family: "In May of 1753 my Mother was so ill that she sent my brother to bring me back to Philadelphia. Actually my heart was opposed, but, because I was not yet entirely free of her [influence], I let myself be persuaded to go; however, the Heiland made amends and soon took her to Himself, and there was nothing to prevent my return to Bethlehem and my beloved Choir house, which, however, I accomplished only after deep reflection and many tears. The Gemeine had to become important to me all over again." Johanette was 30 years old at the time. The Gemeine recognized the "risk and harm" associated with such visits to "relatives in the world" and explicitly warned against such practice in the Synod Minutes.[6]

We have no information about how the separation from parents at the age of 18 months was managed. In fact we have little knowledge about the ideal life of Nursery children in general. There is only one very brief biography from the first period for a child of this age group: since children aged 2 to 4 died much less frequently than did infants, there are fewer funeral biographies for that group. The sources we do have indicate that the Moravians greatly emphasized the toddlers' religious education. Every evening they gathered the Nursery children together for a Singstunde, at other times they organized quarter-hour services with Kinderreden ("children's talks"). Maria Spangenberg wrote, "The little lambs (there are almost 50 in the Nursery who are just beginning to walk) astonish everyone in the whole country. They know nothing except for the Sacrificial Lamb and don't want to know anything else. They think and talk and sing and play and dream of Him. And at the same time they are full of life but their hearts totally depend on the Lamb, and they love Him beyond compare."[7]

When children reached the age of 4 or 5, they graduated into the Boys' and Girls' Choirs. From this point on, they were separated not only from parents but from members of the opposite sex as well, and their education to Moravian life began in earnest. They were now expected to

149

be attentive and interested in the religious services held specifically for them. Juliana Fritsch was "very attentive at the services in general and took everything to heart." Anna Schmik was an "attentive child, especially in Children's Services," and everyone noticed a change in Agnes Schulz: "she became more attentive in the Children's Services." But more was expected than just passive interest. Juliana was noted for her ability to "tell what she remembered from a long time ago in the Children's Services, and she told it with such feeling." Anna "sat down sometimes after she came from the Children's Services and was able to repeat everything." Elisabeth Böhner "affirmed with moist eyes how happy she felt" [after the Children's Services]. Children also organized their own ways of worship. Elisabeth "held beautiful Liturgies." Johannes Sehner "often sang about [the Heiland] and talked of Him to his playmates." Martin Spohn organized a group of children his own age into a band who "gave their whole heart to the Heiland and [promised] to love Him above everything else."

During their years in the Choirs for Little Girls and Little Boys, children were expected to begin understanding their corrupt natures and their dependence on the Heiland as a consequence. Seven-year-old Anna had clearly made such a beginning: "Once she was crying and her Overseers asked why. She said, 'Because the Heiland is still often distressed with me; He can't always be pleased with me, but I will ask Him for a feeling heart'; and she sat down and cried by herself."

During this stage, too, children began to grapple with the concept of death. They thought about it by themselves and talked it over with each other. Some children prayed to the Heiland to please take them home soon. When Juliana "heard that the smallpox was in Bethlehem she rejoiced and said, 'Oh, if only I get it soon because I think the dear Heiland will take me to him' , and she always looked forward to going home." Others declared they wanted to be the first in their Choirs to go home.

When a child succeeded in beginning to deal with these difficult concepts he or she was admitted to the class of children who were allowed to prostrate themselves before the Heiland at the end of the Children's Gemeintag Service. Prostration ("Anbeten") was as important for children as Communion was for adults. Children's biographies sometimes mentioned a particularly meaningful Anbeten: Anna "never forgot the Prostration at the last Children's Festival. She often told with tears in her eyes how happy she felt then."

At the age of 12 or 13 girls and boys were promoted to the Choirs for Older Girls and Older Boys (Grosse Mädgen and Grosse Knaben), where they received an intensive six or seven year apprenticeship into adult Moravian life. When they joined the Choirs for Older Boys and Girls they usually moved into the houses for Single Sisters' or Single Brothers'. Ideally they also became members of the Gemeine during these apprenticeship years—usually at the age of anywhere from 15 to about 19, depending on their religious maturity. If the young person continued to advance as everyone hoped, then he or she was admitted into the group of people who were allowed to take Communion.

The goal of Moravian life during the period of the General Economy was to develop a relationship with the Heiland which was characterized by Einfalt (childlike simplicity) and Sünderhaftigkeit (acknowledgement of one's sinful nature). Simplicity was the ability to trust in the Heiland and believe in Him with the total acceptance of a child. Acknowledgement of one's sinful nature was extremely difficult because it was accomplished initially with a great deal of trauma. When people first became aware of their failings, they usually struggled to become better, all the while agonizing that the Heiland was displeased. Religious maturity was reached when they realized that by themselves they were incapable of becoming better, that they were by nature corrupt, and that their only hope was to depend totally on the Heiland. Once they reached this point, they were usually rewarded with a vision of the Heiland (most often "in His bloody state" on the Cross) and a sense of great relief. Like the Calvinists, the Moravians believed in original sin. Unlike them, they held that *anyone* who gave themselves to the Heiland would be rewarded with forgiveness and eternal life.

But individuals could not attain these goals by themselves. Rather they required the elaborate support system provided by the Gemeine and the various Choirs. Individuals' ability to profit from this support, however, depended upon the degree of their Offenherzigkeit ("openheartedness")—their willingness to describe their religious struggles to their Overseers and their Choir Helpers—for only then could these spiritual advisers help them attain the proper relationship to the Heiland.

Although openheartedness was an important trait in everyone, it was especially so for people between the ages of 12 and 19, for these years were considered crucial ones.[8] On the one hand they held great promise, for past experience among the Moravians had shown that people of this age often underwent awakening and conversion.[9] On the other hand the Moravians recognized danger for this pre-adult age group: the Synod Minutes called this age "the risky years," and declared in the section on Older Boys that "especially in Older Boyhood, the depraved human disposition becomes very active" and warned Older Girls that "with the increasing sense of human depravity, all kinds of inquisitive thoughts and wicked inclinations also make their appearance." [10] A major concern seemed to be the handling of growing sexual awareness: "One must exercise great care with the boys and youths, not to question them too soon about certain things and definitely not to urge certain confessions prematurely, so that they are not exposed too early to things, about which they are sometimes still ignorant and innocent." [11]

Balthasar Köhler's path through these risky years was nearly ideal. His early childhood was not spent in Bethlehem, but with his non-Moravian parents in a neighboring town. Nevertheless, "he already as a little child loved the Brothers [from the Gemeine] with great tenderness and rejoiced whenever a Brother visited at his parents' house." At the age of 17 he received permission to move to Bethlehem where he quickly demonstrated the hoped for signs of religious growth. "The Heiland soon came into his heart, he became openhearted, and one became aware of a special work of grace by the Heiland on his heart." Because Balthasar so quickly demonstrated his openheartedness he was admitted to the Gemeine within six months and to Communion eight months after that.

Ideally, one's First Communion was a rare and memorable experience. So it was for Balthasar: "That was an extraordinary day for him; as he himself expressed it, he could not have imagined that a person could feel and enjoy anything that much. One could read it in his eyes that something remarkable had happened to him there."

Although participation in the ritual of Communion marked a person as a full member of the Gemeine, one could not at this point sit back and rest secure, but must use the new medium to continue to grow. Balthasar's biography implies that it was his Communion experience that caused him to "become from day to day more childlike and more thorough in this relations with the Heiland, so that one always had to comfort him for those faults about which, it seemed to him, the Heiland was dissatisfied." Balthasar's initial openheartedness gave him access to Communion, but Communion itself helped to teach him the proper simplicity and acknowledgment of his own sinful nature.

Not every successful path took the same turns, but the result was the same. Rebecca Weis [12] arrived in Bethlehem at the age of 13 with the proper religious stance already developed, but she too was said to possess the same traits: "She was aware of her sinful state; she was simple and she was openhearted; she had a tender impression of the Heiland's martyrdom; she gradually became more acquainted with her nature and often lamented that she had spent her childhood so badly." She, too, knew that one's being good required believing that one was bad.

Caspar Boekel's biography reflects a life path that contrasted sharply with both Balthasar's and Rebecca's. "His behavior was frivolous, and he spent his boyhood years in that manner, so that one didn't know what would become of him, until last Christmas when a new blessed period began among the Younger and Older Boys; it looked as if something might begin for him, but it got stuck again." His religious state remained a vacuum right up to his final illness, and as a later section will show, in such cases, final illness took on greater significance than for people who already recognized themselves as helpless sinners.

At about the age of 19, young men and women joined the Choirs of Single Brothers and Single Sisters. These Choirs were particularly important, for it was from them that the Unity leaders chose people to take on the various offices and roles necessary to Moravian Society. The Choir principles for both the men and the women explicitly mention this function. The Single Sisters' Choir was a "school [literally "nursery" or "plant-school"] of the Holy Ghost in which he prepares people for all kinds of uses." [13] The Choir houses of the Single Brothers were "not founded or intended as commercial establishments, but as schools of the Holy Ghost, in which servants are summoned . . . to all kinds of offices and employment in the Heiland's . . . kingdom." [14] The main effort in these preparatory "schools" concerned the condition of each person's "heart," for the proper religious state was a requirement for service in the Gemeine or for marriage.

Ideally each Sister and Brother had already become members of the Gemeine, and they had already joined the ranks of those allowed to take Communion before they joined the Single People's Choirs. In addition it was hoped that they had become awakened (aware of their state of depravity) and converted (aware of their dependent relationship with the Heiland). If they had not, this was their task. If they had, they still had to work hard to keep the proper relationship with the Heiland, for it was easy to fall away from the proper stance. The primary dangers were periods of "dryness" (meaning, apparently, "aridity"), of "indifference" to the Heiland, or of "carnality."

In order to establish the proper relationship to the Heiland or to maintain it, members of the Single People's Choirs were encouraged to hold to certain principles which must have seemed quite familiar to the people who had been raised in the Moravian Church. They had to keep their bodies and souls pure by putting themselves totally in the hands of the Heiland,

and they had to be openhearted with their Choir Helpers so that the latter could measure and guide their progress. The goal was not only to convert but to *stay* converted, to get past the nearly universal ups and downs and to reach final stability.[15] People often had had a conversion experience during their years as Older Girls or Boys, but they rarely had found stability before they became Single Sisters or Brothers.

That the state of stability was not thought to be easily reached was demonstrated in nearly every biography of single adults. That it was necessary for a happy and fulfilling life was demonstrated time and again in the biographies of men and women alike, by good examples and by bad. Elisabeth Brazier had already been admitted to the Gemeine and to Communion as an Older Girl, but as a Single Sister and until her final illness, she continued to display, now and then, "vicissitudes in her carriage" because "she was by nature a very doubting type." Likewise, Elisabeth Kannhaeuser was admitted as a Single Sister to the Gemeine and to Communion a few months after her arrival in Ebersdorf but nevertheless had "many difficulties to pass through" in the beginning, and it was nearly two years before a Choir Helper's question about her religious condition "pierced her heart so deeply that she pondered the matter and didn't stop weeping until the Heiland appeared before her heart in his bloody martyred form and she saw her election in his bloody nail marks which so greatly enlivened her that everyone could . . . sense it."[16] From this point on, she apparently had no problems with the condition of her heart for she spent the remaining few years of her life deeply involved in the service of the Choir with numerous responsible positions.

Johanette Salterbach had seemed to overcome her problems before she became a Single Sister. She reported that as an Older Girl she had battled "indifference and lack of feeling for the Heiland," and that when she overcame that "it cost me a great deal until I could escape from my piety and believe that there was nothing good in me." On the basis of the new found sense of her depravity she was admitted to the Gemeine and to Communion. But not a year later she had another bout of indifference and had to discontinue Communion for more than six months. A few days after her public absolution she became a Single Sister and seemed to settle into the mature stability which the Moravians valued. But the subsequent visit to her mother's deathbed in nearby Philadelphia was enough to break her apparent equilibrium. It was not the event of the death which destroyed her hard-won peace, but living even for a short time in the unprotected environment in "the world" outside the Gemeine. She lost her devotion to the Gemeine and had to regain it before she could reappear in Bethlehem and continue the life of a Single Sister.

Mattias Gottschalk also found that he needed the support which comes from membership in the Gemeine. Although he had been awakened at the age of 13, and later studied at Halle, which was well known for its community of Pietists, he "observed a legalistic conduct." That is, he followed the rules of ethical living, but he did not understand the rightful role of the Heiland in his life. It was not until his first visit to Herrnhut that he was "powerfully inflamed and permeated by the Gemeine's redemption through the wounds [Wundengnade]." But a visit was not enough to preserve him, for "he came to a post where he could easily have become enmeshed in the world and stopped in his tracks if the Heiland hadn't torn him loose and brought him to the Gemeine in Marienborn" at the age of 25 years. From that point until the end of his life eight years later he dedicated his energy to traveling and preaching for the Gemeine with single-minded intensity. The message of his story was again that membership in the Gemeine and devotion to the Heiland brought fulfillment and stability.

Johann Müller also found peace in the context of the Gemeine. He had tried to follow the advice of the minister in his home town and lead a pious life, but learned that that was impossible. He "was overcome by the power of natural depravity and fell again and again into sin." He was restless and worried about his repeated failures until he by chance met some Moravian Brothers who told of the Heiland and his service to humankind. He was deeply impressed and kept company from that time on with the Moravian Brothers in Basel. Eventually he went to the Gemeine in Herrnhaag to live, was made a member and admitted to Communion. But like that of others, his struggle for grace was to last a while longer. He writes in his autobiographical account that after being transferred to Zeist, "I had a hard time, which I had caused for myself. But I turned to the Heiland, asked Him for grace and comfort, and since He appeared to me the way He had bled to death for my misery, I was richly reassured and blessed by Him and I spent the rest of my time in the Brothers' House at Zeist very peacefully."

All of these examples are positive ones. The struggles and anxieties are part of the expected lifepath of good Moravians. Only if they experienced how ineffective they were in controlling their natural depravity on their own, could they understand how important was the Heiland's self-sacrificing death on the cross and how necessary was their dependence on him. These repeated examples also give another message: it would have been nice if people could have become awakened, converted, and then stable in their childhood years, but that was unlikely. Most people had to struggle until well into their twenties, only then to find peace. This mes-

155

sage must have been reassuring to the young people listening to these life stories, for chances were, they were still struggling. They had not yet matched the Moravian ideal, and these biographies gave them cause for hope.

Less reassuring, but no doubt effective, were the negative examples like those of Jacob Schoen. So trying was this man that the author of his biography could not resist qualifying his last name (which means "beautiful") with an alias: "Wüst," which translates variously as "desert," "waste," "confused," "wild," "disorderly," and even "filthy" or "vulgar." His life began harmlessly enough. Born in Switzerland into the Reformed Church, he emigrated to America as a young man and served several years as an indentured servant in Lancaster, Pennsylvania. Having been awakened by the message of some Moravian Brothers in the area, he moved to Bethlehem as soon as his indenture was complete. He was 26 years old. Almost exactly a year later Jacob was made a member of the Gemeine. In retrospect the biographer felt the need to answer the question which everyone must have been asking: How could such a man as Jacob Schoen have become a member of the Gemeine? His answer was long and even defensive: " . . . at first his carriage amongst us held promise. Not only was there by nature something special about him (namely he influenced everyone and won their affection with his inexhaustible willingness, acquiescence, diligence and loyalty in external matters), but also in those days the enjoyment of the grace of Jesus' blood and the . . . connection with the Heiland and the close relationship with His People were important to him. That is how it happened that on the 17th of November 1748 he was embodied into the Gemeine. . . ."

The following year, however, the leaders in Bethlehem were clearly shocked to find how mistaken they had been, for "since he didn't value [his membership in the Gemeine] sufficiently . . . and swerved away from the Heiland and from his own heart, . . . he did something seductive [Verführerisches]." Nowhere does the author tell us exactly what Jacob did that was so bad. The word "Verführung" was used frequently in the Synod Minutes in contexts where it was obvious that its meaning was "sexual seduction,"[17] but one paragraph explicitly broadens the concept: "Under the seduction [Verführung] of the youth, not only the seduction to sins of the flesh is understood, but also every significant inducement to [do] anything that could have a harmful influence on the soul of a person and lead it away from simplicity [grounded] in Christ."[18] What seems clear from this definition is that Verführung was a sin which influenced another person to commit a sin.

This is why the leaders in Bethlehem reacted so strongly to Jacob's transgression: their immediate thought was to expel him from the Gemeine so that other people would not be influenced by him. But when he begged not to be sent away, they relented and found instead a place for him to live by himself in nearby Gnadenthal where he at least could not come into contact with others. After a considerable while, he was allowed to move into the Choir house of the Single Brothers at Christiansbrunn. Then in 1753, four years after his transgression, the Moravian leaders were impressed enough with his apparent progress that they finally admitted him for the first time to the sacrament of Communion.

They were to be disappointed a second time, for in 1755 he "again fell into his previous disloyalty to the Heiland, to His People, and to his own heart." Once more the leaders intended to send him away and once more they gave in to his pleas and allowed him to stay because "he . . . was a person who no longer fit into the ways of the world anyway. After all, he had at this point lived in the seclusion of the Gemeine for nearly seven years."

He continued to live in Christiansbrunn, but he was kept, as much as possible, to himself. This time the spiritual leaders were less gullible, and they noted that "he never came to a really serious contemplation of his miserable condition or to a true embarrassment about it, therefore he never achieved a complete cure through the wounds of Jesus." Because of this, nobody was very surprised when five years later he succumbed for a third time to his vice. This time the Moravian leaders expelled him from the Gemeine, their "patience and sympathy . . . at an end."

But Jacob was nothing if not determined. He went immediately to Lititz, another Moravian settlement in Pennsylvania, and begged for someone to intercede for him in Bethlehem. Upon receiving the answer that he should apply on his own, he wrote a letter to Brother Gottlieb, the Single Brothers' Choir Helper, carried it himself to the inn in Bethlehem and asked to speak to Brother Gottlieb in person. In this interview he told how the wretched condition of his heart had become obvious to him. He argued that he had nowhere else to go, that the "Heiland showed mercy to the worst infidels and the greatest sinners when they turned to him" and that "he hoped the Brothers would show him similar mercy." After 3 weeks of waiting without hearing from Brother Gottlieb he wrote a second letter including "an honest and frank confession of [the condition of] his heart and of all his previous bad . . . deeds," an expression of the "remorse and shame" he felt, and a "most humble" request to be allowed to stay in Bethlehem. Almost immediately he was granted his wish. So convinced was everyone that his change of heart was sincere and permanent that he was publicly absolved and allowed to participate again in Communion just two months later. When he died 56 days after that, the biographer rejoiced that Jacob was an "example of the amazing patience of our Lord and proof that . . . He doesn't let the soul go, He loves it too much."

How could the biographer be so sure? Jacob's problem had surfaced in 1749, 1755, and 1760. That is just three times in eleven years and more than five years between incidents. Only six months passed between the time of his last transgression and his death. Perhaps not enough time had gone by; perhaps he would have eventually succumbed a fourth time if he had not died instead. If confronted with this possiblity the Moravians would have assured us that Jacob could not have failed again. They would have pointed to the difference between the content of his interview with Brother Gottlieb and his second letter to him.

Jacob's interview was a challenge to the authorities in Bethlehem. Arguing by analogy Jacob admonished them to show him the same kind of mercy which the Heiland showed to sinners. No doubt the authorities would have agreed that it was their duty to show mercy in a Christ-like way. In fact they had repeatedly done just that, as they wrestled with earlier occurrences of Jacob's problem. But Jacob had overstepped his proper role. Although it was the authorities' duty to show him mercy, it was not his right to insist upon it. His proper role required humility and remorse at the thought of his depraved state. Brother Gottlieb's response to Jacob's ill-conceived interview was to leave him alone and let him contemplate his situation. Jacob must have suffered untold agonies, not knowing his fate, fearing the worst, day after day for three weeks.

We do not know the course of his struggles during that period, but his letter tells us the result: Jacob had undergone a metamorphosis. His arrogance was gone. The letter showed no trace of challenge. Rather it told of new insights into the depths of his depravity, it confessed shame over his past deeds, and it asked in the "most humble" manner if he could be allowed to stay. If the letter was not convincing enough then his subsequent behavior was: "from then on his behavior was entirely changed. He became a Poor Sinner and was greatly embarrassed about his [depraved] situation; his main concerns were the Heiland, the forgiveness of his sin, the cleansing in His blood, and a complete cure of the old injury."

Furthermore, Moravians would have expected such a change because he had survived the ultimate "school of being sent away from the Gemeine." As they had noted earlier, he had been in the Gemeine for so long that they knew a sudden immersion in the outside world would be a severe shock—a shock of the sort needed to force him to think intensely about his desperate situation. Those weeks of insecurity were exactly what he needed for his "cure."

Jacob Schoen was nearly 40 years old when he found the peace sought after by all good Moravians. His biography was a vivid warning of the many years of heartache which young people would have to endure if they failed to establish and maintain a solid relationship with the Heiland. But if Jacob's example was a fearful one, it was also reassuring, for it counseled that no matter how badly people had spent their past lives, they could still reach the Moravian ideal if they would turn to the Heiland for help.

Many people lived out long and fulfilling lives as Single Brothers or Sisters. They served the Gemeine in a variety of ways: as caretakers and teachers of the young people of their own sex, as spiritual advisors to other members of their Choir, as Choir administrators, as caretakers of sick people in their Choir, as launderers, cooks, farmers, and gardeners, and as craftspeople of various sorts. (The Sisters' crafts were confined to spinning, sewing, and fine needlework, whereas the Brothers practiced one of about thirty different crafts ranging from glovemaking to blacksmithing.) From time to time everyone contributed their labor to the harvest efforts in the summer and fall. But through all this activity the main focus was on forming and maintaining the stable relationship with the Heiland which was required for service in the Gemeine and for marriage.

Each person's progress toward this ideal was carefully measured and described by the ever-watchful Choir Helpers in periodic reviews sent to Moravian leaders in Germany. The Choir Helpers were supposed to be "quietly attentive to the direction in which each person is destined" [19] and to point out those people who reflected the Heiland's grace and showed special talent so that the leaders could keep him in mind as they chose candidates for marriage and for office. [20]

Often when people were chosen for office they were at the same time chosen for marriage, for among the Moravians, marriage had a religious purpose. In order for the spiritual leaders to best help individuals in their religious growth they needed to get to know them intimately. Such intimacy was considered improper between people of the opposite sex. Since only men could minister to men and women to women, Zinzendorf invented a version of marriage in which a husband and wife worked together as a team, the husband serving the spiritual needs of the men in the community and the wife those of the women. [21] Moravian workers were called Streiter or "fighters," and marriage was Streiterehe [22] or "marriage militant," which paralleled the concept of the church militant.

Because of its religious purpose, marriage was governed by a number of constraints. Candidates for marriage were nominated by the Choir Helpers of the Single People's Choirs.[23] In order to qualify, Single Brothers and Sisters had to satisfy a number of requirements, the first and most important of which was the proper awakened, converted, and dependent relationship with the Heiland.[24] If a person met this requirement, the other requirements were thought likely to follow automatically, since the Heiland had the ability to improve people as they by themselves could not.

However, the other requirements were thought to be important enough to name and consider separately as well. Choir Helpers were to take into account people's general disposition, their administrative talent and judgment, and their professional bent. When the pool of candidates was identified, the Choir Helpers from all the Choirs matched candidates to each other according to these same qualifications.[25]

Once a Sister and a Brother were matched, the question of their marriage was submitted to the Lot in order to learn the Heiland's opinion.[26] The Synod instructed Moravian leaders to word marriage questions as follows: "The Heiland approves our proposal that Brother So and So marry Sister So and So," and it explicitly prohibited them from using the words: "the Heiland wills it that Brother So and So should marry Sister So and So."[27] The goal was to learn the Heiland's opinion without forcing the Sister and Brother into a marriage they did not want.

If the Heiland gave his approval (i.e. the Lot produced a "yes"), then the Brother and Sister were approached individually for their consent. Even though the Heiland had already sanctioned the match, this step was taken very seriously, for it was one of the Moravians' "primary principles . . . that the certainty of one's heart should be the basis of all [one's] actions, so that even in the face of positive instructions [from the Heiland], what matters most is the joy in one's heart,"[28] and they recognized that "if someone accepted an offer without having the requisite joy . . . simply because it came to him on the instruction of the Heiland through the Lot, then it is not easy to derive a good result."[29] So, although the Heiland's approval was required for a marriage, it was not enough. The individuals involved had the last word.

However, that was not necessarily an easy task. They were supposed to learn "to distinguish between joy in their hearts [Freudigkeit des Herzens] and the inclinations of nature, because experience teaches that these two things can sometimes conflict with each other." Thus "joy in one's heart" corresponded to a sense of what was right to do, while "inclinations of nature" referred to untutored desire. One could attain real joy only

through an understanding with the Heiland. When faced with such a decision as whether to accept a proposal of marriage Brothers and Sisters had
"to negotiate the matter with the Heiland in childlike simplicity and beg
Him for clarity and determination." If they did this, they were assured of
receiving the will of the Heiland into their hearts—a certainty which
caused joy in the hearts of the truly converted. "The instructions to the
heart [as opposed to instructions through the Lot] they *must follow* and, in
conformity with it, accept or reject the offer [emphasis added]." Although
the Heiland was consulted twice, once through the Lot and once through
prayer, the answer received through prayer was considered the binding
one, as long as a person could be certain that the answer came from the
Heiland's will rather than one's natural inclinations.[30]

The several required preliminaries to a Moravian marriage reflected
the great importance of the "marriage militant," but they also had the
effect of helping to make solid marriages. Most biographies of married
adults report marriages that were "happy and blessed." Other evidence
supports the view that marriage lasted. The Synod Minutes, which gave
unusually explicit rules about almost any other topic, were silent on the
subject of divorce. Apparently there was little need for a divorce code:
among all the people who lived and died in Bethlehem before 1844 there
is official evidence of only one divorce.[31]

Probably the most important cause of marital stability was the careful
selection and matching of candidates for marriage in the first place. Im-
mature, unresponsible, and uncooperative people were ruled out. The
leaders of the Single Choirs (who knew the candidates well) were reminded
repeatedly to voice any hesitations they had whatsoever about the character
of any of the candidates. And leaders of the Married People's Choir (who
knew well the requirements for good marriage partners and good office
holders) were to evaluate as forthrightly as possible whether any of the
candidates seemed unsuitable.[32] Any people deemed unfit for marriage
were simply not allowed to marry.

A second encouragement to marital stability was the Heiland's contri-
bution to the marriage decision through the Lot. For people who believed
that the Heiland spoke through the Lot, his "yes" would have had a powerful impact. If the Heiland thought their match was a good one, they
would be motivated to put effort into making it good.

The participation of the candidates themselves also helped to create
marriages which lasted. If they discovered any unsuitability or unreadiness
during their prayerful consideration of an offer of marriage it was their
responsibility to refuse the offer. If, on the other hand, their period of

introspection and prayer resulted in a conviction that they should accept
the offer of marriage they then could enter their new state with a confidence
that could only help them succeed. This filter was made all the more effective by the fact that everyone had a viable alternative: they could remain
single and still lead a rewarding, useful, and economically secure life in
the company of other Single People. The Choir system institutionalized
and legitimized the single life in a way unknown to other colonial groups.
We know that a number of people chose to remain single in the face of
repeated opportunities for marriage, and others married only after considerable hesitation.[33]

If, in spite of these precautions, trouble developed between a Sister
and Brother married to each other, they were urged not to discuss their
problems with friends and relatives, but to ask their Choir Helpers for
assistance. The Choir Helpers in turn were expected to treat all such information in the strictest confidence.[34] Since individuals already knew their
Choir Helpers quite well and were accustomed to seeking their help and
trusting their advice they probably did make use of this built-in system of
marriage counseling. Its easy accessibility no doubt helped to keep existing
marriages viable.

When Single People left their Choirs to join the Married People's
Choir, they were expected to renew their commitment to the Heiland, just
as they had with all earlier Choir changes: they evaluated their relationship
to the Heiland in the old Choir and prayed for the proper commitment as
members of the new Choir. There was a difference though. Usually, when
people graduated from the Choirs of the Older Boys and Older Girls, they
were still struggling and searching, not having yet reached the appropriate
stance. Hence they would ask for success as Single People if they felt they
had failed as Older Children. In contrast, candidates for the Married People's Choir were chosen because they had already developed a stable relationship with the Heiland, so the statement of new commitment struck a
different tone. Catharina Oberlin's biography reports, for instance, that
"she was bound in marriage to our Brother Oberlin . . . and her yearning
immediately aimed toward becoming a joy to the Heiland in the Married
Choir *as well*" (emphasis added). The implication was that she had already
become a joy to the Heiland as a Single Sister, and her challenge was to
maintain his joy about her in her new role as a married woman.

This was not an easy task, even for those considered solid enough to
enter the married state. Catharina commented to a friend after she attended
her first Married People's Liturgy, "That was a weighty lesson! If I hadn't
thoroughly determined with my Best Friend [the Heiland] that my heart

and His completely understood each other about [my marriage], then it would be too heavy for me; but, as it is, I can depend on Him with complete confidence." Marriage meant a great deal more than just a commitment to one's spouse, it meant increasing commitment to the Heiland, not only in maintaining a personal relationship to him but also by carrying out the tasks he required of people "in the Gemeine and among other people outside the Gemeine and on missionary posts." [35]

In practice this meant that most of the power in the Gemeine (and thus the burden of running it) rested in the hands of the Married People, not just by accident, but by design. For instance, the officers for the Married People's Choir usually also functioned as the officers in charge of the whole community. The Married People's Helper was often also the Gemeine Helper, who was in charge of all the Choir Helpers, and the Married People's Overseer was also the Gemeine Overseer who managed the Overseers for the other Choirs.[36] Likewise, in order to qualify for the office of minister or for any of the Unity offices, a man had to be married. Thus the yearning expressed by Catharina Oberlin to "become a joy to the Heiland in the Married People's Choir as well" was not an empty ritual but a heartfelt prayer for assistance in meeting the new challenges which faced her as a talented young married woman.

Among the Moravians during Bethlehem's General Economy, then, marriage was not so much a social institution as a religious one. Several of the principles, included in the Synod Minutes to instruct the Married People, reminded them of this emphasis again and again. "Marriage is an ordinance of God," said one principle, "which He Himself instituted and blessed." And later, "Therefore each married couple in the Gemeine is to look upon themselves as a little church of Jesus, in which He lives and walks." And still later, a married couple's "association is therefore to be neither frivolous, flirtatious, and carnal, nor legalistic and unfriendly, but evangelical so that one is always aware of the close communion . . . which each partner has with the Heiland." [37]

In order to prevent carnality within marriage some of the instructional principles for Married People emphasized the sacred nature of sexual intercourse between marital partners. "The Heiland not only won for our Brothers through his holy circumcision and for our Sisters through his holy incarnation in the body of Mary, [the ability] to keep their body parts pure and blameless but also to make holy and liturgical use of those same [parts] . . . in marriage. . . . Marital union is therefore viewed in our Married People's Choirs as an act which the Lord Himself ordained and sanctified through his blood, [and] which is sure to be accompanied by his blessed presence and by a remarkable peace, if it is done in His name."[38] Moravians used similar words when they spoke of Communion, and like Communion, intercourse was an act of worship to be performed by a married couple as "a little church of Jesus."

The biographies do not discuss the religious nature of marriage as explicitly as do the Synod Minutes, but they do reflect the fact that its focus was more religious than social. For one thing, children played almost no role in the biographies of their parents. Maria Sehnert's biography was typical—the primary reference to her children was genealogical: her marriage "was blessed by the Heiland with 5 little marriage plants, of which 3, namely 2 sons and 1 daughter, are already at home with Him, while 1 son and 1 daughter are still here on earth and in the Children's Institutes of the Gemeine." Except for the premature birth of her last son during her final illness, none of her children were mentioned again. Instead we are told the details of her service to the Gemeine as a chef in various Moravian establishments. The fact that children did play a significant role in the biographies of the Single People who cared for them, indicates that children *were* important to Moravian society—they just were not considered central to marriage.

The adjectives used to describe successful marriages also reflect the religious nature of wedded life: "blessed" (gesegnet), "happy" (vergnügt), "childlike" (kindlich), "simple" (einfältig), and "blissful" (selig). These same adjectives were used to describe one's mood after a memorable religious experience. The particular kind of religious concern in Married People's biographies, however, contrasted with that in Single People's. For Married People, the time of anxious religious searching was past. They had been chosen for marriage precisely because they were stable and mature in every way, including their relationship to the Heiland. Instead of detailing the struggles toward conversion, the biographies of Married People focused upon their steady relationship to the Heiland and upon their service in his behalf.

Although the biographies of Married People usually mentioned their awakening, it was treated summarily. Maria Sehnert "heard . . . the gospel through the service of the Brothers, was awakened and came to Bethlehem for a visit around 1747." Anna Schaaf "was born . . . in the Bern district of Switzerland, where she was awakened in 1738. In July of 1745 she came to Montmirail and in 1749 to the Gemeine in Herrnhaag." Rosina Michler's biography is a little more descriptive. It quotes her as saying, "My conversion proceeded pretty slowly; I often became discouraged, and was heartily ashamed because many went before me, until I gave myself to the Heiland just the way I was." But even this description is more general and emotionally removed than those of Single People. The next sentence in Rosina's biography is: "In the year 1738 she was accepted into the Gemeine." Her biography reports no incidents of backsliding. The topics of awakening and conversion do not come up again. Johann Bernhard Müller's account is similar to Rosina's: "In the year 1739 he was gripped . . . and awakened by the dear Heiland and he fell into a pitiable condition until 1740 when the Heiland appeared before his heart in His bloody state and let him feel His mercy and love for sinners. In October of the same year he came to the Gemeine in Herrnhaag where he was accepted in 1741 into the Gemeine." Again the issue of conversion is completely settled by this summary statement. There is no discussion of backsliding. The rest of Johann's biography is a model of stability.

The one exception among married people is Martin Hirt, whose biography records many ups and downs. When he was in his teens, his widowed mother married a Moravian Brother, so the family "became acquainted with the Gemeine in Heidelberg [Pennsylvania]. However, our Martin avoided this acquaintance for a long time, until Brother Nathaniel came there in 1747; then he learned to love the Brothers, went to Bethlehem and received permission to stay . . . in 1748." A year and a half later he was admitted to the Gemeine and to Communion, "but afterward he fell away from his heart and left the Gemeine during the summer of 1750. In 1752 Brother Nathanael found him again, and he came back to Bethlehem, received absolution and was readmitted to the sacraments of the Gemeine." But that was not yet the end of his conversion story because his "raw and untamed nature" prevented the Holy Ghost from being really effective in the work on his soul. What finally forced a stable relationship was extreme physical disability which began to develop a year before his death. Martin's example stands in sharp contrast to that of all the other Married People, but it does not reduce the effect of theirs. Rather the tardiness of his conversion and the storminess of his adult life make the steady and rewarding but quiet life of the others all the more pronounced.

Upon the death of a spouse, the surviving partner joined the Widows' Choir or the Widowers' Choir. However, Bethlehem's entire population during the period of the General Economy was quite young, so that the majority of the married couples who were separated by the death of one partner were also young. Of the Married People who died during the first twenty years, 85 percent were 49 or less. Their Widows and Widowers were correspondingly young. Even as late as 1764, 12 of the 24 Widows in the Bethlehem/Nazareth area, and 6 of the 10 Widowers, were 49 or less.[39] Because of their youth these Widowed People produced very few funeral biographies during the first twenty-year period in Bethlehem's history, for a number of them remarried and, of the remainder, only four Widowers and no Widows died in Bethlehem during that period. The result is that no biographies exist for the widowed women of the period and only four exist for the widowed men. And these four biographies offer little information on the life of Widowed People, for they concentrate on their lives as Married People.

Perhaps one reason for the de-emphasis on widowed life in the biographies is that in Moravian society the change from married life required an extraordinary amount of adjustment. The transition from the Married People's Choir to the Widowed Choirs was the most difficult of all Choir transfers, not only because it was caused by the death of one's spouse, but also because it was accompanied by radical changes in one's life. The Moravians were conscious of these difficulties, and, as a result, the section in the Synod Minutes concerning the Choirs for Widowers and Widows discusses them at length.

Several of the principles of the Widowed People's Choir were intended to ease the grief of a newly widowed person. The first task of a Brother or a Sister as soon as he or she was widowed was "to spread the whole of his/her now finished marriage before the Heiland and ask [the Heiland] to give forgiveness for all . . . defects and to anoint . . . his/her new state with new grace."[40] Modern psychology suggests that one of the most painful experiences for survivors is a debilitating sense of guilt for all real or imagined wrongs against a deceased loved one. This first task assigned to newly widowed Moravians would have helped to diminish that guilt, for it assumed that everyone makes mistakes, because as humans they are imperfect. Therefore, whatever wrongs a person remembered doing could be depersonalized and generalized as another manifestation of original sin. It was also assumed that anyone who went to the Heiland and sincerely begged for forgiveness and grace would receive it, so a person was assured of finding peace and freedom from guilt.

In the place of guilt the Moravians encouraged positive thoughts about the spouse. Widowers were told "the memory of his wife and marriage is always material for thanksgiving and praise, also . . . humility before the Lord."[41] Furthermore, both men and women were to believe that the death of a spouse gave them an especially vivid sense of the Heiland and the Gemeine in Heaven, and that "the blessing that [the Heiland] shares [in the death of a spouse] will accompany [a person] through the whole widowed state."[42]

In spite of the encouragement to positive thinking the Moravians knew of course that the widowed state was often difficult, but during the rough periods they were advised that they should "hold very close to the Heiland" and that he would "comfort them through all the difficulties."[43] And if that did not help, their well-developed counseling system did. Widows were told, for instance: "To be sure, such a Sister is free to share her heart and her sorrow with her . . . Choir Worker [in the Married People's Choir] before her complete transfer to the Widows' Choir . . . and since it is natural for us to cry with those who cry, her Choir Helper in the Widows' Choir will not refuse her her empathetic heart, whenever something concerning her late marriage should well up which could be hard for her."[44]

Another attempt to help Widowed People to heal their grief was to urge them to "forget what lies behind and stretch themselves towards what lies ahead." The expected future was different for a widowed person depending on his or her age. Younger Widows and Widowers "should surrender to the Heiland in everything, even if He calls [them] into marriage again." In other words, the Moravians realized that people often withdraw from society when stricken with grief and that they must be roused and prompted to reestablish themselves as contributing members of society. For this reason, Choir Helpers were exhorted not to delay the remarriage of young Widows and Widowers.[45]

Older Widowed People, on the other hand, were expected to view their widowed state as a Sabbath period and to look forward to a future with the Heiland. Older Widows were told "to spend their remaining days, like Hannah, in conversation with the Heiland and in the blessed expectation, that they will come home to Him and be with him forever." A Widower was advised that "when he could no longer serve because of old age or weakness . . . [he should] rejoice daily in the God of his Heiland in expectation of the blessed hour, when the Heiland will call him home."[46]

In addition to the pain of losing their helpmeet, Widows and Widowers among the Moravians suffered a unique and unsettling change: the sudden curtailment of their professional life. Since the Moravians required that many of their offices be filled by Married People, theoretically a person holding such an office would have to give it up when his or her spouse died. In practice this rule applied more rigidly to women than to men. Concerning men, the Synod Minutes asked "whether and for how long a Widower should keep a community office and hold services in other Choirs? Nothing can be determined in general about that, rather the matter must be left to the Unity Elders' Conference to decide according to the circumstances each time the case comes up." [47] In contrast, Widows were told: "In the case of those Widows who previously served the Heiland (often for many years) in the Gemeine and in the Choirs, there often arises a painful emotion, because they no longer have access to many special services . . . to the Helpers' Conference, etc. As much as one would like to spare them this [emotion] this is often not possible. It is reasonable that one should do everything that one can for their pleasure and their well-being. Concerning the above-mentioned gatherings, however, we have instructions from the Heiland [through the Lot], which we must follow, and by which such Widows can comfort themselves. The best thing for them is this thought: The Heiland has put us into retirement—we can now no longer desire what others, who still serve Him, have; however, we still have *Him,* and in Him [we have] everything to keep us happy forever." [48] Since the status and role of a married couple resided with the man and not the woman, the cases of Widowed Men were to be decided individually, whereas those of women had already been decided as a class. Women were compelled to accept their sudden retirement with grace. In addition, if a Widower remarried, he could continue in his job, whereas if a Widow remarried, she derived her new status from her new husband. Her experience and talents were always to be considered when the leaders matched her with a new husband, but this practice did not guarantee that she would regain her former status: "If a Sister, who has up till now been a member of a Conference, is married to a Brother who is not a member of the same Conference, then she must resign herself [to the fact] that she must also stay away." [49]

In spite of the unusually equal amount of responsibility given to and shouldered by the Moravian women, these policies suggest an underlying assymetry between the sexes which must have affected other men and women besides those widowed. This was in fact the case. The principles for Married People reflect the sexual hierarchy typical of colonial society in general: "The husband is the head of the wife, just as Christ of the Gemeine; and just as Christ loves the Gemeine, so he should love, nourish and care for his wife. . . . The wife is entrusted to his care in spiritual and physical matters. He must treat her with understanding, in order to give her respect as the weaker part, and to show her love, sincerity, and patience in accordance with Christ." [50] These views about the superiority of males persisted in spite of the fact that Moravians believed all human beings, including men, were by nature too weak to assume such a role without the help of the Heiland. Therefore they hastened to add: "However, because a man is not capable through his own power and reason of behaving in a manner befitting his calling and office, the Heiland must hold him to [his office] . . . and give him the priestly and kingly spirit that he needs."[51]

Interestingly, the biographies of the first period do not reflect these differences in the status of the two genders. The status difference emphasized is that between all humans and the Heiland, and the status difference between men and women is totally lost in the grander comparison. Most of the biographies for females could function quite acceptably as biographies for males if the names and the pronouns were changed.

On the other hand, three of the male biographies would have made unlikely biographies of females: those of Caspar Boekel, Jacob Schoen (alias Wüst), and Martin Hirt. All three were extremely difficult cases, and their negative examples stand in stark contrast to all the other biographies. Was it a coincidence that the only really negative examples were provided by men, or did the Moravians expect that males would have more difficulty in reaching the Moravian ideal?

Since the Single People's Choirs were considered the "schools" in which Moravians were to reach the ideal, let us look at the principles for the Single Brothers' and Single Sisters' Choirs for an answer to this question. Although a number of principles for the two Choirs treat parallel topics, a number take different emphases. I am certain that if we could ask the Moravians about these subtle differences, they would insist that they were not intended. However, the differences show a pattern which is hard to dismiss so easily. I would argue that while the Moravian answer to a direct question would reflect *overt* culture, the actual differences unconsciously written into the Synod Minutes reflect *covert* culture.

A number of the differences indicate that the Moravians unconsciously expected more behavior problems from the men than they did from the women, even though their overt theory would say that *all* people are by nature depraved. Both men and women were admonished to beware of wrong, but with greatly contrasting implications.

A Single Brother was advised to "take care of his body . . . so that he would not become lustful," to guard "against sensuality and worldly phantasies" and was encouraged to "purify himself at every onset and every incident of such weaknesses."[52] These instructions assume, in line with Moravian theory, that people have the seeds of corruption within themselves. A Single Sister, on the other hand, was told to "close her eyes and ears against everything harmful,"[53] as if the danger for her came from corrupting *external* influences. A later principle tells leaders of the Single Sisters that they must "deal strictly with any impurities."[54] Contrasting that brief and vague statement with the detailed worries about Single

Brothers, including possible lustfulness, sensuality, worldly fantasies, and onsets of weaknesses, one is convinced that the Moravians had a much more vivid sense of the carnalities which plagued men than those which threatened women, never mind what their theory dictated.

A similar contrast is implied in the discussion of other behaviors. Single men were admonished to avoid "anger, quarreling, dissension, hate and jealousy" and try to live in "love and harmony" with each other.[55] Single Sisters were merely asked to consider whether "the spirit of joy could be perceived among them."[56] Likewise, when contemplating marriage a Sister was warned not to "give her consent if she wasn't certain that she had found grace in the blood of Jesus,"[57] whereas a Brother must desire "that it happen in the Lord" and not "think about marriage because of a sensual disposition [or] for worldly purposes."[58] Again, the Moravians suspected the Brothers of baser motives than the Sisters.

Since the Synod Minutes so clearly differentiated the expected behavior of men and women, it is likely that the three strongly negative male biographies are no coincidence and that the Moravians of the first period assumed that men would have more trouble reaching the Moravian ideal than women.

This fact, however, should not overshadow the important point that the ideals for men and women were virtually identical during Bethlehem's Communal Period. Both men and women were to find their primary focus in the Heiland and to develop the humble and totally dependent relationship to him expected of humans suffering from original sin. Both men and women were expected to spend their lives serving the Heiland and the Gemeine in whatever way their talents and skills and socially defined limits allowed them to serve. For both men and women, marriage was an institution designed to further that service, and they were to serve as husband and wife teams, doing similar work that served other males and females respectively. Children were no more a focus of everyday life for women than for men. And for both men and women, the period of retirement (the Sabbath, in their words) was devoted to becoming even more intimate with the Heiland and to preparing for death. This focus on developing a relationship with the Heiland was also emphasized across the entire spectrum of ages. Even infants were expected to search after him in their own limited way.

If the primary goal in life was to relate closely with the Heiland, death was its ultimate realization, for death was thought to be a joining with the Heiland. The most common term for dying during the first period was "zum Heiland Heimgehen" (going home to the Heiland). Such imagery was no casual metaphor. The Moravians of the first period talked of "going home" in the personal terms and with the same anticipation that we would expect of people returning to their family home after years of being away. Juliana Fritsch, for instance, "rejoiced greatly when she heard that the smallpox was in Bethlehem, and she said, 'Oh, if only I could get it soon, because I think the dear Heiland will take me to him', and she always looked forward to going home." Martin Spohn "frequently thought about going home and often begged the Heiland . . . to fetch him home soon."

The image of joining the Heiland was developed further in the concept of uniting with him in marriage. Elisabeth Brazier "crossed over into His arms with a truly bride-like appearance." Catharina Oberlin's earthly husband "gave her over . . . to her Eternal Husband, from whom he had received her. And so this blessed soul drew over . . . into the arms of the Bridegroom." Making use of the feminine gender which the German language assigns to the word "soul," the Moravians extended the use of the marriage metaphor to include men. For example, Philip Meurer's autobiography (written in English with a strong German "accent") uses the marriage metaphor to describe Philip's anticipation of death: "And in this sinnerlike happy situation and expectation of his Bridegroom, he continued till the 15th towards eavening."

Another way of joining the Heiland was to embrace his wounds, the primary symbol of his sacrifice for humanity and therefore the symbol of his relationship to human beings. Catharina Oberlin told her husband: "Now I am certain: I am going to the Heiland. [When I get] there I will catch what flowed from His side and I will kiss His wounds for you." The liturgy sung to people as they died often used the Sidewound metaphor. Johanette Salterbach died hearing these words: "You laid yourself into [the place] where the spear split his side." These uses of the wounds image, strange to modern sensibilities, were comforting to the early Moravians because they suggested nurture and protection.

There were numerous other metaphors designed to emphasize the positive experience of death. One such was the notion of completion or perfection—"Vollendung" in German. A second one was the metaphor of ripening: people were identified with fruits or flowers to be picked by the Heiland when they were mature. Another notion reversed the meanings of life and death. Life was called "Sterbensleben" (life of dying) or simply "Sterben" (dying), and death was "das ewige Leben" (eternal life). All these metaphors helped the first period Moravians maintain their positive view of death as they faced its different stages.

Because they understood death as the positive goal towards which life was leading, the Moravians expected that people would be able to anticipate their own death before there was any outward sign of illness. In the Moravian view, even infants were able to predict their deaths in an infant-like way. Johanna Ettwein "was for the whole day on the 26th of May unusually joyful and affectionate towards her parents, which some of the Sisters, who visited her, noticed and (they) talked about the fact that she had something special about her and would probably not be very long on this earth." Ten-year-old Elisabeth Böhner showed similar behavior: "Shortly before the smallpox came into the house, she was especially sweet. It was as if she had a presentiment of her speedy call home."

Often a premonition of death combined with a strong desire for it. We saw an example of that in Juliana Fritsch's joy when smallpox came to Bethlehem and her sense that the Heiland would use that opportunity to take her to him. Johannes Sehner expressed such knowledge and desire when the children received their New Year's texts distributed as a part of the year's end ceremonies: "The one he received read: 'We should love each other, until my heart flows in to His.' The Brother in his room asked him at this opportunity: 'Do you intend to go home this year?' Answer: 'Yes, I want to be the first.' The other children wanted it to happen by turns [according to age]. But he remained steadfast that he intended to be the first." For Anna Schaaf, pregnancy and childbirth planted a desire for death: "This year she bore her first child. She was especially glad and blissful before as well as after her delivery; and she was often occupied with the thoughts of going home. She also gave witness to her husband as to her yearning for it and her imminent expectation of this great happiness."

Although these biographies suggest that the Moravians expected their members to accept and even desire death, they also suggest a carefully balanced attitude. If the Heiland called a person home, he or she was expected not only to be ready but to be grateful for the favor. If, on the other hand the Heiland still required a person's service here on earth, he or she was expected to willingly shoulder the responsibility. Catharina Oberlin's biography illustrates the confusion when the Heiland sent mixed signals. Scarcely five weeks before the onset of her illness, Catharina had married. She had taken the step of marriage only after prayerful consultations with the Heiland. It was her belief that he fully supported her marriage which gave her the courage to face the considerable responsibilities of a married person in Moravian society. Therefore, when she became ill she had difficulty knowing how to react: "When . . . the red pustules appeared, her husband asked her if she was going to the Heiland. She replied, 'I don't know, but I can't yet believe that the Heiland would have appointed us together for such a short time. I think we will still have more blessed times with each other. On the other hand, it does occur to me sometimes, that who knows if maybe I won't go home [after all]; but then I worry about you." Catharina was facing an intense form of the dilemma whether to focus her energy into recovering or into dying.

The key ingredient in a person's attitude about death was the recognition that the timing of one's death was the Heiland's responsibility. People were expected to look forward to death, but they were never to encourage it by their own actions—suicide was *not* an option. The descriptions of people's desire for death always implied that the Heiland was the agent of death. Recall Juliana Fritsch's words: "Oh, if only I could get [the smallpox] soon, because I think the dear Heiland will take me to Him." Catharina Leibert "said to a Sister at our [Choir] festival, '*Oh please beg the Heiland* that I shall soon attain the happiness of going to him.'" Balthasar Köhler said on his death bed, "It would be my greatest joy if the Heiland would kiss poor me to Him [in death], but I don't yet know how soon it will happen. *I have left it up to the Heiland, to do with me what he will*" (emphases added).

The one case of apparent suicide during the first period was handled entirely differently than other deaths. Margaretha Kunz, married just one month before, was reported to have run away from the Sisters' sleeping room and to have fallen into the Lehigh River down by the washhouse, where she was found dead in the morning. A number of statements in the Church Register entry about Margaretha's death indicate that the Moravians thought it was suicide and not an accident. This was called a "rare and depressing case," whereas accidents were described in the same matter-of-fact tone used for illness. Furthermore, "Justice Owen and the Jury viewed her body" and delivered their report to the court—a step not taken in accident cases. As a mark of disapproval about the way she died, the Moravians buried her that evening "in der Stille"—a German phrase which implies that she was buried without the usual liturgy and with few people present.

But even though the timing was the Heiland's to decide, people who were sick struggled to learn if their present illness was to be their last. Some people knew with great certainty that they were about to die. Agnes Schulz told her playmates a few days before her illness "I am going to get sick, and when I go to the sickroom, I won't come back to you again—I'll go to the Heiland instead." Two days into Juliana Fritsch's final illness, "after she had been very still for about half an hour, she called the Sisters to her and she said that it was now settled in her mind, that she would go to the dear Lamb." Johannes Sehner "said to a Brother, that he hurt all over, and when the latter comforted him with the Heiland's pains, he became very quiet and said, 'I will soon go to the Heiland.'"

Other people, like Catharina Oberlin, were not sure for some time about the certainty of their death. But they struggled with the question until the answer became clear. Catharina's answer to her husband's query about her possible death showed that she had been intensely thinking about the issue. A few days after that initial conversation she said to him, "If the Heiland wants to take me home, you won't hold me back, will you?' And upon her husband's response, 'No—if your real and Eternal Husband has destined you for that happiness, I won't stand in the way, and I won't begrudge you your blessed fortune,' she embraced him with the words: 'Don't be depressed,' and asked him to read to her from the liturgy for Good Friday." Two days later "when her husband was alone with her, she motioned to him and said with a very serene look, 'My dear, good heart! Now I am certain: I am going to the Heiland. . . .' Then she embraced him and thanked [him] for all [his] love and [his] faithfulness." Although clarity was slower in coming to Catharina her conviction was just as strong in the end as it was for those who knew at once that they were about to "go home to the Heiland."

Once they knew for certain that they would die, their nurses, their friends, their family, and Bethlehem's spiritual leaders began to envelop them with support. These people visited them and talked with them about their spiritual state and about "going home;" they read inspirational literature to them and sang liturgies with them; they prayed for them and administered Communion in the sick room; and they took care of their physical needs.

This abundant support must have surrounded dying people with warmth and security. Particularly important during this stage were the farewells exchanged as death drew closer. Both the people dying and those around them tried to sense the right time—after they knew their death was imminent, but before they lost their ability to communicate. The farewells expressed the dying person's individuality in their heartfelt and personal wording, but they reflected Moravian values as a whole in their standardized format. Catharina Oberlin's farewell with her husband (quoted in part above) is a good example: "When her husband was alone with her, she motioned to him and said with a very serene look, 'My dear, good heart! Now I am certain I am going to the Heiland; [when I get] there I will catch what flowed from his side and kiss his wounds also for you.' Then she embraced him and thanked [him] for all [his] love and [his] faithfulness, and said, 'I know it is hard for you to leave [sic] me so soon, but the Heiland will bless you, and who knows, but what you'll follow me soon.'" Farewells frequently included the same content as this one: Catharina thanked her husband for all he had done; she encouraged him by suggesting that his turn might come soon; she blessed him vicariously through the Heiland (though a man would have blessed his spouse himself); and she described her mission in heaven to intensify her own relationship with the Heiland and to act as an intermediary for her intimates on earth. People who had been together longer than Catharina and her husband also often reminisced about experiences they had shared on earth.

The farewell was an important step in the process of dying, for it allowed dying people to loosen their ties on earth in order to further tighten those with the Heiland. Many biographies describe this growing intimacy: Rosina Michler "talked with her charming Martyr-man [the Heiland] and sang the hymn: 'What is He to me? My Eternal Husband . . .' and [she] added that she was already more with Him than here." Elisabeth Kannhaeuser felt the Heiland's presence so intensely that a day before she died she thought he had already come: "On the 2nd of June . . . she asked to be blessed [into death] with the words: 'Give me my blessing and let me move on in peace,' and when she was told that this would happen when her hour came and the Heiland [came to] fetch her, she said, "That's fine, but He's already here."

There was even a view that people who showed no signs of illness but who exhibited an unusually close relationship with the Heiland must be close to death. Balthasar Köhler's biography illustrates this idea especially well: "In the middle of July, he was sent with several youths to Christiansbrunn for the harvest. Before he went away, he came to his [spiritual] Helper and said, among other things, that he knew one could easily become distracted during the harvest and, because of that, away from the Heiland, but he had meditated with the Heiland about that [problem] and asked Him to protect him from anything which could disturb his relationship with Him. The Heiland granted him his [request]—so much so that his uninterrupted relationship with the Man of Sorrow caused reflection in [the minds of] all those who had been with him." The next sentence, as if to corroborate the suspicion, tells of the onset of Balthasar's final illness, which occurred even before the harvest was finished.

This extraordinary intimacy with the Heiland drew visitors to the bedside of the dying, for people came not only to give their support to the dying but to reap benefit for themselves. Many biographies suggested this connection. For example: "In this sickness of [Michael Schnall's] the

Friend of Sinners became so intimate with him that he often couldn't express how good his heart felt when meditating about the martyrdom of Jesus, so that it was a joy to visit him." Likewise, "On the last day of his life, [Caspar Boekel] became so sweet and childlike and so [aware of his] shame as a sinner, that no one there could get their fill of looking at him." Even when the dying were unconscious or delirious, their fantasies could offer inspiration: "The last 2 days, [Balthasar Köhler] lay in fantasies, but with such childlike and sinnerlike an essence, that it was a joy to be with him. Whenever anyone talked to him about the Heiland and His wounds, he immediately came to, and in general his fantasies had to do with Communion and going home to the Heiland." For the same reasons that people gladly visited the dying, they also sought after the highly valued office of sick-nurse. Johanette Salterbach wrote in her autobiography: "In October of 1757 I was assigned the office of sick-nurse in the Sisters' House, which I held for 3 years and 2 weeks with all my heart and had the benefit of many a blessed hour and felt in abundance the closeness of the Heiland at the side of His beloved sick ones."

As the final illness took its course, the dying person and the visitors watched carefully for signs that the "blessed moment" was at hand. This vigilance was motivated by the importance of giving a blessing and performing a "going home" liturgy while the person died. Nearly every biography reported such exact timing and coordination. The description of Catharina's last few hours illustrates the concern: "Once again she thanked her husband fervently for all his love. She begged him incessantly to get a little sleep, saying that she felt quite comfortable now, and in the meantime she conversed with Sister Münster, to whom she reaffirmed her inner well-being, which one could also see in her joy-filled countenance. In the afternoon at 2 o'clock she experienced a sudden change, and her dissolution drew near. Her husband, who was immediately summoned, met her already in the process of going home and, with tears in his eyes, [he] imparted the blessing of the Gemeine and of her Choir, and during a blessed liturgy and in the heartrending presence of the Friend, [he] gave her over to her Eternal Husband, from whom he had received her."

The above quotation suggests that the actual death was a stage preceded by a sudden change in the dying person's condition. It was not a mere instant dividing life from death, but a process with duration. Anxious eyes watched day and night, in order not to miss the change which signaled the beginning of this final process. Once it was clear that the dying person had entered this stage, people rushed to the scene in order to pray for and bless the person and to sing a liturgy designed as a background to the event of death and a celebration of it.

Maria Bechtel's biography gives a more detailed description of such a liturgy: "On the morning of February 7th between 4 and 5 o'clock, her most blessed moment arrived while her husband sang, 'Let her see her election to grace in your nail marks and lead her poor soul home through the gaping [wound in your] holy side.' She sang the first 2 verses quite audibly along with [him]; but she began to sink from then on. He said to her, 'Now you will probably go soon to the Heiland,' and she answered in the affirmative with the expressions on her face. And she fell asleep in the arms . . . of the Heiland quite gently and without moving, accompanied by the words: 'Thou Man of Sorrow, so beautiful, toward whom we continue to move, please smile upon her until she can see Thee there.' " Maria and her husband continued to communicate within the framework of the death liturgy as long as Maria could participate. The liturgy gave Maria the support she needed as she left, and it gave her husband the solace he needed as he was left behind.

Maria's last moments also illustrate another theme in the Moravian way of dying during this early period. The terminally ill were active partners in the process of their dying and not just passive recipients. Individuals embraced the entire process of their own death. People predicted it before they took sick, and when they did become sick, they were the ones who knew first if this was to be their last illness. They initiated the farewells with family and friends. They volunteered to act as intermediaries in heaven between the Heiland and those still on earth. They readily talked about their own death, and when they could not longer talk, they continued to communicate their spiritual well-being with facial expressions. They begged the Heiland to come for them, and they organized others to pray for them. They asked for their final blessing, and they joined in with the death liturgy. Even when they were no longer capable, they made their *wish* to join in quite clear. People remained active participants until the very last second, if their strength permitted. When Juliana Fritsch "went toward her Bridegroom with joy, accompanied by the blessing of her Choir, she stretched out her hands three times, if somewhat shakily, in order to receive him." Michael Schnall surprised everyone with the level of his activity immediately before death. "When the final blessing of the Gemeine and the Choir was given to him on the 24th during a liturgy by Brother Münster and no one thought that he was still there, he bared his head himself and received [his blessing] with folded hands and a beautiful countenance."

As the biographies make abundantly clear, death during Bethlehem's first period was intended as a primarily positive experience in spite of the physical pain of final illness and the psychological pain of grief, for death meant a complete unification with the Heiland in heaven. But that was possible only for people who had developed the expected close relationship with the Heiland. For those who had not, the prospect of death was agonizing. Death after conversion meant eternal life. Death without it meant unending death. The threat of death was therefore a powerful force to awaken the unconverted. Jacob Schoen's belated awakening was finally effected by a fear of death just after he was expelled from the Gemeine: "While on the road, the following thoughts occurred to him very emphatically: 'Where are you going? You must turn around and go back; *This will be your last year down here.*' " (Emphasis in the original.) This newly acquired conviction left him shaken because, even though he had not been a good Moravian, he accepted their view that an unconverted person like himself was lost to death. Only people who had developed the expected humble and "sinnerlike" dependence on the Heiland could benefit by his sacrificial death and live in heaven for eternity. Because of Jacob's premonition, he had enough time and motivation to struggle through awakening to conversion before his final illness.

Caspar Boekel was not so lucky: "He was a frivolous person in his carriage and he spent his boyhood years in such a way, that no one knew what would become of him. . . . He became sick at the same time as the blessed Balthasar Köhler, and it dawned on him that he might die. This put him into considerable anxiety concerning his condition. He lamented from the bottom of his heart his lost time, and he couldn't be comforted about the fact that he would now die, his being still neither accepted nor a Communicant. People referred him to the Friend of Poor Sinners." The solution to Caspar's problem lay in his sickness, for the Moravians believed that serious illness could turn the hearts of even the most difficult cases. "His illness increased. He had a lot of pain, but he was patient and resigned. He talked a great deal with the dear Heiland, and soon received assurance that He forgave [him] everything and would accept [him] in grace." Within a few days, Caspar's illness had accomplished the conversion which had eluded him until then.

Martin Hirt was another example of the power of physical afflictions to pave the way for the healing of a person's soul. His "raw and untamed nature [had] hindered the . . . work of the dear Mother [the Holy Ghost] on his heart . . . until the miserable condition of his body brought him to his heart." The physical infirmities required to bring him to conversion were extreme indeed. Over the course of a year he suffered excruciating headaches, gradually lost his sight, and became paralyzed first on one side then on the other. "Then the dear Mother worked on the cure of his soul, and with good success. He became very softhearted, confessed with a thousand tears the previous bad condition of his heart, begged all the Choir Workers to forgive him, [because] he had so often distressed them, and was shamed by the astounding patience and love of the Heiland and the Sisters and Brothers of the Gemeine. He also claimed that he felt so good in his heart that he could never have imagined it before." Because of his conversion it was possible for him to face his death with the "passionate longing" proper to a good Moravian from the first period.

As soon as a person died, the trombone choir assembled in the Bell Tower to announce the death by playing two hymns: first, one which signified that a person had died, and second, one which identified the Choir to which the person belonged. In a town as small as Bethlehem, this was usually enough information to inform everyone who it was that died, for it was well known who was expected to die. The result was that within minutes of a death, even those not at the bedside could participate in a person's "going home."

During the next few hours the body was prepared and transferred to the "corpse chapel" where it was kept for one or two days, depending on the time of year. In the hot months of July and August, funerals usually took place one day after death, whereas in the cooler months, bodies often remained longer in the corpse chapel to give people in the settlements outside Bethlehem a chance to view the body.

Viewing the body was considered an edifying and inspiring experience for much the same reason that visiting the dying was: the body preserved the expression on the person's face in that last moment when the soul joined the Heiland. Elisabeth Brazier's "body . . . had gotten from the Sidewound's kiss [death] an especially sweet and virginal look." Philip Meurer's "last look which was very visible in his corpse testified that he believed." Johanette Salterbach's body "left behind a sweet look." Mattias Gottschalk's body "looked quite sweet and like the body of the Lamb." By viewing the body, those people "left here on earth" were able to experience vicariously the intimate relationship between the dying and the Heiland.

The funeral itself began in the large meeting room (the "Gemein-Saal") with a musical liturgy and a sermon, both of which focused on any of the following themes: the Heiland's death in relation to eternal life for believers, the reunification of the body with the soul at the Resurrection, and the hope which each death gave to survivors of following a similar path to the side of the Heiland. After the sermon, the funeral biography was read, followed by more music which often included verses composed especially for the person who had just died.

The body was then brought in a procession to God's Acre, Bethlehem's graveyard. Sometimes the procession included primarily members of the person's Choir. Little Anna Müller's body, for instance, was "accompanied to the earth by our Children['s Choir]." Frequently, however, the whole Gemeine accompanied the body to the grave, as they did in the case of Father Nitschmann: "Then everyone went in a sizeable and beautiful procession to God's Acre, led by the children of both Institutes [for boys and girls], after them the trombone choir, then Brother Joseph and Brother Peter, the liturgist, followed by the body which was carried by 12 of our ordained ministers and deacons and accompanied by all the Choir Workers, the Widowers' Choir and the rest of the Brothers, after which the Sisters followed in the same order." At the gravesite another liturgy was held while the body was being buried.

NINETEENTH-CENTURY HOUSEHOLDERS

In the year 1762, a date which coincides closely with the end of the first period as defined in this study, Bethlehem underwent the radical change described in Chapter 1. Because of the Moravian financial crisis following the death of Zinzendorf, the Moravian Unity required that Bethlehem end its Communal Economy which had been designed to free up adult labor for religious work in Bethlehem and outside of it. Henceforth virtually all labor was to be devoted to economic pursuits, and families were therefore made responsible for their own economic upkeep. To encourage the new family economy, people were expected to live as nuclear families in separate apartments or in single family dwellings. Such a fundamental change in the social organization was bound to have an equally fundamental effect on how people lived out their lives and what their values and goals were.

The biographies from Bethlehem's fifth period reflect this new emphasis starting with infancy. Whereas the infants from the first period were expected to begin actively cementing a relationship to the Heiland, those of the fifth period were not. It is true that within a few days of birth most babies were "given over in baptism to be the eternal possession of the Heiland," but the greatest concern was to determine the health of the child. "Right after [Joseph Kluge's] birth, he seemed to be a healthy and happy child, for which his parents rejoiced with thanks to the Heiland." Mary Ann Eberman "was from her birth on a very healthy and lively child." Israel Luckenbach was baptized "on the same day as his birth (it appearing doubtful whether his life would long be spared). During infancy this feeble state of health, with occasional changes, continued until the 7th year from which time his constitution gained strength rapidly, and his health became more firmly established."

Connected to these concerns about the health of a child was a judgment about whether the parents could look forward to a future with that child: James Göhring "was a healthy and lively child, and it seemed that one could rightfully hope that he would grow up to be a joy to his parents and also with the proper guidance would prosper for the Heiland." Underneath such statements are suggestions of the psychological toll of high infant mortality. Parents loved and tenderly cared for their little ones, but they refrained from allowing themselves any dreams for their children's future lives until they could depend on their ability to survive.

The kinds of dreams that parents had for their healthy children indicate that life's goals had changed since the first period. No longer was a relationship with the Heiland the only goal in life; instead social goals had, by the fifth period, joined the religious ones. James Göhring's biography expressed the hope "that he would grow up to be a joy to his parents and . . . would also prosper for the Heiland." Individuals were still expected to relate well to the Heiland, but they also had responsibilities to the people around them, in this case, parents. So important were these social expectations that some biographies emphasized them more than the religious ones: "Since [Henrietta Seidel's] birth . . . she had enjoyed almost uninterrupted health, a circumstance which very naturally contributed to all those fond anticipations in which affectionate parents indulge themselves—whilst sympathizing friends and relatives strengthen them in hopes of future pleasing gratifications and accomplishments by which children endear themselves to their parents and friends."

In these parental hopes that their children would grow up to please them lies the seed of the goal which dominated the lives of fifth period Moravians in Bethlehem—that of being socially useful. During the later years of childhood, this theme became more explicit, as is already obvious in 6-year-old Mary Ann Eberman's biography: "She was from her birth on a very healthy and lively child, and caused her parents much joy, especially in her last years, in that she was very diligent in her studies at school and in general gave much hope that she would someday make herself useful and helpful both to herself and to others."

By the teen years the dreams of future usefulness became more closely tied to specific activities which would lead to productivity as an adult. Since the roles of women and men were differentiated in nineteenth-century Moravian society, the particular tasks considered useful for girls were different than the ones deemed useful for boys. For 14-year-old Henrietta Seidel such tasks were ones useful to a life of domesticity. "She . . . enjoyed for an ample time a very good health so that she was able to apply herself without interruption to the learning of useful knowledge and skills. To the joy of her parents and of everyone who took friendly interest in her well-being, it came evident that the effort spent on her was not in vain, and her progress—especially in beautiful handwork—awakened hopes of her future usefulness."

Boys were expected to learn one of the many professions available in Bethlehem. Since there were a number to choose from, an effort was made to match a boy's interests and abilities with a trade so that his productivity level was as high as possible. Israel Luckenbach "made good progress in various branches of knowledge during his course at school under several instructors. After leaving school he was placed in a store at Nazareth; the situation, however, not agreeing with him and his health not being good, after sometime he returned home. Shortly after, he was placed with Br. R. Luckenbach to learn the cabinet-making business. He took an interest in this new employment, and showed diligence and attention."

In the case of Johannes Schmidt this effort to find suitable work required considerable perseverance. "At the age when the basis must be laid for a thorough learning of a particular craft or profession, it seemed that our late Brother lacked the necessary coordination and the requisite talent, even though he had an unusually good memory. Therefore, after several vain attempts in that direction (with the nail smith, the linen weaver, the tailor), no further attempt was made with him toward the learning of a particular profession, rather only toward useful employment, in which area there was never any lack of opportunity from that time on until his last illness: at first in the house of his parents, then for a number of years in the Single Brothers' House, namely in the Single Brothers' gardens and fields, and the last few years as night watchman, along with other small jobs."

Judging from the information in Israel Luckenbach's biography, a boy's training for a profession began after he had left school at about the age of 12, and Johannes Schmidt's biography suggests that the next few years were "the age when the basis must be laid for a thorough learning of a particular craft or profession." It is important to notice that these are the very same years which were, in the minds of first period Moravians, so crucial to the building of a relationship with the Heiland. During that first period, if a young person failed to make religious progress in the teen-age and early adult years, people began to fret and worry. By the fifth period, it was the inability during those years to make progress in the social and economic realms which caused concern. At only two points did the topic of religion come up in the biography of Johannes Schmidt. The first was this brief report: "In 1790 . . . according to the custom of the time he was accepted into the Gemeine and in 1792 [he] came into the enjoyment of Communion after previous instruction." These events no longer were the culmination of agonizing introspection, rather they were the automatic result of custom and instruction. The second mention of religion was the statement that in his final illness "he soon lost consciousness so that he was not able to explain any more about the condition of his soul." While Johannes lived, the main worry among the people around him was his difficulty in contributing economically. It was not until he approached death that they became concerned about his spiritual condition.

The biographies of younger single men suggest that remaining single was no longer a desirable option for men by the end of Bethlehem's first century. In contrast to the samples of biographies in every other group of men, all four of the younger single men were described as social misfits. Samuel Peysert and Lewis Schmidt were abnormally withdrawn. Johannes Schmidt was the young man, discussed already, who was unable to develop any economic stability. Daniel Hauser "fell with increasing age into the evil habit of drinking brandy and in that way destroyed his health and his happiness." Because of his drinking problem he was able to work only as a day laborer, and the last few years of his life he ended up under the care of the township and living in the poor house.

The descriptions of the younger married men were a striking contrast: Johann Kern "showed industry and ability in his . . . craft, the weaving of stockings, and during the years he spent here in the Single Brothers' House [before marriage] he enjoyed the friendship and respect of all those who knew him." Marcus Fetter was not only a trained blacksmith, but a talented musician: "Until the end of his life it gave him joy to serve the Gemeine with the talent that had been bestowed upon him and, without tiring, to contribute to the glorification of our dear Lord in the beautiful worship services." Jacob Bush became a master shoemaker. And Carl Dober served the Gemeine as a gifted teacher of young boys, then as a minister and finally as a teacher of ministerial students. All four of the younger married men were socially and economically successful, whereas every one of the younger single men was handicapped either by a social or economic deficit or by both. By the end of Bethlehem's first century virtually every young man married unless he showed himself to be socially or economically unable to meet the responsibilities of marriage.

The biographies of younger women do not indicate so clear a distinction between married and single women. It is true that one young single woman, Sophia Kitschelt, was left lame from a childhood disease (probably polio) which "also made her unable to do heavy work." But with that exception there was no obvious difference between the young single women as a class and the married ones. Sophia Kitschelt, Sabine Schropp, and Rebecca Cist all became teachers. The biography of Mary Cist, Rebecca's sister, indicates nothing about how she earned a living, but it also reports no physical, mental, or social problem. These women, with the possible exception of Sophia, all appear able to have carried out responsibilities similar to those in married life. Sabine Schropp, in fact, did take on the duties of a mother when she took her orphaned niece, "a child of about 6 years . . . and raised her with motherly attention and concern (Angelegenheit)" and even when in later years she lived alone, she "served her brothers and sisters and her friends whenever and however she could, for it was important to her, whenever possible, to live for and be useful to others, not herself."

The difference between the biographies of young single men and young single women underscores and elaborates a point made in Chapter 2: by the fifth period the Single Brothers' Choir had ceased to exist as a setting for men to live out their lives; virtually every single man who was able to marry did so. Single Sisters, on the other hand, still had the option to remain single, for the Single Sisters' Choir continued to be a viable institution from which normal, active, and healthy women could lead rich and useful lives.

By the fifth period, however, nuclear family life had become much more important in the lives of both men and women. Even single people valued intimate family relationships. They lived with their parents until they died, and then they joined the family of a sibling or they moved in with foster parents. Sabine Schropp was taken as a daughter by the Loskiels after the death of her father and she "amply fulfilled the duties of a child's love and deference, which she demonstrated especially well in Brother Loskiel's long and painful last illness. . . . She remained with Sister Loskiel until her blessed end a few years ago. This loss cut her deeply, for she loved and honored her as a mother."

Family life was even more important in the lives of married people. During the first period, children had hardly figured in the lives of parents, since they were raised from an early age in Choir houses. By the fifth period all children were raised by their parents and the biographies reported whether people performed well in their roles as parents. Johann

Kern was "tenderly concerned about [his children's] well-being" and they paid him back "for his devotion with filial love and dutiful obedience." When Marcus Fetter died, his children "lost in him a devoted father whose tenderness and caring about their welfare left an inextinguishable impression with them." Sarah Hüffel was noted for her "conscientiousness, orderliness, and carefulness . . . which were also demonstrated in the way she related to [her] children, toward whom she also proved herself a tender mother."

As the above examples indicate, both men and women were expected to be concerned about their families, but the biographies also suggest that men and women supported their families in different ways. The men's biographies explicitly name the profession, sometimes describing in great detail a whole career path. Johann Kern learned the craft of stocking weaving as a young man, but "after [he] had run his business . . . for a number of years with God's blessing on his industriousness he [began] to finish gravestones as well as conduct a silk business on the side, for which he had all the more time and opportunity as his stocking weaving business decreased." Carl Dober began his career as a teacher at the Boys' Institutes in a number of Moravian settlements in Germany and he "won everywhere not only the love of the parents but also that of his students through his good nature and through [his] . . . instruction, which he knew how to make just as understandable and pleasant as it was informative." But he yearned for a position as a minister, and after teaching for eighteen years he finally decided to emigrate to America where he was more likely to get such a post. Within a year of arriving in America he was called to be a minister first in York and then in Schoeneck. He served as a minister for five years before he was called to teach at the seminary in Nazareth where future ministers were trained. Marcus Fetter's career as a blacksmith was only briefly mentioned but the development of his other career as a church musician was described in some detail.

In contrast to the lengthy descriptions of married men's careers, discussions of married women's work life are brief or nonexistent. Louise Herpel's career is not mentioned. Sarah Luckenbach was "industrious in her profession," but we are not told what that profession was. Perhaps the reason for this lack of information is that it was assumed that every married woman did the housework, fed and clothed her family, and raised her children.

There are hints that women sometimes helped their husbands in their work. Two married women's biographies use plural pronouns to describe the married couple's work: "In the year 1832 [Maria Kluge] accompanied her husband to Bethlehem, in 1836 *they* were called to serve the congregation at Emaus, [and] in 1838 *they* retired to Nazareth" (emphasis added). Catharina Weinland's biography (written by her husband) reports: "After *we* worked the farm on the other side of the Monocacy for 24 years, *we* moved in 1830 to our children Charles and Elisabeth Kummer." (Emphases added.) But even these descriptions lack the detail characteristic of the biographies of married men. Contrast the information in Catharina's biography with that in her husband's who died eight years later: "After [David Weinland] came to Bethlehem [in 1773] in order to learn the craft of stocking weaving, he took Communion for the first time. . . . In about 1781 he became Master of his craft. . . . In 1798, since he could no longer continue his craft because of bad eyesight, he assumed the management of Bethlehem's [communal] farm. When it was dissolved, he took over a private farm on Bethlehem land, on which he, with God's blessing, found ample support, until the work became too difficult for him because of increasing age and he turned the farm over to his son." Although David recognized that Catharina had worked the farm with him, the wider community clearly thought of the farm as his operation and took some pains to describe his connection with it.

Sarah Hüffel's biography is a clear demonstration not only of the difference in careers of married men and married women, but also of the radical difference in the work activity of single and married women. Sarah was a woman of unusual talent: "Already in her girlhood years the opportunity presented itself . . . to use her talents and her skills; she was appointed as a teacher in the Girls' Institute, and because she had proved even more since her acceptance into the Single Sisters' Choir in 1784, that she was willing and able to serve the Lord in any number of ways, she was accepted soon after the Synod of 1789 as an acolyte along with several other Brothers and Sisters . . . [D]uring [a trip visiting the Moravian settlements in Lausitz and Silesia] she received an offer to take on the office of Overseer for the Single Sisters in Gnadenfeld, which she willingly agreed to, and she began her duties in the year 1795. Our dear Heiland was with her and blessed her loyal service, in which she won the love of all her sisters through her mild, gentle carriage, although she also strove to be exact and orderly." Sarah had obviously found fulfillment in this position because when a call to marry came to her three years later she was unprepared for it and at first even unwilling, "because she felt so happy with her station and her service, that she had no reason to wish for a change." However, she became convinced that "the call was from the

Lord . . . and therefore she gave her hand [in marriage], trusting that the Heiland would make everything good."

From that point in her biography to the beginning of the discussion on her final illness we hear little of Sarah's work life and considerable detail about the career of Sarah's husband, both in Germany and later in Bethlehem. He was by turns the "conference scribe of the Overseers Department for the Unity," the minister and head of the Boys Institute in Niesky, the spiritual head ("Gemeinarbeiter") of the Gemeine at Barby, a member of the Overseers Department, and holder of an unspecified office in Bethlehem. We are told little of Sarah's work life, apparently because it was focused around the domestic care of her family and it was assumed that everyone knew what was involved. Even during the period when they lived in Herrnhut and she had "for 9 years . . . something of a vacation" from carrying out the domestic activities, she did not turn her energies to the running of any of the business affairs of the Gemeine as she did when she was single. Rather she spent her time "in pleasant and useful relations with her acquaintances and friends here in Herrnhut." She apparently did not even share her husband's responsibilities in Herrnhut as a member of the Unity Overseers Department. Clearly a married woman's role was quite different from a married man's by the fifth period. This finding is hardly a surprising one for a group of people living in nineteenth-century western society, but it is a remarkable change from the first period in Bethlehem in which women's biographies portrayed lives as filled with community responsibility as the men's. The earlier women were given these responsibilities not because Pilgergemeine Bethlehem had intended to provide equal opportunity for women but because the separation of sexes had required women as leaders and providers of service for the female part of the community. Once the sexes were no longer kept separate and religious progress no longer required intimate counseling, the double provision of services became unnecessary. The new Ortsgemeine in Bethlehem quite naturally reverted to the traditional work patterns which had continued in other Moravian settlements where women's roles were primarily domestic.

Just as there was a change over Bethlehem's first century in the ways people lived, so there was a matching change in the ways they died. When Bethlehem began, the goal in life was to develop an intimate relationship with the Heiland, and death was the sought-after and joy-filled realization of that goal. By the end of the period under study the primary focus in life was to develop a responsible and "useful" relationship with one's family and community, and death meant the painful severing of that relationship. In contrast to first period biographies, those of the fifth frequently mentioned

187

the "pain of separation from loved ones." Even when a dying person was widowed and alone, as in the case of Joseph Till, his death was referred to as the "end of his pilgrimage down here" or in David Weinland's case, simply as "his end." Maria Kluge's biography repeatedly refers to "her departure." Death was in general no longer conceived as a positive event. Johannes Schmidt's biography even uses the words "terror-filled moment of death."

This more negative view of death was expressed in the biographical treatment of the various stages of final illness and death. The portion of the biographies concerning death was no longer introduced by a premonition of death, but by a discussion of the general state of health or a description of how the final illness began. For example, "Some time before [Maria Kluge] removed here the first symptom of the disease which finally became the occasion of her departure, had made its appearance, but the progress of the complaint was very slow and gradual."

This sort of introduction was appropriate, because in contrast to the first period emphasis upon the death to come, biographies from the fifth period focused primarily on the final illness itself and the details of its pain. With the exception of the first sentence, Dorsey Stout's biography is entirely devoted to an account of his many afflictions: "Dorsey Syng Physick Stout was born on the 9th of October, 1824. He enjoyed uninterrupted health till he arrived at the age of four years and a half when he got an attack of the measles from which he retained an affection of his lungs and his digestive organs which were soon accompanied by an effusion of water in the head, or dropsy of the brain. To this formidable disease was added, in the course of last summer, a white swelling of the knee-joint, from which he suffered much pain. Though he had intervals of ease and comparative comfort, yet it was obvious from the frequent and violent paroxysms of pain and fever, that he was gradually approaching his dissolution. His constitution being wracked and nearly exhausted by such a combination of diseases, he became yet afflicted, on the fourth instant, with cholera morbus which speedily produced mortification of the stomach, and in the morning of the 14th instant, death closed the scene of the very patient but unfortunate sufferer, after an illness of two years and two months."

This focus on the physical condition of the sick and dying as opposed to their spiritual condition reflected a new attitude toward sickness. No longer was it a medium to help bring people closer to the Heiland, but an affliction to be battled. Nearly every fifth period biography included a reference to medical treatment. In obviously hopeless cases the treatment was an attempt to relieve pain: Christina Hübener, for instance, "suffered indescribably from tightness in her chest, which, in spite of all the medical aid, brought her some relief for only a short time." But in most cases it is clear that the hope was not merely for relief but for a complete cure. Survivors battled to keep their loved ones with them. Joseph Kluge's biography reflects anguished attempts to save him: "Last Wednesday . . . as his mother held her beloved and seemingly healthy and happy little son on her lap, he suddenly got convulsions or powerful cramps (as the doctor called it), which was heart-breaking to look at and against which all treatment applied by the doctor was in vain."

During the first period, a long sickness was invariably interpreted as a "school" in which the Holy Ghost was able to improve a person's spiritual condition. By the fifth period protracted illness no longer had any positive purpose. It was simply thought to cause suffering and hinder normal living, and it was actively fought with medical treatment. Sarah Hüffel suffered for over ten years from a painful skin disorder to which she paid little heed since it appeared only during cold weather. "But when it in the following years spread further on her body during the periodic recurrence and caused more inconvenience, it appeared necessary to use remedies, various sorts of which were tried almost without interruption, but without the desired success. [She and her loved ones] harbored the hope that the long trip from Europe to here and the character of the climate and lifestyle in this country could effect an improvement, and until 1820, this still seemed quite plausible; but from then on the disorder spread to the parts of her body which had previously been spared. . . . [She] therefore decided to submit to the cure of a physician in Philadelphia and spent several months in his house in 1821. When she returned from there to Bethlehem at the beginning of November, she found herself considerably improved, and [she] seemed to lack little for a complete cure. This positive impression disappeared however in the first months of the following year, and since then her troubles and sufferings have gradually increased, until they reached the highest possible degree at the beginning of this month."

Not only did people no longer find serious illness a positive experience in itself, they also no longer welcomed the death that it implied. Instead of looking forward to death, seriously ill people and those around them concentrated on finding a cure so that they could avoid death. Carl Dober was an especially poignant example because his final illness began shortly after he entered a new and absorbing profession as a teacher in the Seminary: "This his new calling he commenced with the warmest interest . . . in the hope that he could contribute a great deal to the future usefulness [of the Gemeine's servants] in the House of the Lord. But all too soon he was hindered by powerful attacks of . . . headache, which he however at first dismissed as temporary, and through which he didn't allow himself to be deterred from diligently preparing and giving his lectures at the seminary in the most thorough and conscientious manner whenever he was able. In the spring of 1838 he moved here, when the seminary was relocated [from Nazareth] to Bethlehem, and in so doing, [he] felt sincerely happy and thankful to be able to fulfill his professional duties in the midst of this beloved Gemeine. But the Lord had decided otherwise. All too soon the disorder reappeared which had already revealed itself in Nazareth, and [it] gradually forced him to give up his lectures entirely, because any effort at thinking increased his pains. These increased so much, in spite of all the medical treatment, that hardly a day passed without them. His left eye was particularly badly affected, so that after a few months he completely lost the use of it. Through all this, he and his loved ones hoped, and with them many empathetic friends, that he would eventually recover. Their hopes were frequently strengthened by the appearance of an improvement, and his faithful doctor repeatedly encouraged them in these hopes. Unfortunately the betterment proved to be of no duration. Rather, worse pains settled in different parts of his body and one could plainly see, that a disease which wouldn't bend under all the remedies of medical science had gripped his entire system. It was agonizing for him to have to remain idle for so long, and very often he prayed fervently to the Heiland for a cure."

What makes Carl Dober's example so striking is that he, more than any other person in the fifth period sample, had devoted his life to the service of the Heiland. He was beyond doubt a very religious man, yet, in contrast to the spiritually committed people of the first period, he wished not to be with the Heiland in heaven, but to serve him here on earth. He continued to strive for a cure in the face of much evidence that he could not survive, because he, like most other fifth period Moravians, focused his energies among the people around him—family, parishioners, and students. He valued his role of spiritual service to others and was loathe to give it up before his work was done.

In spite of the general fifth period desire to overcome illness and prolong life, a person was obviously expected to accept death when it became clear that medical treatments were having no effect. But the meaning of acceptance had changed over Bethlehem's first century. During the first period, people yearned for death before it came and embraced it when it arrived. By the fifth period, acceptance meant resignation to the will of the

Lord. Sophia Kitschelt came home sick from her job as a governess, "went right to bed and didn't rise again from this painful confinement. She shouldered her pains with patience and submission to the Heiland's will." In Lewis Schmidt's case, "the tightness in the chest increased so that he had many difficult times of suffering, during which he remained patient and trusting in the Lord, and although even in the last days he spoke (as was the nature of his illness) of getting well again, yet he submitted . . . with willing resignation to the will of the Lord."

The ambivalence which Lewis Schmidt showed was fairly widespread, for it was not easy for fifth period Moravians to give up their earthly existence. Time and again biographies juxtaposed human plans and wishes against the will of the Lord. Carl Dober envisioned a full career as a teacher of ministerial students, "but the Lord had decided otherwise." Marcus Fetter "was especially happy to see his family . . . increased with the [addition of] his beloved in-laws. According to human reason, one would think that he would be granted the enjoyment of an intimate family circle for a long time to come. But the Lord, on whom our lives and actions depend, had decided otherwise." Maria Luch "was a healthy child . . . so one thought it safe to give space to the hope, that she would prosper to the joy of her parents and to the glory of the Lord as she grew older, but the Lord, who alone is wise, decided to tear this dear and beloved child from all earthly trouble already at a most tender age."

But in the trauma of separation from earthly existence and loved ones, another factor besides the Lord's will encouraged dying people and those around them to accept death: as an illness dragged on and the pain grew, they welcomed and even yearned for death as an end to suffering. Sarah Hüffel, whose suffering reached "the highest degree" learned "to follow [the Lord's] example of patience . . . to the amazement and edification of many, who saw her circumstances . . . but it was not surprising that her situation and her feelings often drove her to hot tears and heartfelt yearnings for her final dissolution from this wretched life." Likewise Christina Hübener "showed [through her suffering] exemplary patience. . . . We couldn't look at her suffering without the most heartfelt sympathy; she herself used every lighter moment to raise up our courage, but she often prayed urgently to the Heiland to bring her suffering to an end through a blessed consummation."

The result was that by the time death came, people were generally ready for it. Even Carl Dober who so desperately wished to stay here on earth to serve the Heiland as a teacher in the Seminary—even he was thoroughly ready when the time came: "On the following evening a partial paralysis of his body took away the still cherished hope of his recovery and soon it was apparent that his end drew near. He himself seemed to be convinced of that, and he declared repeatedly that he was sure of his salvation and was ready whenever the Heiland would come to lead him into Paradise. Frequently he seemed to have bright visions of [heaven], when he called with folded hands and eyes directed upward, "Oh, how beautiful, how bright—how heavenly!"

As was the case during the first period, the dying were surrounded with people at the bedside giving support and comfort, but what motivated the visitors was no longer their desire to benefit from the intimacy between the Heiland and people about to die. Rather visitors and the dying sought to preserve the social ties which had bound them together in active life. Christina Hübener remained concerned about her family right up to the hour of death. "Because her youngest grandson became seriously ill during [her last] night, the parents had to bring him to her deathbed, and she frequently inquired about his condition, in spite of the severe compression [in her chest]. In the 8th hour of the morning . . . she died in a very gentle manner." Israel Luckenbach's mother continued her motherly role with great intensity during his final illness, and he that of a son in need: "During his long and for weeks helpless confinement he enjoyed the unremitting care of his tenderly solicitous mother, to whom he often expressed his most affectionate and grateful feelings, to her he also frequently opened his mind reflecting freely upon the doubtful issue of his case." Joseph Oerter "remained conscious most of the time, and in between the periods of delirium [literally 'fever fantasies'] he could converse sweetly and satisfyingly with his loved ones." During the first period, the content of people's fantasies had often helped people to judge the quality of their relationship with the Heiland. In the later period, Joseph's loved ones jealously guarded the time in between his fantasies in order to maintain their connection to him, and they held the fantasies themselves to be hindrances to that connection.

So strong was this need to maintain the connections between loved ones and a dying person that two biographies reflected a new taboo: the avoidance of the topic of death in conversations between the dying and their families. Fourteen-year-old Henrietta Seidel "told a close friend with whom she often spoke of her bouts with illness . . . that the last time she was sick she had dreamed she saw the dear Heiland. 'Oh, he looked so beautiful,' she added, 'that I wanted never to leave him.' At the same time she begged her not to say anything about it to her parents." Marcus Fetter also apparently tried to shield his family from discussions about death: "It was generally suspected that his end was drawing near, but he himself seemed not to be certain of that—at least he did not suggest anything clearly about that, rather he expressed his hope for recovery—probably in order not to hurt his dear family." Such avoidance of the topic of death would never have been accepted during the first period when a dying person and the survivors were expected to embrace and look forward to death. By the fifth period Moravians openly acknowledged that death meant the severing of meaningful social ties. The development of the taboos described above were a response to this new attitude.

Another response was the open display of grief. Survivors during the first period thanked the Heiland for giving their deceased loved ones time to live here on earth and for rescuing them from the dangers of the sinful world. Although these themes continued into the fifth period, they were accompanied by expressions of anguish unheard of during Bethlehem's first period. The parents of 4-year-old Henrietta Seidel described their grief in a poem:[59]

> To grave the chaplet of the blessed
> full oft is pluck'd a tender bud
> bedew'd by parents sore distressed
> with bitter tears in copious flood
>
> But oh! The hand that pluck'd the flower
> Tho' wounding meant in truth to bless;
> Heav'ns sunshine will dispel the shower—
> The ways of God are Happiness.
>
> In this vain world of care and sorrow
> a child, that bloom'd as flow'r of spring
> Our joy today may fade tomorrow
> pierc'd by temptations venom'd sting.
>
> But, to yon realms of bliss and glory
> transplanted by the Saviours hand
> with heav'nly charms not transitory
> The lovely flowret will expand
>
> Be then our tears of deep affliction
> transform'd to tears of grateful joy!
> Henrietta blooms—O blest conviction
> where nothing can our hopes destroy—

Hark—hark—we hear her angel spirit
Thus sweetly lisp—Oh! weep no more!
I'm blest—by the Saviours merit
you'll follow—where I went before!

This poem includes all the stages of grief expressed in fifth period
biographies: the bitterness and sense of loss, the struggle to understand the
ways of the Lord, the acceptance of his better judgment, and the hope for
coming together again in heaven. Because the Moravians of the first period
focused their lives on developing an intimacy with the Heiland and because
they de-emphasized ties among family members, they found it comparatively easy to accept his decisions about life and death. By the fifth period
the importance of family relationships had grown substantially, and Moravians now had to struggle through stages of grief to an acceptance of the
loss of their loved ones.

This process required considerable adjustment in survivors' relationship to the Heiland. They were frank about their desire that their sick loved
ones recover, while their world view told them that the decision was the
Heiland's to make, not theirs. At the same time they were used to seeking
comfort from the Heiland when they needed it. This combination of values
and behaviors required them to find solace from the very being they held
responsible for taking their loved ones away from them. The struggle involved is evident in many biographies, but especially so in that of Lucien
Wolle: "In spite of all the doctor's care, none of the remedies were effective, and to our great distress, we had to give him over to the Friend of
Children, who really does know what is best and most beneficial for his
poor little children: for he never once made a mistake in his entire reign,
no! Whatever he does or causes to happen always comes to a blessed end.
This is also for us, his parents and remaining brothers and sisters, the only
comfort." These words read as if Lucien's family members were trying
hard to convince themselves of what they knew they should believe—that
God's inexplicable ways are the best.

Once the loved ones died, the survivors attempted by various means
to reestablish the broken connection. They called after them with poems
similar to Henrietta Seidel's quoted above, and they frequently looked forward to the time when they could rejoin their loved ones in heaven.

Behind the changed understandings about the contents of a good life
lay a changed view of the Heiland's nature. During the first period the
Heiland was a friend who ideally played an important role in even the
earliest stages of a person's life. By the fifth period the Heiland was a

194

remote authority figure who required submission, but who rarely was even mentioned in a biography until the sections dealing with serious illness and death. And even the conception of the Heiland's role in sickness and death had changed. When Bethlehem was first established, the Heiland played the welcoming Bridegroom or the affectionate Gardener who picked a lucky flower. One hundred years later the Heiland had become a much more distant Lord who caused illness and pain and who separated loved ones by death against their wishes. In both periods the Heiland's acts were considered good ones, but during the first period he did what was best for human beings as an intimate and compassionate friend, while for the Moravians of the fifth period he was the wise ruler who made decisions impartially and without feeling as a part of a grand plan beyond the comprehension of human beings.

Although some of the themes described here as characteristic of one period were found to a degree in the biographies of the other, their relative emphasis was so different that it would be hard to mistake a biography from one period for that of another. First period biographies reflected lives structured around a person's growing relationship with the Heiland. All other aspects of life on earth were subordinated to that end. By the fifth period, a person's development was structured around his or her usefulness to family and society—even lives devoted to religious concerns used religion as the means to serve the needs of other people. The Moravians in Bethlehem had clearly experienced in their own individual way the very process of secularization which they had sought to avoid by separating themselves from "the world."

Notes

1. The reader will remember from Chapter 3 that married women and men lived, for the most part, in separate houses during the General Economy.

2. Babies frequently begin losing interest in nursing between 9 months and a year, and gradually they wean themselves over the course of the next year. See Karen Pryor, *Nursing Your Baby* (New York: Harper & Row, 1963).

3. Quoted in Erbe, p. 44.

4. The remarkable biography of this child, who was only 13 months old when he died, gives us many details about the process of birth and about the raising of babies. My account of infancy leans heavily on this biography, but draws from others as well where appropriate.

5. Erbe, pp. 44–45.

6. Verlass, §158.

7. Hamilton, *History of the Moravian Church*, p. 37; Erbe, pp. 44–45; The Bethlehem Diary, p. 168.

8. Verlass, §175:13; §180:11.

9. Numerous biographies of adults report the first significant religious awakening during the period of "youth," which corresponds roughly with the period spent as Older Girls and Older Boys.

10. Verlass, §179:9; §180:10, 11.

11. Verlass, §178.

12. Rebecca Weis's biography (1768) actually belongs to the period beginning after the General Economy dissolved, but since children of her age continued to live in Choir groups until well into the 1770s her life was still representative of the Choir-oriented living system. I have used her biography in the absence of any biographies for Older Girls during the first period proper (1744–1763).

13. Verlass, §152:12.

14. Verlass, §120:14.

15. Verlass, §120:2,4,10; §152:1,8,14.

16. The question which shook her so was "whether she had experienced the blood of the Heiland on her heart and was washed clean by it?"

17. See for instance, Verlass, §465 and 466.

18. Verlass, §507.

19. Verlass, §152:12.

20. Verlass, §168.

21. Erbe, p. 36.

22. Erbe, p. 36.

23. Verlass, §152:13.

24. Verlass, §152:14; §116.

25. Verlass, §116.

26. Verlass, §629.

27. Verlass, §593, §631.

28. Verlass, §593:3.

29. Verlass, §594.

30. Verlass, §593:4.

31. Johanna Dorothea Miller is listed in the Bethlehem Church Register as "geschieden" in the 475th entry of the section on deaths. Her husband had been Johann Heinrich Miller.

32. Verlass, §116; §152:13; §316.

33. See Erbe, p. 38, who quotes letters from Spangenberg to Zinzendorf describing his frustrated attempts to extract the necessary consent from many a Single Brother or Sister. Biographies of Married People sometimes report the hesitations at the time of a marriage proposal.

34. Verlass, §115.

35. Verlass, §113:9.

36. Verlass, §225; §247; §251; §325; §329. The Helpers (*Pfleger* or later

Helfer) directed for spiritual affairs, whereas the Overseers (*Vorsteher* or later Diener) managed external ones.

37. Verlass, §113:5–8.

38. Verlass, §113:17, 18.

39. Church Register and Census Catalogs.

40. This passage is repeated word for word (except for gender changes) in the principles of both Widows and Widowers, Verlass, §93:2; 98:3.

41. Verlass, §93:6.

42. Verlass, §98:4.

43. Verlass, §93:7.

44. Verlass, §106.

45. Verlass, §93:8; §98:11; §107.

46. Verlass, §93:8 and 10; §98:12.

47. Verlass, §95.

48. Verlass, §108.

49. Verlass, §302.

50. Verlass, §113:11 and 13.

51. Verlass, §113:12.

52. Verlass, §120:8, 9, 10, 15.

53. Verlass, §152:4.

54. Verlass, §152:10.

55. Verlass, §120:16.

56. Verlass, §152:15.

57. Verlass, §152:14.

58. Verlass, §120:15.

59. The fifth period sample includes two girls named Henrietta Sophia Seidel, one 4 years old and the other 14.

Chapter Six

Secularization of Consciousness

We have seen evidence of the decreasing focus on religion in Bethlehem's political and institutional history, in the changing demographic patterns, in the evolving shape of the town plan, and in the different structures for individual lives. This chapter will treat the theme of secularization directly, using a perspective suggested by Peter Berger in *The Sacred Canopy*. He points out that most studies of secularization concentrate on its external aspects: the separation of church and state, for instance, and the changes in social structures which de-emphasize religion. He urges a consideration of "the secularization of consciousness" as well, by which he means "the process in which an increasing number of individuals . . . look upon the world and their own lives without benefit of religious interpretation." [1] A study of secularization from this point of view not only entails different content but a different scope as well. The separation of church and state represents the broad sweep of changes in western society. A process by which individuals change their religious world view suggests a smaller and more local form of secularization which takes place at the community level. Such an approach is particularly appropriate for a study of the Moravians in Bethlehem, who in the beginning were a good deal more separated from the "world" and more focused on their religious practice and their missionary work than any other colonial group.

The topic of secularization can be a sensitive one, especially for a society like the one in Bethlehem: no society which was built for a religious purpose likes to admit that it is growing more secular. If we could ask the Moravians whether the Heiland should be the primary focus in a person's life, I feel certain that most of them would say "yes," regardless of whether they lived in 1744 or 1844. However, I am equally certain that, if those same people were asked to describe a particular person's life, the emphasis they would give to that person's religious life *would* be different, depending on the period in which they lived. I would argue that this unconscious emphasis is more representative of the actual emphasis in Moravian culture than a direct answer to our question would have been.

Historians often envy social scientists whose subjects are available for direct interviews. They would do well to remember that even experimental social scientists often design their experiments so that their subjects are unaware of the topic being studied. Social linguists and psychologists, in particular, have learned to distrust direct opinions about language and mental states. Likewise, documents which were not intended to answer the questions historians ask may in the end give more dependable information than those which were.

The biographies discussed in the previous chapter are an excellent source of unconscious emphases. Although they were originally written to describe and judge the lives of particular individuals, we know that they were also used as tools of socialization. As such, they transmitted Moravian values about family, community, and religion, but they did so in subtle and unintended ways. In order to make use of these rich documents, I needed to develop a dependable method for finding these subtleties and measuring them. The one I settled upon was adapted from a method developed by Zellig Harris as a formal means for discovering the underlying logic of a text.[2] I have adopted it as a means of regularizing the biographical text so that it answered certain questions about its subject which would not have been obvious from an informal reading of the original biography.

The biographical form described individuals, told what they did, and named the other individuals they related to. Since these general functions parallel certain properties of language, I was able to reformulate the original text to make each sentence represent one of the above functions. I simplified complex sentences. I changed nouns that came from verbs back into verbs and attached them to their subjects. If I found a pronoun, I searched for its antecedent. In short, I diagrammed sentences and resolved ambiguities. Next, I stacked the resulting statements over each other so that all the subjects were in one column, all the verbs in another, all the personal objects in a third, and all the predicate adjectives and predicate nouns in the fourth. The hypothetical text shown in the Illustration was constructed to show all the sentence types. It shows just how straightforward the reformulation process is. (See Appendix I for an actual biography from each period, translated into English from the original German.) Statements enclosed in square brackets do not refer to Sister Bechtel. All others do. Items enclosed in parentheses indicate information that was implied but not stated directly. The verbs without personal objects tell us what

Illustration

After she had lived in Nazareth for two years, Sister Bechtel was called to be the Leader of the Single Sisters in Bethlehem. She accepted the call willingly, trusting that the Heiland would bless her service among them. Having had no Leader for some time, the Sisters received her with warmth. As their Leader, Sister B. was strict and at the same time loving, so that within a short time she had earned the love of the Sisters in her care.

Conj	Subject	Verb	Personal Object	Predicate Adjective/ Noun
After	she	had lived in Nazareth for two years		
	Sister Bechtel	was called	(by the Gemeine)	
that	she	be	of the Single Sisters	the Leader.
	She	accepted the call		
in that	she	(was)		willing
while	(she)	trusted	(the Heiland)	
that	she	would be blessed	by the Heiland	
while	she	served among	them (Single Sisters).	
Since	[(the Sisters)	had had no leader for some time]		
	she	was received	by the (Single Sisters)	
in that	[they (Sisters)	had		warmth].
While	she	was	of them (Single Sisters)	the Leader
	Sister Bechtel	was		strict
and	she	was at the same time		loving
so that	she	earned within a short time		
that	she	was loved	by the Sisters	
whom	she	cared for	(the Sisters).	

kinds of things she did: she lived in Nazareth for two years, she accepted a call, and she earned something. The column of predicate adjectives and nouns informs us that she was willing, warm, strict, and loving and that she played the role of a Leader. The personal object column lists the Gemeine, the Single Sisters, and the Heiland as her relationship partners, and the verbs belonging to each relationship partner tell us how she related to each one. Thus, each reformulated biography consists of verb statements, attribute statements, and relationship statements.

As it turns out, verb and attribute statements support but add little to the pattern drawn by the relationship statements. The relationship statements are clearly the richest source of information on the secularization of consciousness in Bethlehem because Moravian religious culture focused so heavily on expected interactions between partners. For these reasons, the following discussion is based on an analysis of the relationship statements.

Relationship statements can be further subdivided according to the type of relationship partner, they can be classified as active or passive (depending on whether or not the subject of the biography initiated the action described), and they can be grouped according to the type of action.

Since the biographies identify individuals according to their age, sex, and marital status, we can find out which kinds of statements applied to all Moravians and which were specific to certain sub-groups. We can also measure how these patterns changed during Bethlehem's first one hundred years. Because the biographies are idealized positive and negative examples, these results cannot be construed as indicators of actual behavior. Rather, in line with their socializing role, they will tell us about behavioral *expectations* for the various sub-groups of the Moravian community.

The methodology described above has two characteristics which suit the kind of analysis proposed: (1) The reformulations regularize the texts into sets of simplified statements, at the same time keeping each statement and each element of each statement in context. This means that they can be analyzed formally without losing the richness of the originals. (2) The simplified statements make it possible to be consistent when measuring the frequency of different types of statements. Such consistency is nearly impossible to apply to the original texts because of their complicated linguistic structures. My assumption here is that the frequency of different elements in a text reflects the unconscious emphases of its author. Authors of biographies would surely not have counted how many statements they used to describe their subject's relationship with the Heiland. Rather, if their subject's relationship to the Heiland were considered important, authors unconsciously would have given it more space than if it were not.

Since an important ingredient in the religious conception of the Moravians was each person's relationship to the Heiland, an analysis of these relationship statements is the central focus of this study. In order to judge the importance of relationships with the Heiland, it is obvious that they must be compared with the other relationships described.

I have classified the relationship partners into three categories (sacred beings, relatives, and unrelated community members) on the basis of distinctions made in Moravian literature. In line with good Protestant tradition, Moravian sermons made a clear division between sacred beings and human ones. The category "sacred beings" included the Heiland, God, the Holy Ghost, and the Angels. During both periods under discussion, however, nine-tenths of the references in the biographies to sacred beings were to the Heiland. Therefore, for most purposes, this category stands for the Heiland, and I will refer to it with his name except where the discussion requires otherwise.

The Moravians further divided the category of human beings into two subcategories: relatives and non-related members of the Gemeine. They developed a social structure and a vocabulary to help people make this distinction. The Choir living system helped to build ties with non-related members of the Gemeine and to discourage those with family, and the practice of using the words "Brother" and "Sister" to name fellow members of the Gemeine transferred some of the power of kinship ties to relationships between community members.[3] Poignant proof that these techniques were successful is found in the example of Johannette Salterbach who feared that any commitment to her dying mother would result in diminished commitment to the Heiland and to the Gemeine, even though it was her mother who encouraged her to join the Gemeine in the first place.

Tables 6-1 and 6-2 compare the Period I emphasis on relations with the Heiland to those with kin and those with community members. They convert the raw numbers into group percentages. Each individual's relationships with these three partner types contributed to group totals for their age group. For instance, in the biographies for girls aged 5–19, there was a total of 51 relationships, of which 27 were with the Heiland, 2 were with kin, and 22 were with members of the community. I used these group totals to compute group percentages. Thus 53 percent of these girls' relationships were with the Heiland, 4 percent were with kin, and 43 percent were with community members.

The reader will notice that figuring the group percentages in this manner weights the effect of the biographies in proportion to their lengths. An extreme example is found in the case of the males aged 0–4 (see Table 6-2). The biographies of Johann Schlegel and Ludwig Cammerhoff boasted only three relations and one relation respectively, while Anton Böhler's included 164. Obviously the group percentages for males aged 0–4 are completely dominated by Anton's biography. Ordinarily a statistician would take pains to give equal weight to each case, and this would certainly be the required strategy if my interest were individual behavior. But since I am using these biographies in their role as socializing tools (i.e. as reflections of guidelines and expectations), they should not be treated as equal to each other in importance. Surely the long and information-laden biography of Anton Böhler would have had more influence than the biography of Ludwig Cammerhoff, which told little more than that he lived and died.

Since the patterns in a table of numbers are hard to see, it is useful to convert these group percentages into horizontal bar graphs like Figures 6-1 and 6-2, with the percentages for each age group lined up in a separate row: the percentages of relations with the Heiland on the left, those with kin in the middle (shaded bars), and those with community members on the right.[4]

By making symmetrical columns such as these it is possible to compare intuitively the emphasis on relations with each partner type for all the men and for all the women. Figure 6-2 shows clearly that the male biographies from the first period (1744–1763) stressed relations with community members more than with either the Heiland or with kin. It also shows little difference between relations with the Heiland and relations with kin. The female biographies, in contrast to those of males, show nearly equal emphasis on relations with all three kinds of partners (see Figure 6-1).

These symmetrical bar graphs also show how the columns mesh with each other. That is, they help us see for each age group which partners form the "tongues" of emphasis and which ones the matching "grooves" of de-emphasis. A generalization which we can make about both male and female biographies is that the percentage of relations with community members remained comparatively steady and strong for all age groups— there are no noticeable "grooves" in that column. In contrast the relations with the Heiland and with kin show a great deal of fluctuation from one age group to another. Furthermore the shapes of the symmetrical graphs for the Heiland and for kin are similar for males and females. Relations with kin form hourglasses with the narrow part representing the kin relations for youth and younger single people. Relations with the Heiland on the other hand are shaped like Christmas trees with the wider branches fitting into the neck of the hourglass. Thus the biographies emphasized and thereby encouraged young people—especially females 5 to 19—to focus more on their relationships with the Heiland than on those with kin, while the biographies of Single People of both sexes stressed relations with community members even more than those with the Heiland.

TABLE 6-1 Partner Types for Females—Period I (1744–1763)

| Name | | Relationship Partners | | | |
	Heiland	Kin	Community	Total
CHILDREN, 0–4					
Ettwein	3	0	2	5
Müller	0	1	0	1
Ohneberg	0	2	0	2
Total	3 (38%)	3 (38%)	2 (25%)	8 (101%)
YOUTH, 5–19					
Schmik	12	0	5	17
Schulz	2	1	6	9
Böhner	9	0	9	18
Fritsch	4	1	2	7
Total	27 (53%)	2 (4%)	22 (43%)	51 (100%)
SINGLE, 20–59					
Brazier	2	1	8	11
Leibert	6	3	17	26
Salterbach	20	21	42	83
Kannhaeuser	10	12	30	52
Total	38 (22%)	37 (22%)	97 (56%)	172 (100%)
MARRIED, 20–59					
Oberlin	14	5	11	30
Sehnert	6	19	14	39
Schaaf	3	5	10	18
Michler	5	34	7	46
Total	28 (21%)	63 (47%)	42 (32%)	133 (100%)
MARRIED, 60+					
Bechtel	4	14	9	27
Total	4 (15%)	14 (52%)	9 (33%)	27 (100%)

TABLE 6-2 Partner Types for Males—Period I (1744–1763)

		Relationship Partners			
	Name	Heiland	Kin	Community	Total
CHILDREN, 0–4	Schlegel	2	1	0	3
	Böhler	32	55	77	164
	Cammerhoff	0	1	0	1
	Total	34 (20%)	57 (34%)	77 (46%)	168 (100%)
YOUTH, 5–19	Sehner	4	1	7	12
	Spohn	7	2	11	20
	Boekel	0	1	1	2
	Köhler	12	6	17	35
	Total	23 (33%)	10 (14%)	36 (52%)	69 (99%)
SINGLE, 20–59	Kapp	2	2	7	11
	Gottschalk	3	0	18	21
	J. Müller	11	4	11	26
	Schoen	18	0	52	70
	Total	34 (27%)	6 (5%)	88 (69%)	128 (101%)
MARRIED, 20–59	Hirt	3	7	9	19
	J. B. Müller	10	10	9	29
	Schnall	2	3	14	19
	Jorde	1	14	20	35
	Total	16 (16%)	34 (33%)	52 (51%)	102 (100%)
WIDOWED, 20–59	Meurer	36	14	31	81
	Total	36 (44%)	14 (17%)	31 (38%)	81 (99%)
MARRIED, 60+	Tanneberger	3	8	10	21
	Hantsch	0	15	8	23
	Total	3 (7%)	23 (52%)	18 (41%)	44 (100%)
WIDOWED, 60+	Klemm	10	21	62	93
	Nitschmann	8	38	93	139
	Total	18 (8%)	59 (25%)	155 (67%)	232 (100%)

Partner Type as Percentage of Total Relationships Period I

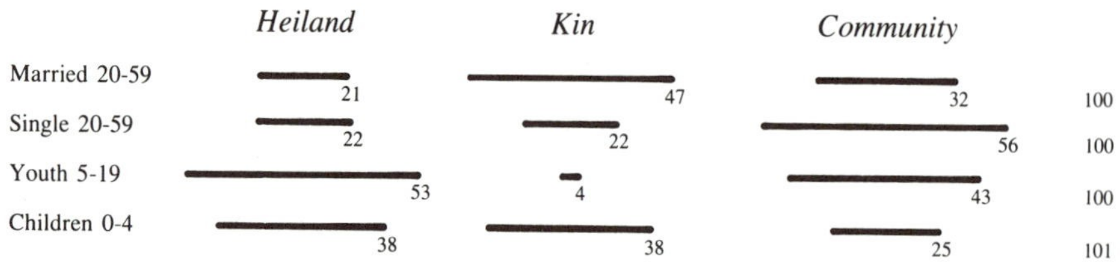

FIGURE 6-1. Females

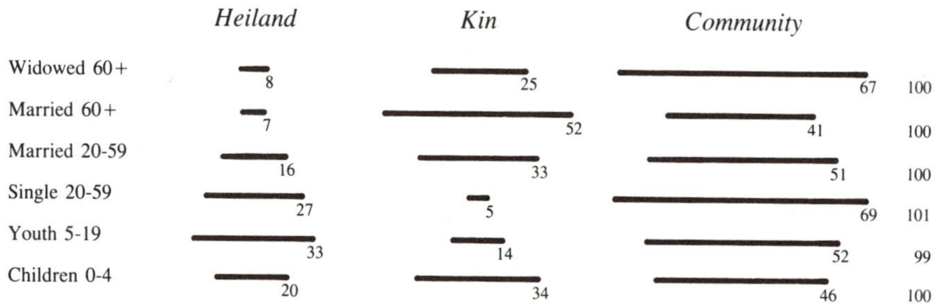

FIGURE 6-2. Males

As we would suspect, marital status also played a role in the pattern of relationships. Unmarried people (single and widowed) from both sexes emphasized relations with community members a great deal more than they did relations with kin. In contrast, all the married groups, except one, emphasized relations with kin more than those with community.

Figures 6-1 and 6-2 indicate that there were many similarities in the patterns for men and women. In order to refine this comparison, I reorganized the information into a set of vertical bar graphs which place the male and female bars side by side for each of the three partner types. The resulting graphs (Figures 6-3 through 6-5) show marked similarities. The hills and valleys appear to match each other closely, and the relatively high Pearson correlations (.65, .77, and .93) prove that they do. The hills on the graph characterize relations with the Heiland and the community for both women and men, while kin relations form a valley for both genders.

These graphs not only point out the similarities between male and female relationships, they also allow us to generalize the differences. For

Gender Comparisons of Relationships Period I

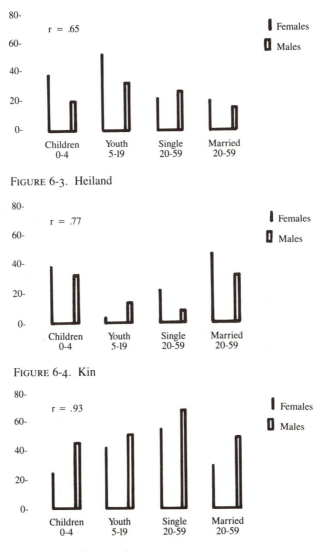

FIGURE 6-3. Heiland

FIGURE 6-4. Kin

FIGURE 6-5. Community

every age group the percentage of men's relations with community members was higher than those for women's. And for most age groups, women's relations with the Heiland and those with kin were higher than men's. Thus in spite of the explicit attempts of the Moravians to free women from the responsibilities of family so that they could direct their efforts more intensely toward community goals, female biographies still focused more on family and less on community than male biographies did. And in spite of the explicit attempt to encourage men and women equally to focus their lives on the Heiland, these biographies suggest that men were thought to be less religious than women.

But the really surprising message from all these bar graphs is that the Heiland was not the central focus in these documents of socialization that we would expect given the explicit intent of Bethlehem's founders and leaders. If we assume that religious focus is accurately measured by the percentage of relations with the Heiland,[5] then we have to conclude that Bethlehem was from the outset more secular than the documents from the first period would lead us to believe. Before settling on such a surprising conclusion, we need to consider other interpretations of the data.

First it is important to realize that secularization is a relative term. It does not specify a particular high level of religious commitment beforehand nor a particular low one afterwards. It does suggest a lessening of religious focus over a period of time. Therefore one way to explore the process of secularization in Bethlehem is to turn to the fifth period (1824–43) and compare its focus with that of the first period.

Using a set of tables and graphs which parallel the ones describing Period I, let us look at the emphasis on different kinds of relationships in the biographies of the last period. Tables 6-3 and 6-4 show the data from individual biographies and the group data upon which the subsequent bar graphs are built. These tables are organized in the same way that Tables 6-1 and 6-2 were. As before, it helps us to interpret this data if we convert these tables into symmetrical, horizontal bar graphs (Figures 6-6 and 6-7). The most obvious message of these graphs is that with the exception of Single People, both males and females emphasized relations with kin more than those with the Heiland and with community. The demographic and social organizational changes from a communal society to one focused on nuclear families is clearly reflected in these documents of socialization: people of all ages were getting the message that family relations were of primary importance. Only the Single People received a different message: for them, relations with community continued to be more important than those with kin. Of all the age groups, only older single women emphasized relations with the Heiland more than those with any other partner type, and that only just barely so—43 percent of their relations were with the Heiland and 42 percent with community.

Just how this data compares with the data from the first period is best shown in vertical graphs with the percentages from the two periods lined up side by side for each age group (Figures 6-8 through 6-13).[6] The most striking development from the first period to the fifth was a decrease for most age groups in relations with community members and an increase in relations with kin, a change which reflects quite straightforwardly the change in social organization. During the first period people lived with and related to members and leaders of their respective Choirs. During the last period they lived with and depended on family members.

The change in relations with the Heiland are harder to interpret, but we can generalize to a degree: 5 of the 6 unmarried groups (children, youth, and single) showed a decrease in the percentage of relations with the Heiland from the first period to the fifth, whereas all four groups that had ever been married (younger and older Married People and Widowed Men) showed an increase.

In order to judge these results in terms of secularization, let us first return to the idea which introduced this comparison between Periods I and V. Was there in fact a lessening of religious focus? The graphs of relations with the Heiland show a change in focus, but not necessarily a lessening of it—at least not one which can be attributed to all Moravians. The biographies of Bethlehem's young people, however, do suggest a diminished religious focus by the fifth period. This fact offers a clue to the nature of the change experienced by all of Bethlehem.

During the early years of Bethlehem's existence, young people were assigned the intense and often arduous task of developing a stable relationship with the Heiland. It was expected that they would struggle with this task—in fact the more committed they were, the more they agonized over their failings and their inability to please the Heiland. Anna Schmik, a very serious 7-year-old, cried "because the Heiland [was] still often distressed with [her]; He [couldn't] always be pleased with [her]." And the overseers of Balthasar Köhler often had to "console him about his faults . . . he was especially worried that he didn't love well enough." As committed as Balthasar was, he worried that the intensity of the upcoming harvest might cause him to stray from his close relationship with the Heiland. He prayed that the Heiland would "protect him from everything which could disturb his relationship with the Heiland."

The biographies from the first period also stressed the joyful side of a

TABLE 6-3 Partner Types for Females—Period V (1824–1843)

	Name	Relationship Partners			
		Heiland	Kin	Community	Total
CHILDREN, 0–4	Grünewald	0	2	0	2
	Andres	0	2	0	2
	Luch	3	7	3	13
	Seidel	5	22	12	39
	Total	8 (14%)	33 (59%)	15 (27%)	56 (100%)
YOUTH, 5–19	Eberman	3	6	2	11
	Schneller	0	0	0	0
	Luckenbach	5	4	0	9
	H. S. Seidel	20	23	18	61
	Total	28 (35%)	33 (41%)	20 (25%)	81 (101%)
SINGLE, 20–59	Kitschelt	1	8	7	16
	R. Cist	0	17	7	24
	M. Cist	0	7	4	11
	Schropp	2	13	31	46
	Total	3 (3%)	45 (46%)	49 (51%)	97 (100%)

					Total
MARRIED, 20–59	Herpel	0	11	1	12
	Kluge	1	13	1	15
	S. Luckenbach	0	10	2	12
	Hüffel	53	64	56	173
	Total	54 (25%)	98 (46%)	60 (28%)	212 (99%)
WIDOWED, 20–59	Schroeder	0	16	0	16
	Total	0 (0%)	16 (100%)	0 (0%)	16 (100%)
SINGLE, 60+	Kunz	4	2	21	27
	Kremser	7	0	7	14
	Pyrlaeus	85	41	48	174
	Beroth	35	5	52	92
	Total	131 (43%)	48 (16%)	128 (42%)	307 (101%)
MARRIED, 60+	Till	10	6	7	23
	Bourquin	21	19	12	52
	M. Luckenbach	2	11	2	15
	Weinland	5	17	1	23
	Total	38 (34%)	53 (47%)	22 (19%)	113 (100%)
WIDOWED, 60+	Cist	3	13	4	20
	Hübner	2	30	1	33
	Maslich	0	7	5	12
	Schindler	0	7	11	18
	Total	5 (6%)	57 (69%)	21 (25%)	83 (100%)

TABLE 6-4 Partner Types for Males—Period V (1824–1843)

		Relationship Partners			
	Name	Heiland	Kin	Community	Total
CHILDREN, 0–4	Jungmann	0	2	0	2
	Kluge	4	9	3	16
	Knauss	2	0	0	2
	Brickenstein	3	0	1	4
	Total	9 (38%)	11 (46%)	4 (17%)	24 (101%)
YOUTH, 5–19	Göhring	4	15	6	25
	Wolle	2	5	2	9
	Stout	0	0	0	0
	Luckenbach	1	0	2	3
	Total	7 (19%)	20 (54%)	10 (27%)	37 (100%)
SINGLE, 20–59	L. Schmidt	1	0	14	15
	Peysert	0	5	1	6
	Hauser	0	0	2	2
	J. Schmidt	1	11	9	21
	Total	2 (5%)	16 (36%)	26 (59%)	44 (100%)

MARRIED, 20–59	Dober	27	10	13	50
	Bush	0	8	2	10
	Fetter	5	17	4	26
	Kern	15	23	14	52
	Total	47 (34%)	58 (42%)	33 (24%)	138 (100%)
SINGLE, 60+	Beitel	0	5	11	16
	Hennig	23	30	49	102
	Total	23 (19%)	35 (30%)	60 (51%)	118 (100%)
MARRIED, 60+	Braun	0	5	1	6
	Weiss	18	14	15	47
	Bischoff	0	5	1	6
	A. Schmidt	1	13	3	17
	Total	19 (25%)	37 (49%)	20 (26%)	76 (100%)
WIDOWED, 60+	Till	6	10	2	18
	Oerter	9	30	15	54
	Weinland	1	25	3	29
	Total	16 (16%)	65 (64%)	20 (20%)	101 (101%)

Partner Type as Percentage of Total Relationships Period V

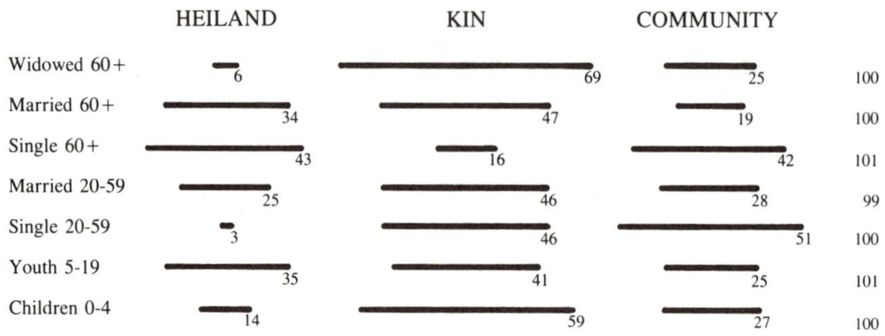

	HEILAND	KIN	COMMUNITY	
Widowed 60+	6	69	25	100
Married 60+	34	47	19	100
Single 60+	43	16	42	101
Married 20-59	25	46	28	99
Single 20-59	3	46	51	100
Youth 5-19	35	41	25	101
Children 0-4	14	59	27	100

FIGURE 6-6. Females

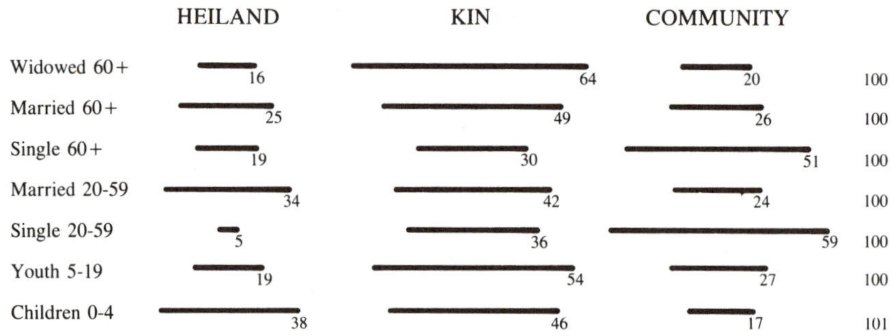

	HEILAND	KIN	COMMUNITY	
Widowed 60+	16	64	20	100
Married 60+	25	49	26	100
Single 60+	19	30	51	100
Married 20-59	34	42	24	100
Single 20-59	5	36	59	100
Youth 5-19	19	54	27	100
Children 0-4	38	46	17	101

FIGURE 6-7. Males

person's relationship with the Heiland. Anna, for example, shared such joy with an intimate playmate. "Right now I feel so close to the Heiland, that my heart is burning up. Oh, how much I love the Heiland; I want to take Him in my arms and embrace Him right now." Reactions and struggles such as these dominated the biographies of young Moravians from Period I and in doing so they gave a powerful message to their young comrades to follow their example and struggle with similar intensity to develop close ties with the Heiland.

The biographies of the young people from Bethlehem's fifth period also expressed concern about their relationship to the Heiland, but with a completely different set of implications. For one thing, most references to young people's ties to the Heiland are actually religious rituals performed

Period Comparisons of Relationships, by Gender (in percentages)

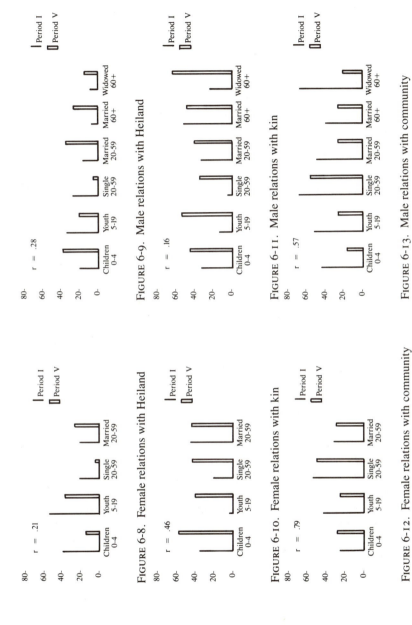

FIGURE 6-8. Female relations with Heiland

FIGURE 6-9. Male relations with Heiland

FIGURE 6-10. Female relations with kin

FIGURE 6-11. Male relations with kin

FIGURE 6-12. Female relations with community

FIGURE 6-13. Male relations with community

by parents for their children. Soon after Lucien Wolle was born, his parents "dedicated [him] in Holy Baptism to the Possession of the Lord." In Lucien's biography and in those of many other young people from the last period, this ritualistic statement was the only reference to a relationship to the Heiland. James Göhring's biography shows continuing concern on the part of his parents. The Göhrings had moved to Hellertown, several miles from Bethlehem, and when James was four years old they sent him to Bethlehem for an education: "He was an active and healthy child, and one apparently had the right to hope that he would live to bring joy to his parents and that with the proper guidance, he would also prosper for the Lord, to whom he was dedicated. In order to better reach this goal he came . . . here to be cared for by his dear grandparents." But even this example suggests that children's relationships with the Heiland are no longer wrought by their own intense and introspective efforts. Rather it is the responsibility of parents to bring their children to the proper religious stance through rituals and education.

Two biographies from the fifth period do reflect more personal ties with the Heiland but they again contrast with those from the first period. Seven-year-old Sarah Luckenbach was afflicted with ill health "which gradually increased upon her, causing often much pain. She . . . showed much patience even under severe sufferings. Her heart was early drawn in love to the Saviour; she took pleasure in learning hymns, and often thought more deeply on her soul's concerns, than she expressed in words. Thus the Good Shepherd gradually prepared this Lamb of His flock for the mansion above." Henrietta Seidel, who had not always been quite so sickly, became so ill in her eleventh year, that her parents thought they would lose her, "but the Heiland, who had allotted her a few more years, permitted her . . . to recover. . . . She acknowledged with fervent thanks . . . the . . . gift of renewed health, and often declared herself [grateful] with great feeling and tenderness for the untiring constancy and care with which her dear mother tended her by day and by night. At the same time she felt that she must make it her main concern to live for the joy of the Heiland and to repay her parents for all their pains through obedience and hard work." In both of these cases from Period V, it was serious illness which encouraged the more personal relationship, whereas during Period I a personal commitment to the Heiland was expected of everyone, sickly or not.

Moreover, the character of the relationship was different in the later period. During Bethlehem's first years young people's relationships with the Heiland were filled with inner turmoil and constant struggle, punctuated with moments of exultation and joy. Sarah and Henrietta on the other hand attained their relationships with the Heiland easily and apparently maintained them without conflict, the one having been "early drawn in love to the Savior" and the other having simply resolved "to live for the joy of the Heiland." And in Henrietta's case, the parallel syntax suggests a commitment to her parents which equalled her commitment to the Heiland: "to live for the joy of the Heiland and to repay her parents for all their pains." A relationship to the Heiland no longer shook people's souls. It became instead a routine and taken-for-granted part of young people's lives.

If it is true that young people's commitment to the Heiland decreased over Bethlehem's first century, what explains the increased emphasis among married people on relations with the Heiland? As a start let us use the clue offered by the discussion above about Bethlehem's young people. Perhaps the responsibilities of parents to act as religious intermediaries for their children translated into an increased dependence on ministers and other religious professionals. Such positions had previously been filled by married couples who acted as teams to care separately for the spiritual needs of males and females. But by the nineteenth century, girls, boys, men, and women commonly lived together as families, and Moravians no longer considered it necessary to care separately for the spiritual needs of females. Since the primary responsibility for professional duties had always rested with the men (women losing it if their husbands died, men keeping it if their wives died), the responsibility for religious education remained with the men once the religious education of the two genders was no longer done separately. The result was that religious professionals were by that time nearly all married men.

Looking again at Table 6-4, we see that of the 11 married and widowed men, 6 had a significant relation with the Heiland (defined operationally as a 15 percent portion or better of all their relations); they were Dober, Fetter, Kern, Weiss, Till, and Oerter. Of these 6, 4 were tied in a professional way to the church: Carl Dober and Paul Weiss were ministers, and Johann Kern and Joseph Oerter were church musicians. The 5 men whose relationship with the Heiland was minimal had no professional ties to the church.

If we make a 2 × 2 table summarizing the above information, we can measure the degree to which religious professionalism explained men's relationships to the Heiland during the fifth period (see Table 6-5). Since ϕ^2 is equivalent to R^2 for dichotomous variables, this table shows that 48

TABLE 6-5 Correlation Between Profession and Relation to Heiland

	Religious profession	Non-religious profession	
Significant relation with Heiland	4	2	Phi = .69
Insignificant relation with Heiland	0	5	Phi Square = .48

percent or nearly half the variance is explained by a man's profession. Another more intuitive way to look at this table is to note that all men who had religious professions also had significant relations with the Heiland whereas only 29 percent of the laymen did.

These first-period/fifth-period comparisons of proportions of people's relations with the Heiland indicate that the Moravian Church had undergone an institutionalization. The experience of religion was no longer so much a personal relationship with the Heiland as a regularized participation in rituals performed by professionals.

If this is the case, then there ought to have also been a change in their images of the Heiland. In order to test this idea we can compare the terms applied to the Heiland in the biographies of both periods. Tables 6-6 and 6-7 summarize the results, classifying the separate terms into six image sets: sacrifice, intimacy, service, authority, name, and origins. Although the Moravians themselves did not supply this classification, I am certain they would have agreed with a similar division, because the terms belonging to each image set often appeared in close context with each other: biographies or sermons which called the Heiland "Lamb" were also likely to refer to him as "Sidewound," for example.

The columns on either side of the image sets in Tables 6-6 and 6-7 give the percentages for each term in each period. For example, Table 6-6 tells us that of all the Period I references to the Heiland in female biographies, 14 percent were images of sacrifice. That is, 2 percent of the references to the Heiland conceived of him as a Martyr, 2 percent as a Sidewound, and 10 percent as a sacrificial Lamb. In contrast, only .4 percent of the Period V references to the Heiland were sacrificial ones.

Tables 6-6 and 6-7 both indicate that some of the image sets were emphasized in one period but not the other. In order to show these different emphases in a formal way I have figured for each individual image the

TABLE 6-6 Images of the Heiland—Females

Period I	Percents	Image Sets	Period V	Percents
14%		*Sacrifice*		.4%
	(2%)	Martyr	(0%)	
	(2%)	Sidewound	(0%)	
	(10%)	Lamb	(.4%)	
18%		*Intimacy*		6.4%
	(1%)	Child	(0%)	
	(7%)	Bridegroom	(0%)	
	(6%)	Eternal Husband	(0%)	
	(1%)	Sole Heart	(0%)	
	(3%)	Friend	(4%)	
	(0%)	Lover	(.4%)	
	(0%)	Friend of Children	(2%)	
9%		*Name*		10%
	(8%)	Jesus	(7%)	
	(1%)	Christ	(3%)	
0%		*Origins*		1%
	(0%)	Son of God/		
		Son of Humans	(1%)	
53%		*Service*		51.2%
	(51%)	Savior (Heiland)	(47%)	
	(1%)	Creator	(1%)	
	(1%)	Redeemer	(2%)	
	(0%)	Hand	(.4%)	
	(0%)	Ever Good Will	(.4%)	
	(0%)	Vine (Nuturer)	(.4%)	
5%		*Authority*		31.2%
	(1%)	Chief Elder	(.4%)	
	(1%)	God	(22%)	
	(2%)	Lord	(6%)	
	(0%)	Shepherd	(1%)	
	(0%)	Head of the Gemeine	(.4%)	
	(0%)	High Priest	(.4%)	
	(0%)	Divinity	(1%)	
	(1%)	King	(0%)	
99%		Totals		100%

TABLE 6-7 Images of the Heiland—Males

Period I	Percents	Image Sets	Period V	Percents
21%		*Sacrifice*		1%
	(2%)	Pale Lips	(0%)	
	(1%)	Wounds	(0%)	
	(1%)	Martyr	(0%)	
	(1%)	Sidewound	(0%)	
	(1%)	Man of Sorrow	(0%)	
	(15%)	Lamb	(1%)	
7%		*Intimacy*		2%
	(1%)	Bridegroom	(0%)	
	(1%)	Open Arms	(0%)	
	(4%)	Friend	(1%)	
	(1%)	Lover	(0%)	
	(0%)	Friend of Children	(1%)	
14%		*Name*		17%
	(12%)	Jesus	(15%)	
	(2%)	Christ	(2%)	
1%		*Origins*		1%
	(1%)	Son/Son of God	(1%)	
50%		*Service*		33%
	(49%)	Savior (Heiland)	(25%)	
	(0%)	Redeemer	(2%)	
	(0%)	Creator	(1%)	
	(1%)	Conciliator	(1%)	
	(0%)	Heavenly Physician	(1%)	
	(0%)	Man of Mercy	(1%)	
	(0%)	Intercessor	(1%)	
	(0%)	Expiator of Sins	(1%)	
8%		*Authority*		48%
	(2%)	God	(9%)	
	(6%)	Lord	(38%)	
	(0%)	Shepherd	(1%)	
101%		Totals		102%

ratio between its Period I and Period V percentages. The resulting ratios are graphed along a continuum which increases from zero to one on the Period I (or left-hand) side of the graph and decreases from one to zero on the Period V (or right-hand) side. If the percentage for Period I was the larger of the two, then it became the denominator of a ratio which was plotted on the Period I side of the graph. When the Period V percentage was the larger, *it* became the denominator, and the resulting ratio was plotted on the Period V side of the graph (see Figures 6-14 and 6-15).[7] This means that the terms located to the far left of the graph are associated solely or mostly with Period I, whereas those on the far right are associated solely or mostly with Period V. Those located exactly in the middle are associated with both periods equally.

The results for females and males are shown separately in the two graphs, but they represent a similar picture and can be discussed jointly. Although all six image sets were used during each period, the strong clustering of terms on the right and left edges indicates that some image sets were more closely associated with one of the periods than the other. Both periods conceived of the Heiland in terms of his service to humanity. This common thread was rooted in the term "Savior" (Heiland), which is located in the central portion of the graph, showing that it was used quite equally in the biographies from both periods. (Note also the high percentages for the term "Savior" in Tables 6-6 and 6-7.) However, the common thread of service was interpreted in contrasting ways. The Moravians of the first period dwelt upon the great cost to the Heiland of his service, that is, upon his sacrifice. The Heiland was for them the Martyr, the Man of Sorrow, and the sacrificial Lamb. So focused were they on his physical sacrifice that parts of his body became synecdochic metaphors for his whole being: his Pale Lips in death and his wounds, especially the Sidewound. On the other hand the Moravians of the last period emphasized the positive benefit to humanity of the Heiland's services. They saw in him the Creator, Physician, Man of Mercy, Intercessor, Conciliator, Expiator of Sins, Redeemer, Hand (of help), Ever Good Will, and Vine (of nourishment.)

Alongside these contrasting interpretations of service were other image sets, conceptually related to them. The biographies of the first period emphasized images of intimacy along with sacrifice. The Heiland was a Lover, Sole Heart, Bridegroom, or Eternal Husband. Put together, these image sets form one unified picture of the devoted intimate willing to serve by the ultimate self-sacrifice.

The fifth period biographies posited the image of the Heiland as an authority figure alongside the image of beneficial service. He was Lord, God, Divinity, Shepherd, Highest Elder, Head of the Gemeine, and High Priest. The unifying notion for the fifth period was the protective leader, the benevolent lord who serves his subjects out of a high sense of duty.

These conceptions fit well the kinds of relationships with the Heiland described in the previous section of this chapter. The Moravians' first pe-

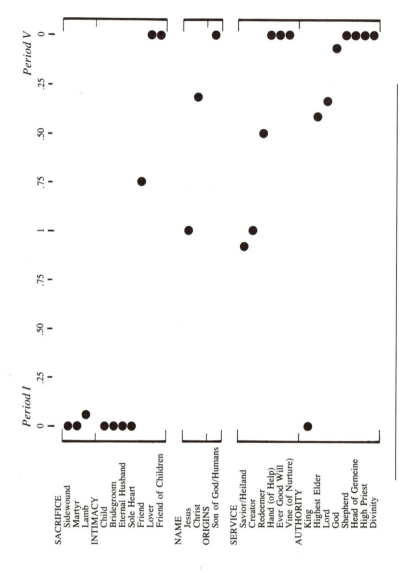

FIGURE 6-14. Females' images of the Heiland: Ratios of Period I and Period V percentages

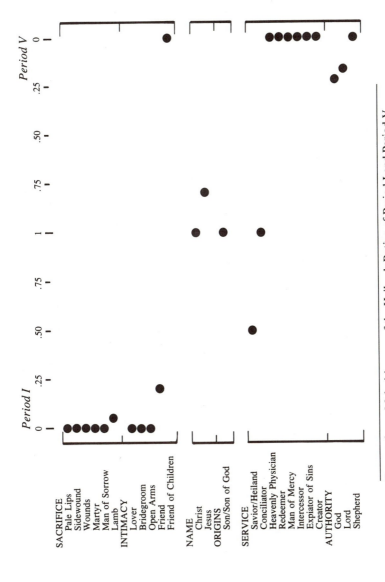

FIGURE 6-15. Males' images of the Heiland: Ratios of Period I and Period V percentages

riod image of the Heiland as an intimate, willing to sacrifice himself to save those close to him, bred the sense that they were unworthy of such great sacrifice and fed their needs to ferret out the wretchedness in the depths of their souls. A personal sacrifice on the part of the Heiland required intense personal commitment and never-ending gratitude in return.

In contrast the fifth period image of the Heiland as the protective lord (in the feudal sense) encouraged a more relaxed and regularized relationship with him. They still understood that the Heiland acted in ways which benefited them as human beings, but because they did not dwell on his sacrifice, they could accept his service without guilt or anxiety. The Heiland as a helping Hand, as a Vine of nourishment, as the Head of the Gemeine, as the Heavenly Physician, as a Man of Mercy, as an Intercessor, as a Shepherd could be repaid by ritual and by praise.

Until this point we have looked for signs of secularization in a dwindling or changing of people's relations with the Heiland, but surely in a community focused on religion, relations with family and community members would also have religious content. Table 6-8 shows that during the first period, there was in fact considerable emphasis on religion in the

TABLE 6-8 Religious and Secular Relationships
with Kin and Community—Period I

	Kin Relations		Community Relations	
	Religious	*Secular*	*Religious*	*Secular*
FEMALES				
0–4	67%	33%	100%	0%
5–19	0%	100%	68%	32%
20–59				
Single	49%	51%	87%	13%
Married	68%	32%	83%	17%
60+				
Married	75%	25%	89%	11%
MALES				
0–4	58%	42%	46%	54%
5–19	70%	30%	97%	3%
20–59				
Single	67%	33%	97%	3%
Married	45%	55%	92%	8%
Widowed	33%	67%	97%	3%
60+				
Married	78%	22%	100%	0%
Widowed	57%	43%	85%	15%

TABLE 6-9 Religious and Secular Relationships with Kin and
Community—Period V

	Kin Relations		Community Relations	
	Religious	*Secular*	*Religious*	*Secular*
FEMALES				
0–4	33%	67%	7%	93%
5–19	21%	79%	10%	90%
20–59				
Single	32%	68%	30%	70%
Married	39%	61%	37%	63%
Widowed	11%	89%	—	—
60+				
Single	23%	77%	46%	54%
Married	25%	75%	41%	59%
Widowed	16%	84%	33%	67%
MALES				
0–4	36%	64%	0%	100%
5–19	25%	75%	20%	80%
20–59				
Single	0%	100%	12%	88%
Married	31%	69%	47%	53%
60+				
Single	34%	66%	42%	58%
Married	8%	92%	60%	40%
Widowed	10%	90%	55%	45%

relations with both family and community. The relations with kin were predominantly religious for 8 out of 12 cohort groups. Relations with community made an even stronger statement: 11 out of 12 cohort groups had a religious emphasis.

By the fifth period, as Table 6-9 shows, the situation was exactly the opposite. Nearly all cohort groups emphasized secular content in their relations with kin and community: all 15 cohort groups had relations with kin which were more secular than religious, and 12 out of 14 had mostly secular relations with community members. Clearly relations with family and community had become more secular.

To obtain a more finely tuned picture of this secularization let us look at the content of religious relations. Tables 6-10 and 6-11 show how the biographies portrayed the different kinds of religious interactions with family members and with community members respectively. If a particular kind of relation was found in the biographies for a certain age group, an X

TABLE 6-10 Religious Relationships with Family Members

| | Period I | | | | | | | | | | | | Mode* | Period V | | | | | | | | | | | | | | |
| | Females | | | | | Males | | | | | | | | Females | | | | | | | | Males | | | | | | |
	Children	Youth	Young Single	Young Married	Older Married	Children	Youth	Young Single	Young Married	Young Widowed	Older Married	Older Widowed		Children	Youth	Young Single	Young Married	Young Widowed	Older Single	Older Married	Older Widowed	Children	Youth	Young Single	Young Married	Older Single	Older Married	Older Widowed
Connections with kin made by Heiland				×					×			×	P							×					×			×
Baptized, blessed by parents	×					×							P	×	×							×						
Cared for spiritually by parents	×		×			×		×		×		×	P	×	×							×						×
Come to Gemeine with parents			×			×							A	×	×	×										×		
Come to Gemeine with spouse				×	×				×	×	×		A				×	×							×			
Discuss religious topics with spouse				×	×				×		×		A				×											
Serve in religious post with spouse				×					×	×	×	×	A				×								×			
Prayed for by kin													P						×	×		×						
Preceded by kin into Heaven												×	P						×	×	×				×			×

*A = active, P = passive

was placed in the appropriate space. If not, it was left blank. And if the subject of a biography initiated an action, it was classified as "active," whereas actions which the partner initiated (or which a third party initiated for the individual and the partner) were labeled as "passive."

Comparing Tables 6-10 and 6-11 makes it clear that during Period I religious relationships with family members were far less substantial than those with community members. This is especially true for religious relations between parents and children. Even line 3 (spiritual care by parents) for Period I refers only to early religious instruction, before the individual joined the Gemeine, with the single exception of 1-year-old Anton Böhler. An individual's religious interactions with non-Moravian parents stopped as soon as he or she joined the Gemeine. Even Moravian parents were not supposed to affect their children's religious life beyond the years of infancy. Religious relations with spouses were more significant, however. Couples joined the Gemeine together, and they were expected to work together as a religious team and to support each other by religious discussion. By Period V the picture was reversed. Religious relations between family members were focused primarily in parent-child relationships. Only a few spouses were described as having religious relationships. The practice of religion had become the giving and receiving of a religious education and had ceased to be a collaboration between a husband and wife.

As the above discussion indicates, the main locus of religious activity during Period I was not the family but the community; therefore, individuals' relations with community members are more likely to reflect the drama of secularization in Bethlehem. With that in mind let us look at Table 6-11. The immediate impression is that the system of religious interactions was more detailed and developed for the first period than for the fifth. Furthermore, during Bethlehem's early period, individuals and community acted back and forth on each other. Note that in this table some actions are active, some are passive, and others are both active and passive. The third type occurred when the subject initiated a kind of action on some occasions, and the community initiated that same kind of action on others. For instance, an individual could initiate the first contact with the Gemeine by visiting it, or the Gemeine could initiate the first contact with an individual through missionary work. During the first period the give and take of these active and passive relations was well balanced: of the 16 types of action in which members of three or more age groups from Period I participated, 5 were active, 8 were passive, and 3 were active and passive.

These actions obviously reflect the religious stages outlined for first

TABLE 6-11 Religious Relationships with Community Members

	Period I												Mode*	Period V													
	Females					Males								Females							Males						
	Children	Youth	Young Single	Young Married	Older Married	Children	Youth	Young Single	Young Married	Young Widowed	Older Married	Older Widowed		Children	Youth	Young Single	Young Married	Older Single	Older Married	Older Widowed	Children	Youth	Young Single	Young Married	Older Single	Older Married	Older Widowed
Baptism	×												P														
Previous religious experiences			×	×				×	×	×		×	A/P														
Awakening				×				×				×	P														
First contacts with Gemeine			×		×		×	×	×	×		×	A/P	×		×		×	×				×			×	
Arrival at Gemeine			×	×				×					A/P							×							
Request for permission to stay			×	×			×	×	×	×			A			×											

Item							A/P*					
Receipt of permission (Erlaubnis)				x	x		P					
Admission to Gemeine			x	x	x	x	P	x	x	x	x	x
Admission to Choirs		x	x	x		x	P	x	x			
Spiritual care by Gemeine	x	x	x	x	x	x	P	x	x	x	x	
Work on own conversion with community	x	x	x	x	x		A				x	
Admission to communion			x	x		x	P	x	x	x	x	x
Religious commitment		x	x	x	x	x	A		x	x	x	x
Call to religious service		x	x	x	x	x	P		x	x	x	x
Religious service		x	x	x	x	x	A	x	x	x	x	x
Deviance			x	x	x	x	A			x		
Deviance control	x		x	x	x	x	P					

*A = active, P = passive, A/P = active and passive

period Moravians in the previous chapter: most Moravians had found their pre-Moravian religious experiences greatly lacking and they usually agonized about it, until by some chance or another they came into contact with the Gemeine. Once they understood the renewal implied in its message, they responded with a request to stay. If everything proceeded as it should, they became more and more a part of the Gemeine through a series of steps which made them members, encouraged their religious growth, allowed their participation in religious sacraments, and engaged their service in the Moravian cause. If they strayed from the prescribed path with deviant thinking or some other kind of nonconforming behavior, they had to undergo appropriate deviance control measures.

The above process is reminiscent of the early stages of Anthony Wallace's theory of revitalization movements.[8] This theory locates the motivation for cultural change in the clash between an individual personality and his or her cultural context. As a psychological misfit in the old culture, the individual becomes a catalyst for therapeutic change, creating a new and better-fitting culture from the old. If his or her creation is attractive and helpful to other distressed souls as well, then the individual's vision becomes a social movement, gathering force with growing membership. As the movement grows it must deal with challenges from the old social order and control any continuing evolutions of its new ideas or any deviant behavior from within its own membership. A movement which survives these stages eventually matures into a stable culture and the new ideas become a taken-for-granted part of a complete cultural system. Although Wallace's description views revitalization from the standpoint of a movement's founders, it also applies well, as Table 6-11 indicates, to the first generation followers as well.

With Wallace's revitalization theory in mind, let us now look at the relationships between individuals and community in the biographies from Bethlehem's fifth period. By that time, people were no longer required to be as actively involved in their own religious growth. Instead of actively searching for religious maturity, they passively received the ministrations of the community. Of the 8 kinds of relations in which three or more fifth-period age groups participated, 6 were passive and only 2 were active.

Even the kinds of religious relations now had different meanings. Admission to the Gemeine, admission to the Choirs, and admission to Communion were no longer yearned-for events before they happened and joy-filled memories afterward. The mechanical manner in which they were reported in fifth period biographies argues that they had become an automatic part of growing up. The biography of Maria Kunz lists them all in one breath: "On May 25, 1782 she entered the Older Girls' Choir; on September 22nd of the same year she was accepted into the Gemeine. On the 21st of December, 1783 she was admitted for the first time to Holy Communion. . . . On the 4th of May, 1787 she was taken into the Single Sisters' Choir." Recall in contrast the lengthy description of Balthasar Köhler's first Communion: "On July 9, 1758 he was admitted to Holy Communion. That was an extraordinary day for him; as he himself expressed it: he could not have imagined that a person could feel and enjoy anything that much. One could read it in his eyes that something remarkable had happened to him there."

Clearly religious fervor had decreased. However, religion had not lost all its significance by the end of Bethlehem's first century. Religious rituals were still thought worthy of mention. The community still offered spiritual care and asked people to serve the church. People still were expected to respond with commitment and service. How, then, can we characterize the difference? The last stage of Wallace's revitalization theory suggests an answer: nineteenth-century Bethlehem represented a revitalization movement matured. The Moravian conception of community and religion—new, exciting, and healing to the first generation—became the status quo to their children and grandchildren. Gradually the new spiritual ideas became a religious institution with a recurring rhythm of sacrament and service. No longer was religion the glass through which everything else was viewed. Religion was contained in a separate sphere, and life as a whole was interpreted according to other, more secular guidelines.

The people who experience secularization frequently view the process as a decline from an earlier and better period. Wallace's theory helps us to understand that the process of secularization—the smaller and more local kind anyway—is not a failure, but the inevitable last part of a mature revitalization movement. If a revitalization movement fails, it does not last into a second generation. If it succeeds, the descendants of the founders inherit the new system of ideas, but because it is all they have ever known, it does not excite them. They are apt instead to develop their own emphases which overshadow the ideas that once inspired their parents.

What were the new emphases of fifth period Moravians in Bethlehem? To discover these let us look at the relations which Moravians engaged in that were secular in nature.

Tables 6-12 and 6-13 show the significant secular relations (those which involved at least three age groups) with community and kin respectively. Both periods placed considerable emphasis on emotional connections with community members (see Table 6-12). The striking difference

231

TABLE 6-12 Secular Relationships with Community Members

	Period I Females					Period I Males							Mode*	Period V Females								Period V Males						
	C	Y	YS	YM	OM	C	Y	YS	YM	YW	OM	OW		C	Y	YS	YM	YW	OS	OM	OW	C	Y	YS	YM	OS	OM	OW
Be friendly with member			×									×	A	×					×	×	×			×	×	×		×
Make oneself loved by member								×					A	×			×		×	×			×	×	×	×		×
Love member	×					×							A			×			×	×				×		×		
Loved by member			×					×				×	P	×	×		×		×	×	×		×	×	×	×		
Known and understood by member								×	×				P	×	×		×			×	×							
Cared for physically by member						×							P	×	×	×	×		×	×		×			×	×		
Interest shown by member													P	×	×	×	×		×	×				×	×	×		
Live with member						×							A	×			×		×	×								
Serve or make oneself useful to member													A		×	×	×		×	×	×			×	×	×	×	
Served by member													P			×	×		×	×				×		×		
Thank member													A		×	×			×	×				×		×		
Thanked by member													A				×		×	×							×	
Taught profession by member													P										×	×		×		×

* A = active, P = passive

is the development by Period V of a network of social services: people were cared for and taught by fellow members of the community, and they repaid this service in kind or in gratitude. We know that Period I Moravians performed these functions with each other as well, but the biographies reported them not as service to fellow humans, but as service to the Heiland. By the fifth period these services were reported as performed directly for other humans without the mediating religious purpose.

Table 6-13 shows a similar intensification of secular relations with family members. During Period I secular relations with kin were primarily confined to a few demographic facts: people came to Bethlehem or moved to different Moravian settlements with family members, and they got married. By Period V secular relations with kin had developed into a much more complex web of affection and service. Family members provided physical care, now that communal arrangements for such care no longer existed. Children obeyed their parents instead of Choir leaders, and family members worked together. In addition, young people had become the center of parents' hopes for the future. They saw their children as providers of joy and as potentially "useful" members of the community at large. Most biographies of children tells of such expectations. James Göhring, for example, "was a healthy and lively child, and it seemed that one had the right to hope that he would grow up to be a joy to his parents and, with the proper guidance, would also prosper for the Heiland, to whom he was dedicated." Likewise, "to the joy of [Henrietta Seidel's] parents and of everyone who took a friendly interest in her well-being, it became evident that the effort spent on her was not in vain, and her progress—especially in beautiful handwork—awakened sweet hopes of her future usefulness." Whereas expectations for the future had focused during Period I on the development of intimate relations with the Heiland on earth and a cementing of them in heaven, by Period V hopes for the future were firmly rooted in one's children here on earth. In addition, as Table 6-13 demonstrates, family members had developed strong ties of love and affection. It is no wonder, then, that death had evolved into a much more important part of the interactions between family members and that the meaning of death had changed. Death was no longer the happily anticipated event that it was during Bethlehem's first years. By Period V death had become the unwished-for separater of loved ones. Death was also less often interpreted in religious terms. People talked less about the "eternal life" of their loved ones or about their "going home to the Heiland." Instead, their loved ones were "lost" to them, they "preceded" them, they "went to sleep" or they simply "died." In this increasingly more secular society, even death was becoming a secular event.

TABLE 6-13 Secular Relationships with Family Members

| | Period I | | | | | | | | | | | | Mode* | Period V | | | | | | | | | | | | | | |
| | Females | | | | | Males | | | | | | | | Females | | | | | | | | Males | | | | | | |
	Children	Youth	Young Single	Young Married	Older Married	Children	Youth	Young Single	Young Married	Young Widowed	Older Married	Older Widowed		Children	Youth	Young Single	Young Married	Young Widowed	Older Single	Older Married	Older Widowed	Children	Youth	Young Single	Young Married	Older Single	Older Married	Older Widowed
Future with, anticipated by kin													P	×	×		×					×						
Be obedient towards parents													A		×								×			×		
Travel or move with kin			×	×	×		×	×	×			×	A					×		×	×			×			×	
Live with kin				×					×				A			×	×	×	×	×	×			×		×	×	×
Give oneself in marriage to spouse					×						×	×	A				×			×	×				×		×	×

	*A/P
Be married to spouse by someone else	P
Lead marriage with spouse	A
Be blessed with children	P
Love kin	A
Be loved by kin	P
Serve kin	A
Cared for physically by kin	P
Work with kin	A
Leave or lose kin in death	A
Preceded in death by kin	P

*A = active, P = passive

Part II

This study has shown a number of subtle and highly connected ways
that secularization affected the Moravian world view. The changes that
occurred from Period I to Period V were characterized not so much by a
decreasing amount of emphasis on the relationship with the Heiland as by
a shift in the kind of relationship: from one of personal intensity to one of
more impersonal ritual and from a relationship which required individual
responsibility to a more passive one that required only the services of religious professionals. Alongside this shift, the conception of the Heiland
underwent parallel changes. For early Moravians in Bethlehem he was the
intimate friend or loving spouse, willing to sacrifice himself for those who
devoted themselves to him. A century later, he had become the benevolent
authority figure who served his followers out of a sense of duty.

The community contexts which maintained these contrasting conceptions of religion changed as well, for the abstract ideas of a religion must
be expressed in everyday practice. Because a very demanding relationship
with the Heiland was the central emotional and mental experience in the
lives of first period Moravians, individuals required considerable psychological support to help modulate their many ups and downs, and the community required stringent social controls to prevent the creative flux from
becoming a chaos of religious ideas and standards. Both of these requirements were satisfied by three systems in Bethlehem: by the intricate structure for admittance to the Gemeine, by the deviance control procedures,
and by the counseling program inherent in the Choir system and the pre-
Communion "speakings." Control systems help to support, and support
systems help to control. By the fifth period, religion was more routine and
less emotional. It required neither the intensive psychological support nor
the tight social control. Religious matters could now be effectively managed
by a few religious professionals.

The love and devoted service which had been directed during the first
period towards the Heiland, just as if he were flesh and blood, was now
turned towards other human beings, especially family members, and the
result was a new conception of life and death which focused on this world
and not the next.

NOTES

1. Peter L. Berger, *The Sacred Canopy: Elements of a Sociological Theory
of Religion* (Garden City, New York: Doubleday & Company, Inc., 1967), p. 108.
2. Harris, "Discourse Analysis."

236

3. See Appendix II for a more complete description of these uses for kin terms. Moravians also frequently distinguished Moravians from non-Moravians in other kinds of documents, but so few relationship partners in these biographies were non-Moravians that it was not useful to add a non-Moravian category.

4. Only four of the female age groups and six of the male age groups are shown in these graphs because fewer than two cases represent the missing categories.

5. Alternative and conceptually more suggestive ways of looking at religious focus will be developed later in the chapter.

6. Only four of the age groups for fifth period females and six of those for fifth period males are represented in these graphs. This is because only these four age groups had enough cases in the first period, which limited the number of comparisons that could be made.

7. If the value for one period were always the denominator, then the value of the ratio would approach infinity as the value of the denominator approached zero. By always making the denominator the larger value, this problem is avoided and the graph is symmetrical around a ratio of 1 which occurs when the Period I percentage is equal to the Period V percentage.

8. Anthony Wallace, "Revitalization Movements," *American Anthropologist,* LVIII (April, 1956), pp.264–81.

Conclusion

The Moravians in early Bethlehem underwent revolutionary social change twice in twenty years. The first change was clearly uplifting. The Bethlehem Diary from that period fairly shouted with joy and excitement. Individuals gratefully gave credit to the Gemeine—especially to Bethlehem—for their sense of inner peace and general well-being. They energetically built buildings, established flourishing trades, and spread their spiritual message. The second change, just twenty years later, was quite another matter. This time the Bethlehem Diary described the change quietly and matter-of-factly, and people reacted with demographic signs of stress. The population of permanent residents in Bethlehem shrank by 20 percent within five years. The marriage rate fell by 44 percent. The birthrate dropped 39 percent. Not only were these changes substantial, they also lasted for several decades. The decline in population and lowered rates of marriage continued for about fifty years. The low birth rate lasted for thirty years. The second change was as upsetting as the first was invigorating.

In both cases the amount of change was substantial. During the years when Bethlehem was first being developed, people gave up their private economies and began to participate in communal ones, they stopped living as families and began living in communal groups organized around age, gender, and marital status, and they increased the religious emphasis in their lives. Twenty years later they reversed all those same changes: they changed their economy from communal to private, their social organization from communal to familial, and their cultural focus from religious to economic. In spite of the similar amount of change, the formation of communal Bethlehem was a positive experience, whereas the dissolution was not.

A number of factors made the difference in how the people in Bethlehem were able to absorb so much change: the motivation behind it, the authority for it, and its physical setting. The *motivation* for the original building of Bethlehem came from the people who underwent the change involved. Zinzendorf was the inspiration behind Bethlehem, but the people who built it were wholehearted participants and were there by personal choice. For them Bethlehem was the end of a long and anguished search for spiritual focus and meaning. In contrast, most of the people who endured the dissolution of the communal economy felt no need for such a radical change. The motivation for the dissolution came from Johann Friedrich Koeber and the other leaders of the Moravian Unity who were faced with a financial crisis of heavy debts and unforgiving creditors. In their view, financial responsibilities had to take precedence over religious mission if the Moravian Church were to survive. Their strategy was to require contributions from every Moravian community including Bethlehem. But residents of Bethlehem had no surplus, since they already had to stretch in order to support a large community without the economic contributions of their many "pilgrim" Brothers and Sisters. The logical conclusion was to change the economic system in Bethlehem so that all the adults could contribute money-producing labor. Forced change, however, is never as easy as self-motivated change. If people feel the need for a change, it heals. If they do not, it causes stress.

The *source of authority* for cultural change also affects how easily people can absorb that change. The authority for the building of communal Bethlehem came from the highest possible source—the Heiland himself, who confirmed through the Lot his agreement with each new step. At this point in their history, Moravians wholeheartedly relied upon the Lot. They had just accepted the Heiland as their Chief Elder, and because they possessed in the Lot a means for learning his wishes on any weighty matter, they took his administration quite literally. The dissolution of the General Economy, on the other hand, was held to be the work of human beings, the leaders of the Unity. In actual fact they, too, had received approval from the Lot, but by then the efficacy of the Lot was being doubted. Spangenberg, for one, commented: "Perhaps the Heiland will allow it, but it is not His first thought."[1] People can endure a difficult change more easily if they believe that their supernatural authority figures sanction and require it of them. Change that is requested by other human beings—especially if they are thought to be outsiders—is more subject to doubt.

The *physical setting* for cultural change can also either support or hinder cultural change. Although the lack of living quarters during the first years must have been difficult, residents in early Bethlehem were fortunate. They had the opportunity to start with a clean slate and to organize their community from scratch. They were able to build buildings that supported their communal idea and their religious focus, and they could locate them in a way that encouraged the necessary separation of the sexes. The plan grew with the ideas, and it in turn helped greatly to make the ideas a reality. However, when the Moravians tried to change the communal system to a private one, these same buildings made their job much harder. The Moravians had to spend many years converting their large buildings into apartments (years which ate into Bethlehem's profitability), and even then they did not achieve the degree of private living typical of towns built for nuclear families to begin with. One hundred years later Bethlehem residents still shared housing to a greater degree than did residents in neighboring townships. If the physical setting fits the ideas behind cultural change, it can help to make them work. If it does not, it will work against them.

The question which arises in the face of this discussion is: why did Koeber and his associates choose to require so much change of Bethlehem? This problem was a financial one. Why did they need to abolish the Choirs of married couples and their children and require that nuclear families live together? Was it necessary to change the communal economy to a private one? If they needed more help from Bethlehem for paying the Unity's debts, why did they not merely encourage more productivity by requiring Bethlehem's adults to spend more hours on economic labor and fewer on spiritual work? Such a plan would have left the communal economy and Choir social organization intact to help support the already weighty change in cultural focus.

Erbe suggests that homogeneity was the issue. In the Moravian world, Bethlehem was something of an exception. Most Moravian settlements were based on the Ortsgemeine form. Of the few that were Pilgergemeine communities, Bethlehem was the most significant and inspiring example and was therefore "a thorn in the eye" to the leaders of the Unity because it was "a completely inorganic structure in the body of the Unity." [2] So, in Erbe's view, these men sought to make Bethlehem a more integral part of the Moravian world. Wallace's revitalization theory (discussed in Chapter 6) suggests why they might want a more conventional Bethlehem. Most revitalization movements encounter resistance from the outside world when they become threatening to it. Moravians had experienced their share of criticism and unrelenting pressure from sources outside of Moravian society. It is highly possible that Koeber sought not only to make Bethlehem a more organic part of Moravianism, but that he wished to cleanse Moravianism of its more extreme characteristics in an effort to make the

Moravian Church as a whole more acceptable and trustworthy to outsiders—particularly to the outsiders who were sources of credit.

Another reason lies in the Unity leaders' commitment to established Moravian culture. Zinzendorf and his early Moravian followers were in an entirely different situation. They had searched for new ways to relieve the religious stress they were experiencing. They had realized that they needed regular support and everyday interaction with people in similar spiritual stages. To achieve this, they had gone beyond the already existing cultural forms to create a conception of society and community that was new to them. In contrast, Koeber and his associates looked for answers to their problems in the choices already available in their cultural world. According to Moravian logic, a community was either an Ortsgemeine or a Pilgergemeine. There were no choices in between. An Ortsgemeine was a group of nuclear families who lived in close proximity and shared a religious belief system. They worshipped together and ran community affairs together, but they lived as separate social and economic units. A Pilgergemeine was a community of individuals whose major focus was missionary and spiritual work. In order to free one group of adults to do the spiritual work, another group, the Hausgemeine, worked to support the whole community: spiritual workers, children, and themselves. They lived in large communal houses, and they centralized all their domestic and economic functions, including the care of their children. Although the residents of Bethlehem grew to greatly appreciate their communal way of life, the leaders of the Moravian Unity had always considered it merely a necessary support for spiritual work. They had never accepted it as a value in its own right. Then, when in Koeber's view the Unity could no longer afford Bethlehem's heavy emphasis on religious mission, Bethlehem had to become an Ortsgemeine—the only alternative to a Pilgergemeine in the Moravian conception of things. Whereas Zinzendorf and his followers had conceived Bethlehem as a new and curative solution to personal stress, Koeber and his associates were not seeking to make a cultural change, but merely to repair the deteriorating financial condition of the Moravian Church. As leaders of a well-established culture, they in fact had an investment in maintaining it. They were not about to reject their cultural logic in order to solve their problem—rather, they needed to use it. Their cultural logic insisted that a communal economic and social system was justified only if the cultural focus was spiritual. Therefore, since Bethlehem's religious work was to be discontinued, the communal system had to be abandoned as well. A Pilgergemeine form without the pilgrim emphasis was unthinkable.

Conclusion

In spite of the extremity of Koeber's solution, it was eventually successful. Bethlehem did indeed become productive enough to contribute to the repayment of the Unity debt, and it did become a community of families. However, the dissolution of the General Economy brought some unintended results as well. It changed not only the economic and social structure of the Moravians in Bethlehem, but also their beliefs about how people should live and what values they should hold. By 1844 people in Bethlehem no longer did their work to serve the Heiland but to serve their friends and families. Intimate friendship with the Heiland was replaced by a growing need for close relations with family and community. And the former requirement for a simple and egalitarian style of life gave way to an easy acceptance of the unequal distribution of Bethlehem's wealth. The simple life had encouraged religious commitment, whereas the ability to accumulate wealth inspired economic success, just as Spangenberg had feared. Religion was no longer the lens through which all of life was viewed and judged. Although the religious mission continued, by 1844 it had taken a more routine place along side everyday social and economic responsibilities. Zinzendorf's original Bethlehem had been completely transformed. His band of "tent dwellers" whose hearts were centered on the more permanent world beyond this one had become a community of families who cherished their time together here on earth.

NOTES

1. Erbe, p.129.
2. Erbe, p.132.

243

APPENDIXES

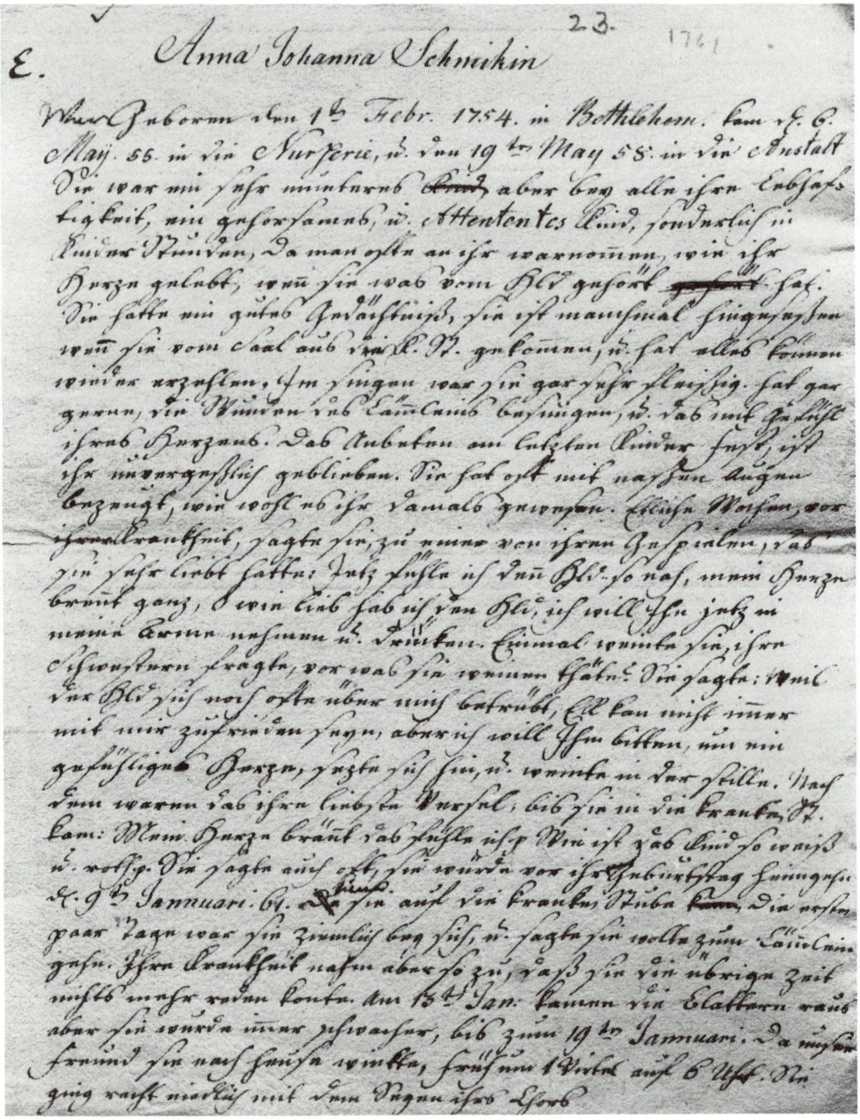

E. 23. 1761

Anna Johanna Schmikin

Ward geboren den 1ten Febr. 1754. in Bethlehem. kam d. 6. May. 55. in die Nurserie, u. den 19ten May 58. in die Anstalt. Sie war ein sehr munteres aber bey aller ihrer Lebhaftigkeit, ein gehorsames, u. attententes Kind, sonderlich in kleiner Stunden, da man öfter an ihr warnehmen, wie ihr Herze gelebt, wenn sie was vom Hld gehört hat. Sie hatte ein gutes Gedächtniß, sie ist manchmal hingesessen wenn sie vom Saal aus d. Kl. St. gekommen, u. hat alles können wieder erzehlen, im singen war sie gar sehr fleißig. hat gar gern, die Wunden des Lämmleins besingen, u. das mit Gefühl ihres Herzens. Das Anbeten am letzten Kinder fest, ist ihr unvergeßlich geblieben. Sie hat oft mit nassen Augen bezeugt, wie wohl es ihr damals gewesen. Etliche Wochen vor ihrer Krankheit, sagte sie, zu einer von ihren Gespielen, das sie sehr liebt hatte: Jetz fühle ich den Hld. so nah, mein Herze brennt ganz, o wie lieb hab ich den Hld., ich will Ihn jetz in meine Arme nehmen u. drücken. Einmal weinte sie, ihre Schwestern fragte, vor was sie weinen thäte. Sie sagte: Weil der Hld sich noch öfter über mich betrübt, Er kan nicht immer mit mir zufrieden seyn, aber ich will Ihn bitten, um ein gefühligers Herze, sezte sich hin, u. weinte in der stille. Nach dem waren das ihre liebsten Verse, bis sie in die kranken St. kam: Mein Herze brennt das fühle ich Wie ist das Kind so weiss u. roth. Sie sagte auch oft, sie würde vor ihrem Geburtstag heimgehen. d. 9ten Januari. 61. kam sie auf die kranken Stube, die ersten paar Tage war sie ziemlich bey sich, u. sagte sie wolle zum Lämmlein gehen. Ihre Krankheit nahm aber so zu, daß sie die übrige Zeit nichts mehr reden konte. Am 13ten Jan. kamen die Blattern raus aber sie wurde immer schwächer, bis zum 19ten Januari. da unser Freund sie nach Hause winkte, früh um 1 Viertel auf 6 Uhr. Sie ging recht niedlich mit dem Segen ihres Chors

FIGURE I-1. Biography of Anna Johanna Schmik

Appendix I: Biographies

Anna Johanna Schmik was born February 1, 1754 in Bethlehem. She came into the Nursery the 6th of May, 1755 and into the Institute on May 19, 1758. She was a very cheerful, but in spite of her liveliness, an obedient and attentive child, especially in Children's Services, where one often observed in her how full of life her heart was whenever she heard something about the Heiland. She had a good memory. She sat down sometimes after she came from the Children's Services and was able to repeat everything. She was very diligent in singing and she loved to celebrate the wounds of the Lamb in song and with such feeling in her heart. She never forgot the Prostration at the last Children's Festival. She often told with tears in her eyes, how happy she felt then. A few weeks before her sickness she said to one of her playmates, whom she loved very much: "Right now I feel so close to the Heiland, that my heart is burning up. Oh how I love the Heiland; I want to take Him in my arms and embrace Him right now." Once she was crying and her Overseers asked why. She said, "Because the Heiland is still often distressed with me; He can't always be pleased with me, but I will beg Him for a feeling heart;" and she sat down and cried by herself. After that and until she entered the sick room, these were her favorite hymns: "My heart burns, that I feel. . . ," "How white and red that child is. . . ." She also often said that she would go home [die] before her birthday. On the 9th of January 61 she entered the sick room. The first few days she was quite conscious and she said she wanted to go to the Lamb. However, her sickness increased so much that for the rest of the time, she could no longer talk. On the 13th of January the smallpox came out, but she became weaker and weaker until the 19th of January, when our Friend beckoned her home, early in the morning at a quarter past five. She left quite sweetly with the blessing of her Choir.

early in the morning at a quarter past five. She left quite sweetly with the blessing of her Choir.

SAMPLE BIOGRAPHY, PERIOD V

Our tenderly beloved little girl Mary Ann Amalia Eberman was born in Litiz the 1st of November, 1830 and was dedicated soon thereafter to our Lord and Savior in Holy Baptism to be his eternal possession. She was from her birth on a very healthy and lively child and she caused her parents much joy especially in her most recent years, in that she was very diligent in learning at school, and in general gave much hope that she would some-day make herself useful and serviceable to herself and to others. However her career in this world was destined to be of only a short duration, in that it pleased the Lord over Life and Death to call her very early out of time and into her only homeland.

She took sick on Tuesday the 14th of this month, but got somewhat better on the following day. However the croup disorder, with which she was overcome, recurred with renewed strength and soon became so vio-lent, that one could have little hope of her recovery, in spite of all the physical remedies which were applied. It pleased our dear Lord to bless-edly complete our dear child already by Sunday morning of this week and to call her dearly bought soul away to her eternal rest after brief but very difficult suffering—just after the blessing of the Lord for her homeward journey was administered to her. Her career down here on earth lasted 6 years, 4 months, and 19 days.

> (1) What happiness was yours
> After suffering a short while!
> Your Savior beckoned you
> Into eternal joys!

> (2) Your shepherd tends you
> On green meadows;
> Your blessed eyes
> Will behold him eternally!

> (3) Among blessed rows of children
> You will praise him
> And sweetly join in
> With heavenly melodies.

TABLE I-1 List of Biographies—Period I

Name	Age	Marital status	Date of death
FEMALES			
Johanna Ettwein	0		1756
Anna Maria Müller	1		1756
Susanna Ohneberg	3		1758
Anna Johanna Schmik	7		1761
Agnes Schulz	8		1762
Elisabeth Böhner	10		1761
Juliana Fritsch	12		1761
Elisabeth Brazier	21	Single	1750
Catharina Leibert	22	Single	1760
Johanette Salterbach	30	Single	1762
Elisabeth Kannhaeuser	40	Single	1763
Catharina Oberlin	23	Married	1763
Maria Sehnert	35	Married	1761
Anna Schaaf	36	Married	1756
Rosina Michler	40	Married	1755
Maria Apollonia Bechtel	67	Married	1758
MALES			
Johann Friedrich Schlegel	1		1752
Anton Peter Böhler	1		1744
Ludwig Friedrich Cammerhoff	1		1749
Johannes Sehner	5		1758
Johann Martin Spohn	12		1758
Caspar Boekel	16		1758
Georg Balthasar Köhler	19		1758
Johannes Kapp	24	Single	1759
Mattias Gottlieb Gottschalk	33	Single	1748
Johann Müller	33	Single	1761
Jacob Schoen	39	Single	1760
Martin Hirt	41	Married	1760
Johann Bernhard Müller	41	Married	1757
Michael Schnall	48	Married	1763
Johannes Jorde	54	Married	1760
Phillip Meurer	52	Widowed	1760
David Tanneberger	64	Married	1760
Georg Hantsch	64	Married	1753
Johann Gottlieb Klemm	72	Widowed	1762
David Nitschmann	82	Widowed	1758

TABLE I-2 List of Biographies—Period V

Name	Age	Marital status	Date of death
FEMALES			
Iduna Concordia Grünewald	1		1833
Maria Elisabeth Andres	2		1832
Maria Cornelia Agnes Luch	3		1840
Henrietta Sophia Seidel	4		1840
Mary Ann Amalia Eberman	6		1843
Hannah Amalia Schneller	7		1832
Sarah Adelaide Luckenbach	10		1838
Henrietta Sophia Seidel	14		1825
Sophia Christiana Kitschelt	27	Single	1833
Rebecca Cist	39	Single	1825
Mary Cist	41	Single	1829
Charlotte Sabine Schropp	46	Single	1833
Louise Herpel	35	Married	1833
Maria Eliza Kluge	47	Married	1842
Sarah Luckenbach	55	Married	1842
Sarah Elisabeth Hüffel	59	Married	1824
Tabea Elisabeth Schröder	35	Widowed	1840
Maria Elisabeth Kunz	67	Single	1836
Anna Catharina Kremser	68	Single	1829
Benigna Caritas Pyrlaeus	79	Single	1829
Marie Elisabeth Beroth	83	Single	1825
Elisabeth Till	67	Married	1835
Susanna Bourquin	72	Married	1839
Maria Magdelena Luckenbach	76	Married	1837
Catharina Elisabeth Weinland	69	Married	1836
Mary Cist	69	Widowed	1831
Christina Hübener	69	Widowed	1829
Justina Maslich	75	Widowed	1834
Maria Magdelena Schindler	84	Widowed	1825
MALES			
Edward William Jungmann	0		1832
Joseph Augustus Kluge	1		1833
Maurice Christian Knauss	1		1838
Maurice Arthur Brickenstein	3		1841
James William Göhring	5		1840
Lucien Wolle	7		1832
Dorsey Syng Physick Stout	7		1831
Israel Lewis Luckenbach	15		1842
Lewis Schmidt	35	Single	1842
Samuel Jacob Peysert	38	Single	1840
Daniel Hauser	55	Single	1839
Johannes Schmidt	57	Single	1831
Carl Christlieb Dober	47	Married	1839

TABLE I-2 *continued*

Name	Age	Marital status	Date of death
Jacob Bush	52	Married	1825
Marcus Fetter	55	Married	1826
Johann Christian Kern	56	Married	1844
David Beitel	71	Single	1825
Gottfried Hennig	81	Single	1825
Gottlieb Braun	65	Married	1825
Paul Weiss	77	Married	1840
Johann David Bischoff	78	Married	1827
Anton Schmidt	85	Married	1834
Joseph Till	72	Widowed	1831
Joseph Oerter	77	Widowed	1841
David Weinland	85	Widowed	1844

Appendix II: Taxonomies and Sources

Taxonomy of Relationship Partners

In order to make sense out of the many relationship pairs represented in the Moravian biographies we need to classify them into a smaller number of categories. Wherever possible we want these categories to come from the Moravian cultural system and not from ours.

James Spradley has developed a methodology in *The Ethnographic Interview* for discovering a group's classification system. It involves finding terms used by members of the group as they talk to each other, write to each other, or use words in any other way. Sometimes several terms will seem to belong to each other. Take for example the following sentence: "His people—especially his wife and his children—remained hopeful that he would recover." The words "his people" form a cover term for "his wife" and "his children"; that is, "his wife" and "his children" are included in the group called "his people." The word "especially" implies that there are other included terms besides "wife" and "children." As Spradley suggests, routine interactions give only partial taxonomies (the cover term with all its branches and layers of included terms). Spradley has developed sorting techniques and series of questions that help fill out an incomplete taxonomy. These techniques help anthropologists who can question their subjects directly, but historians must settle for the incomplete information found in surviving documents. In the absence of complete taxonomies, historians, to be safe, should use the terms found in their subjects' documents and resist the temptation to finish the taxonomies themselves, for they will probably interject too much of their own ways of interpreting the world. In practice, this usually means working with terms at a lower level than the cover term. For example, in the Moravian biographies, relationships are described with close relatives, with distant relatives, with friends, and with Gemeingeschwister (literally, "siblings of the Gemeine").

In line with the above discussion I should have analyzed relationships with close relatives and distant ones separately; however, so few distant relatives were mentioned that no conclusions could be based on a separate analysis and I have included them in the analysis of kin relationship partners.

Figure II-1 shows a taxonomy of Moravian relationship partners. The cover term "relationship partner" is mine, not theirs, but the concept is defined by all the types of people mentioned in the Moravian biographies who related to the subjects of the biographies in any way whatsoever. The other terms are Moravian ones.

In general the cover terms are to the left of the included terms. Thus the cover term "Menschen" included "Gespielen," "Bekannten," "Freunde," "Gemein und Chor Geschwister," "Anverwandten," "Nachkommen," and "Angehörigen." In turn, "Angehörigen" includes "Eltern," "Geschwister," "Mann," "Frau," "Kinder," "Kindeskinder," "Tante," and "Niece." "Kinder" and "Kindeskinder" overlapped. In some cases "Kinder" referred to both children and to grandchildren, but in others "Kinder" contrasted with "Kindeskinder" which grouped grandchildren with greatgrandchildren.

The terms in the taxonomy did not all refer to relationship partners of any one person at the same time. The term "Gespielen" referred only to the young children who were acquaintances of child subjects of biographies. "Bekannten" and "Freunde" were always adults, but they were relationship partners for children as well as adults. "Mann" and "Frau" were relationship partners just for adults (since only adults married) and only adults had children and grandchildren. In addition, in this sample only single women considered aunts and nieces as "Angehörigen." Figure II-2 shows that the meaning of "Familie" changed with age and marital status. Children's families included parents and siblings, but when children grew up and got married, their family included only their spouses and children. Parents and siblings of married adults *were* still considered "Angehörigen" but not "Familie." The cover term "Familie" could not be included in the larger taxonomy because, although a brother-in-law was considered a sibling, he was not a part of a child's family. Similarly a son-in-law was a child, but not a part of one's family.

This taxonomy was developed primarily from the biographies for the

Relationship Partners	Gott (God)					
	Heiliger Geist (Holy Ghost)					
	Heiland (Savior)					
	Menschen (Human Beings)	Gespielen (Playmates)				
		Bekannten (Acquaintances)				
		Freunde (Friends)				
		Gemein und Chor Geschwister (Community and Choir Siblings)	Schwester (Sister)			
			Bruder (Brother)			
		Anverwandten, Verwandten (Distant Relatives)				
		Nachkommen (Descendents)				
		Die Angehörigen, Die Ihrigen, Die Seinigen (One's People or Next of Kin)	Grosseltern (Grandparents)	Grossmutter (Grandmother)		
				Grossvater (Grandfather)		
			Eltern (Parents)	Mutter (Mother)		
				Vater (Father)		
				Stiefvater (Stepfather)		
			Geschwister (Siblings)	Bruder (Brother)		
				Schwester (Sister)		
				Schwager (Brother-In-Law)		
			Mann (Husband)			
			Frau (Wife)			
			Kinder (Children & Children's Children)	Kinder (Children)	Sohn (Son)	
					Tochter (Daughter)	
					Son-In-Law* (German term not given)	
			Kindes-Kinder (Children's Children)	Enkel, Enkelkinder (Grandchildren)	Enkelin (Granddaughter)	
					Enkel (Grandson)	
				Urenkel (Great-Grandchildren)		
			Tante (Aunt)			
			Niece** (Niece)			

* A man whose surname was Weinland wrote, "Wir zogen zu unsern Kindern Charles u. Elisabeth Kremser . . ." (We moved to our children Charles and Elisabeth Kremser), referring obviously to his daughter and son-in-law, but the title of the son-in-law was not given separately.

** The German word "Nichte" never occurs, but two German-language biographies use the word "Niece".

FIGURE II-1. Taxonomy of Moravian relationship partners

For Minors:

Familie	Eltern (Parents)	Mutter (Mother)
		Vater (Father)
		Stiefvater (Stepfather)
	Geschwister (Siblings)	Schwester (Sister)
		Bruder (Brother)

For Married Adults:

Familie	Mann (Husband)	
	Frau (Wife)	
	Kinder (Children)	Tochter (Daughter)
		Sohn (Son)

FIGURE II-2. Relative meanings of "Familie."

last period. During the first period, consanguineal relationship partners are comparatively rare. Most references to relatives of any type concern events which happened before the first period began. During the first period, references to blood relatives served mostly to locate the subject of the biography on a family tree, and they usually gave only the names of the parents and spouses and the number of children. I have assumed that the kin system during the first period was extremely simple because the population was comparatively young and because the social organization of the General Economy abbreviated the more complicated system which these people had apparently been a part of before they came to Bethlehem. Since I wanted to compare the system of relationships for the two periods, I needed to decide on one taxonomy for both. It therefore made sense to choose the more fully developed taxonomy as the basis for the analysis of relationships.

EXTENSION OF KIN TERMS FOR CO-MEMBERS OF THE GEMEINE

The Moravians were accustomed to thinking of themselves as members of one large family, and in an effort to make that idea more concrete, they used some of their kin terms to classify other Moravians who were not actually related to them by blood or by marriage. Thus, "Chorfamilie" (Choir family) or "Chorverwandten" (Choir relatives) were cover terms for people who lived in the same Choir. Likewise the term "Geschwister" (siblings) was used to refer to other members of the Gemeine, as were the terms "Schwester" (Sister) and "Bruder" (Brother). Variations of the sister/brother terms were also used: Single People were called "Ledige Geschwister," "Ledige Schwestern," and "Ledige Brüder," Married People were "Verheiratete Geschwister" or "Ehegeschwister," and Widowed People were "Verwitwete Geschwister," etc. The terms "Geschwister," "Schwester," and "Bruder" also became titles of address, used along with people's proper names.

When used in the above ways, to name unrelated co-members, the terms "Schwester" and "Bruder" never referred to children. Children were called "die Kinder" or "Mäglein" and "Jünglein" (Little Girls and Little Boys). As they got older they became "Grosse Mädgen" and "Knaben." Only when people joined the Single Sisters' Choir or the Single Brothers' Choir were they called "Brüder" and "Schwestern." In contrast, the words "Bruder" and "Schwester" *were* used to refer to blood-related siblings below the age of twenty. If they were very young they might be affectionately called "Brüdergen" or "Schwestergen." Sometimes, especially when there was danger of confusion, a blood-related sibling was called a "leibliche Schwester" or "leiblicher Bruder."

Kin terms other than "Schwester" and "Bruder" were not generally used to name unrelated co-members. The notion of parenthood rarely referred to anyone except one's consanguineal mother and father.[1] Likewise the terms "Sohn" and "Tochter" (son and daughter), "Grossmutter" and "Grossvater" (grandmother and grandfather), "Enkeln" (grandchildren), as well as the terms for cousin, aunt, uncle, niece, and nephew were used only to describe people related by birth or by marriage.

The idea of marriage extended beyond a person's human marriage partner as a metaphor for one's relationship with the Heiland. Theoretically the Heiland was the bridegroom for females *and* males of all ages since they all possessed a feminine soul ("Seele" takes the feminine gender in German). When a person died, the Heiland became his or her Eternal or "real" Husband.

TRANSLATION OF TERMS FOR THE HEILAND

Bridegroom	Bräutigam, Blut-Bräutigam
Child	Kind

Christ	Christus
Conciliator	Versöhner
Creator	Schöpfer
Divinity	(original in English)
Ever Good Will	(original in English)
Expiator of Sins	Sündentilger
Friend	Freund
Friend of Children	Kinder Freund
God	Gott
Guardian	Hüter
Hand	(original in English)
Heavenly Physician	Himmlischer Arzt
Highest Elder	Ältester
Husband	Mann, Ewiger Mann, Eigentlicher Mann
Intercessor	Fürsprecher
Jesus	Jesu, Jesulein
Lamb	Lamm, Lämmlein
Lord	Herr
Lover	Liebhaber, Liebhaber der Seele
Man of Mercy	Erbarmer
Man of Sorrow	(original in English)
Martyr	Marter-Mann
Open Arms	Offne Arme
Pale Lips	Blasse Lippen
Redeemer	Erlöser
Savior	Heiland
Shepherd	Hirt
Sidewound	Seitenhölchen, Seitelein
Sole Heart	Einiges Herz
Son	Sohn
Son of God	Gottesohn
Son of Humans	Menschensohn
Vine	Weinstock
Wounds	Wunden

SOURCES FOR TABLES

Table 2-5

Total migration was obtained directly from the Memorabilia.
Net migration was computed according to the formula:

$P_2 - P_1 - B + D = M_N$, where P_2 = Population at End of Decade, P_1 = Population at Beginning of Decade, B = Number of Births, D = Number of Deaths, and M_N = Net Migration.

The raw scores under the section labeled "Immigration/Emigration" were computed from the equations: $X - Y = M_N$ and $X + Y = M_T$; where X = Immigration, Y = Emigration, M_N = Net Migration (see Chapter 2, note 8, p. 84) and M_T = Total Migration as reported in Memorabilia. X correlates with immigration as reported at .96, and Y correlates with Emigration as reported at .97. The assumptions behind the formulas are that M_T and M_N are correct.

The information on conversion, withdrawal, and transfer migration was obtained from Memorabilia reports.

Table 3-2

The catalog of children was derived from different sources. The numbers of infants and nursery age children were computed by subtracting the number of deaths from the number of births in the appropriate years. The total number of children came from the year's end Memorabilia for the years given. The number of children aged 5 or over was computed by subtracting the number of infants and nursery-aged children from the total number of children.

The location of children came from the Memorabilia for the given years. The percentages were figured from the raw scores reported.

The number of children over 5 with parents was estimated by subtracting the number of infants and nursery-aged children from the reported number of children living with parents.

NOTES

1. The one exception is the term "Choreltern" (Choir parents), used sometimes during the Communal Period to name the married couple designated as leaders of the Children's Choir, but the Single Sisters and Brothers directly in charge of raising the children were always referred to as their "Schwestern" or their "Brüder."

Bibliography

PRIMARY SOURCES

Bernhard, Charles, Duke of Sachse-Weimar-Eisenach. *Travels Through North America During the Years 1825 and 1826 by His Highness Bernhard, Duke of Sachse-Weimar-Eisenach*. Philadelphia: Carey, 1828.

Bethlehem Church Register; Volume I, 1742–1756; Volume II, 1756–1801; Volume III, 1802–1837; Volume IV, 1838–1854. Bethlehem Moravian Archives MSS.

Br. Petri Rede an der Ehe Chor Versammlung nach der Trauung der 3 Paar Geschwistern Gerners, Skangels [?] u. Clavens am 5. Juni, 22. Woche, Number 2, 1767. Bethlehem Moravian Archives.

Br. Reichels Rede an die Kinder zu ihrem Gemein Tag, 42. Woche, Number 4, 1767. Bethlehem Moravian Archives MSS.

Catalogues of the different Choirs, 1747–1845. Bethlehem Moravian Archives MSS.

Diarium der Gemeine zu Bethlehem. Bethlehem Moravian Archives MSS.

Hamilton, Kenneth G., ed. *The Bethlehem Diary. Volume I, 1742–1744*. Bethlehem: The Archives of the Moravian Church, 1971.

Inventarium derer Mobilien in Bethlehem 1758. Bethlehem Moravian Archives MSS.

Johannis Rede an die Kinder am Weynachtsfeste, 51. Woche, Number 4, 1767. Bethlehem Moravian Archives MSS.

Johannis Rede an die Kinder an ihrem Gemein Tage, 46. Woche, Gemeinnachrichten, 1767. Bethlehem Moravian Archives MSS.

Johannis Rede an die Kinder und Gebet bei ihrem Anbeten am Ältesten-Fest 13. November, 45. Woche, Number 2, 1767. Bethlehem Moravian Archives MSS.

Johannis Rede an die Kinder vor ihrem Anbeten, 2. Woche, Number 7, 1767. Bethlehem Moravian Archives MSS.

Johannis Rede an die Knaben an ihrem Chorfest bey der Aufnahme von 5 Kindern in dasselbe, 2. Woche, 1767. Bethlehem Moravian Archives MSS.

Johannis Rede an die ledigen Brueder, 4. Woche, Number 1, 1767. Bethlehem Moravian Archives MSS.

Johannis Rede an die ledigen Schwestern, 2. Woche, Number 3, 1767. Bethlehem Moravian Archives MSS.

Bibliography

Johannis Rede an die Mädgen an ihrem Chor-fest den 17. August, 33. Woche, Number 2, 1767. Bethlehem Moravian Archives MSS.

Johannis Rede an die Mädgen an ihren Feste den 25. März, 12. Woche, Number 1767. Bethlehem Moravian Archives MSS.

Josephs Rede an die Kinder an ihrem Gemeintage, 39. Woche, Number 2, 1767. Bethlehem Moravian Archives MSS.

Lebenslaeufe, 1744–1844. Bethlehem Moravian Archives MSS. See list in Appendix I.

Memorabilia, 1742–1845. Bethlehem Moravian Archives MSS.

Return of the United Brethren of Bethlehem Township delivered to the Constable, December 9, 1756. Bethlehem Moravian Archives MSS.

Spangenberg, August Gottlieb. *Idea Fidei Fratrum oder kurzer Begriff der Christlichen Lehre in den evangelishchen Brüdergemeinen.* Barby: Christian Friedrich Laur, 1779.

The Text-Book of the Protestant Church of the United Brethren (or Moravians) for the Year 1865. Bethlehem, Pa.: H. Ruede, 1864.

U.S. Census, Northampton County, Pennsylvania, 1850.

Verlass der vier Synoden der evangelischen Brüder-Unität von den Jahren 1764, 1769, 1775, und 1782. Bethlehem Moravian Archives MSS.

SECONDARY SOURCES

Blankenburg, Walter. "Die Musik der Brüdergemeine in Europa." In *Unitas Fratrum: Moravian Studies*, edited by Mari P. van Buijtenten, et al. Utrecht: Rijksarchief, 1975.

Brock, Peter. *Pacifism in the United States: From the Colonial Era to the First World War.* Princeton, N.J.: Princeton University Press, 1968.

———. *The Political and Social Doctrines of the Unity of Czech Brethren in the Fifteenth and Early Sixteenth Centuries.* The Hague: Mouton & Company, 1957.

Demos, John. *A Little Commonwealth.* New York: Oxford University Press, 1970.

de Schweinitz, Edmund. *The Financial History of the Province and Its Sustention Fund.* Bethlehem, Pa.: Moravian Publications Office, 1885.

Dreydoppel, Otto. "Rising Patriotism and Declining Pacifism." (Typewritten, Bethlehem Moravian Archives 1975.)

Erbe, Helmut. *Bethlehem, Pa.: Eine kommunistische Herrnhuter-Kolonie des 18. Jahrhunderts.* Stuttgart: Ausland und Heimat Verlags-Aktiengesellschaft, 1929.

Fries, Adelaide L. *The Moravians in Georgia, 1735–1740.* Raleigh, N.C.: Edwards & Broughton, 1905.

Gollin, Gillian. *Moravians in Two Worlds: A Study of Changing Communities.* New York: Columbia University Press, 1967.

Hamilton, J. Taylor, and Hamilton, Kenneth G. *History of the Moravian Church.*

Bibliography

Bethlehem, Pa.: Interprovincial Board of Christian Education, Moravian Church of America, 1967.

Hamilton, Kenneth G. *John Ettwein and the Moravian Church During the Revolutionary Period.* Bethlehem: Times Publishing Company, 1940.

Hayden, Dolores. *Seven American Utopias: The Architectures of Communitarian Socialism, 1790–1975.* Cambridge, Mass.: MIT Press, 1976.

Jordan, Albert F. "Some Early Moravian Builders in America." *Pennsylvania Folklife,* XXIV (Fall 1974), pp. 2–17.

Kroeger, Karl. "Moravian Music in America." In *Unitas Fratrum: Moravian Studies,* edited by Mari P. Buijtenen, et al. Utrecht: Rijksarchief, 1975.

Levering, Joseph Mortimer. *A History of Bethlehem, Pennsylvania, 1741–1892, With Some Account of Its Founders and Their Early Activity.* Bethlehem, Pa.: Times Publishing Company, 1903.

MacMaster, Richard K. et al. *Conscience in Crisis: Mennonites and Other Peace Churches in America, 1739–1789, Interpretation and Documents.* Scottsdale, Pa.: Herald Press, 1979.

Molnar, Amedeo. "Die Böhmische Brüderunität. Abriss Ihrer Geschichte." In *Unitas Fratrum: Moravian Studies,* edited by Mari P. van Buijtenen, et al. Utrecht: Rijksarchief, 1975.

Müller, Joseph Th. *Geschichte der Böhmischen Brüder.* 3 vols. Herrnhut: Verlag der Missionsbuchhandlung, 1931.

Murtagh, William John. *Moravian Architecture and Town Planning; Bethlehem, Pennsylvania and Other Eighteenth-Century Settlements.* Chapel Hill: University of North Carolina Press, 1967.

Nelson, James David. "Herrnhut: Friedrich Schleiermacher's Spiritual Homeland." Unpublished Ph.D. dissertation, University of Chicago, 1963.

Nelson, Vernon. "The Moravian Church in America." In *Unitas Fratrum: Moravian Studies,* edited by Mari P. Buijtenten, et al. Utrecht: Rijksarchief, 1975.

North, Douglass C. *The Economic Growth of the United States 1790–1860.* New York: W. W. Norton & Company, 1966.

Pryor, Karen Wylie. *Nursing Your Baby.* New York: Harper & Row, Publishers, 1963.

Reichel, Gerhard. *August Gottlieb Spangenberg: Bischof der Brüderkirche.* Tübingen: Verlag von J. C. B. Mohr, 1906.

Říčan, Rudolf. *Die Böhmischen Brüder: Ihr Ursprung und Ihre Geschichte.* Berlin: Union Verlag, 1961.

Sawyer, Edwin Albert. "The Religious Experience of the Colonial Moravians." *Transactions of the Moravian Historical Society,* XVIII (1961), Part I.

Sessler, Jacob John. *Communal Pietism Among Early American Moravians.* New York: Henry Holt and Company, 1933.

Vacovsky, Adolf. "History of the Hidden Seed." In *Unitas Fratrum: Moravian Studies,* edited by Mari P. van Buijtenen, et al. Utrecht: Rijksarchief, 1975.

Wagner, Murray L. *Petr Chelčický: A Radical Separatist in Hussite Bohemia.* Scottsdale, Pa.: Herald Press, 1983.

Weinlick, John R. *The Moravian Church Through the Ages*. Bethlehem, Pa.: Comenius Press, 1966.

Wells, Robert V. "Quaker Marriage Patterns in a Colonial Perspective." *William and Mary Quarterly,* XXIX (July 1972): pp. 415–42.

Yates, Ross. "The Period of Questioning, Bethlehem, 1850–1876." *Transactions of the Moravian Historical Society,* XXII (1975), Part III, pp. 193–212.

METHODOLOGICAL AND THEORETICAL SOURCES

Berger, Peter L., *The Sacred Canopy: Elements of a Sociological Theory of Religion*. Garden City, New York: Doubleday & Company, 1967.

Berger, Peter L., and Luckmann, Thomas. *The Social Construction of Reality: A Treatise in the Sociology of Knowledge*. Garden City, New York: Doubleday & Company, 1967.

Bogue, Donald. *Principles of Demography*. New York; Wiley, 1969.

Coale, Ansley J. and Demeny, Paul. *Regional Model Life Tables and Stable Populations*. Princeton, N.J.: Princeton University Press, 1966.

Hallowell, A. Irving. *Culture and Experience*. New York: Schocken Books, 1967.

Harris, Zellig S. "Discourse Analysis," *Language,* XXVIII (1952), pp. 18–23.

Kish, Leslie. *Survey Sampling*. New York: Wiley, 1965.

Kübler-Ross, Elisabeth. *On Death and Dying*. New York: Macmillan Publishing Co., 1969.

Murphey, Murray G. *Our Knowledge of the Historical Past*. New York: The Bobbs-Merrill Company, 1973.

Nadel, S. F. *The Theory of Social Structure*. London: Cohen & West, 1969.

Redfield, Robert. *The Little Community*. Chicago: The University of Chicago Press, 1971.

Spradley, James. *The Ethnographic Interview*. New York: Holt, Rinehart & Winston, 1979.

Sudnow, David. *Passing On: The Social Organization of Dying*. Englewood Cliffs, N.J.: Prentice-Hall, 1967.

Tufte, Edward R. *The Visual Display of Quantitative Information*. Cheshire, Conn.: Graphics Press, 1983.

Wallace, Anthony F. C. *Culture and Personality*. New York: Random House, 1966.

———. *Religion: An Anthropological View*. New York: Random House, 1966.

———. "Revitalization Movements," *American Anthropologist* LVII (April 1956), pp. 264–81.

Index

Acceptance. *See* Admission process

Admission process, 22–23, 135

Adolescence, 12, 151–52. *See also* Older Boys; Older Girls

Adults, 131–32, 134, 135

Age: dimension of contrast, 136–37; treatment of in biographies, 142

Age distribution. *See* Population, composition by age

Age-groups, 127, 143 n.1

Agriculture, 86, 97, 100

American Revolution, 52, 83; allegiance during, 39, 40, 50 n.79; Americanization of Bethlehem during, 40; independence of Bethlehem during, 38; location of Continental Army hospital in Bethlehem, 40–41; pacifism during, 39

Americanization, 40–42

Anstalten, 137, 143 n.4. *See also* Institutes

Apartments, formation of, 107

Apothecary, 91–92

Apprenticeships, 182

Architecture and cultural values, 95, 121 n.19

Assimilation, 40

Aufnahme. *See* Admission process

Augsburg Confession, 48 n.25

Autobiographies, 130–31

Awakening, 151, 153, 155, 196

Backsliding from religious stability, 164–65

Balance between religious mission and economic development, 94–95

Baptism, 180, 214–17, 248

Bar graphs, horizontal, explanation of, 203

Barn, 89, 90

Battle of White Mountain in 1620, 5

Bechtel, Maria, 177

Beds in married women's dormitory, 103–105

Behavior: actual, 201; expected, 146, 201

Behavioral norms: Period I–Period V comparisons, 142; reflected in biographies, 129

Bell House, 89, 90, 92, 120 n.6; East Extension, 89, 90; West Extension, 89, 91

Berger, Peter, 198

Berthelsdorf, 6

Bethlehem: centennial celebration of, 46; early growth of, 27; first Constitution of, 36; founding of, 9; Herrnhut as model for, 33; involvement in county government, 40; move to, 135; as Pilgergemeine, 25–26, 33–34; plans for restructuring of General Economy, 33; relationship to other Moravian settlements, 52–53, 66, 71; special nature of, 24–25; transition of, 34–36, 105–120; Unity and, 35–36, 37, 38, 42–44, 101; value of buildings in, 36

Biographies: as documents, 129–32; list of Period I sample, 249; list of Period V sample, 250–51; original purpose of, 125–26; sampling design, 126–29; source of unconscious emphases, 199; structure of, 132–42; unequal weighting of in statistics, 202–203

Birth, 75, 133, 137, 146–47

Birth control, 75

Birth rates, 74, 76, 103

Blacksmith: log, 89, 90; stone, 91

Blahoslav, Jan, 5

Boarding school for girls, 41

Boekel, Caspar, 153, 176, 178

Böhler, Anton Peter, 146–47, 148, 202–203

Böhler, Peter, 26, 180

Böhner, Elisabeth, 150, 172

Bonnet ribbons and Choir membership for females, 146

Boys' Institute, 94

Brazier, Elisabeth, 154, 171, 179

Breast feeding. *See* Nursing
Bridge across Lehigh River, 109
Broad Street, 109
Brother Joseph. *See* Spangenberg, August Gottlieb
Brother Peter. *See* Böhler, Peter
Brotherly Agreement, 31
Buildings: and cultural values of builders, 95; flexible uses of, 92–93, 120n.13; ownership of, 45
Burial, 135, 180
Burnside, James, 95
Bush, Jacob, 183

Cammerhoff, Anna, 29
Cammerhoff, Johann Friedrich, 29
Cammerhoff, Ludwig, 202–203
Canal, 44, 109, 112
Catalogs (Census), 53
Centennial celebration of Bethlehem, 46
Change, cultural, 46, 119–20, 125–26
Chapel, 120n.6
Character description, in biographies, 133, 137–38
Chelčický, Petr, 3–4
Child rearing. *See* Children, rearing of
Children's Choir: Choir parents for, 258n.1
Children: biographies of, 131–32; census sources for, 258; character descriptions of, 138; concern about health of, 180–81, 248; concern for future of, 181; death experience of, 150, 247–48; education of, 138, 148; integration of, into parents' home, 107, 113, 115–16; mortality of, 81–83; premonition of death, 135; rearing of, 13, 34, 145, 146; relation with community, 149, 150; relationship with Heiland, 133–34, 247; relationship with parents, 138, 148, 214–17, 225–27, 248; religious experiences of, 16–17, 150, 247; social usefulness of, 248; topics in biographies, 137; weaning of, 145, 146, 148. *See also* Adolescence; Infants; Older Boys; Older Girls
Choir Helpers, 151, 157, 160, 162
Choir system, 10, 11, 81–83, 151, 230
Christ. *See* Heiland
Christian Renatus, son of Zinzendorf, 29
Christiansbrunn, 53, 86
Church (Central), 109
Church register, 53
Church Street, 109. *See also* Sisters' Lane
Cist, Mary, 184
Cist, Rebecca, 184

Civil courts, 43
Close regime, 37, 44, 52, 83, 127
Coal, 44
Coale and Demeny's Life Table Models, 79–81
Comenius, Jan Amos, 5
Commerce, 86; expansion of, 44–45; regulation of, 36, 43, 44. *See also* Industries
Communal Economy. *See* General Economy
Communal life style: equality of, 95; religious focus and, 242; simplicity of, 95
Communalism, waning of, 30–31, 34, 49n.54
Communion, 17–18, 158; abstention from, 18; admission to, 22–23, 151, 152, 230; First, 135, 137, 152; preparation for, 17–18; Single Peoples' Choirs and, 153
Community: importance of Period I, 209; relationship with, 202, 203, 208–209, 231–36, 243; secularization of relationship with, 224–31; service to, 231
Compactata in 1434, 3
Conflict, community, 42–43
Construction, 86–95, 105–112; apothecary, 91, 92; barn, wood, 89, 90; Bell House, 89, 90; Bell House, West Extension, 89, 91; Bell House, East Extension, 89, 90; blacksmith, log, 89, 90; blacksmith, stone, 91; bridge across Lehigh River, 109; commercial buildings, 87, 89; Crown Inn, 89, 91; dyeworks and clothiers, 91; First House, 87; flax breaking house, 91; fulling mill, 91; Gemeinhaus, 87; Girls' Seminary, 109; grist mill, log, 89, 90; grist mill, stone, 91; Horsefield House, 89, 91; Indian Hotel, 91–92; locksmith, stone, 91; Married Men's House, 89, 90, 91; materials, 87, 89, 90; Men's Infirmary, 90; millwork, 89, 90; nailsmith, stone, 91; oil mill, log, 89, 90; Old Chapel, 91; pottery, log, 89, 90; pottery, stone, 91; residential, 87, 89; sawmill, 89, 90; sequencing of, 87–92; during 1760s, 105–109; from 1790s and later, 109–112; Single Brothers' House, Eastern Annex, 91; Single Brothers' House, First, 89, 90; Single Brothers' House, Second, 89, 90; Single Sisters' House, North Extension, 91; stables, 90; store, first, 91; store, second, 91–92; Sun Inn, 91–92; tannery, stone, 91; tannery, wood, 89, 90; techniques of, 87; waterworks, 91–92; Widows' House, 93

Continental Army hospital in Bethlehem, 40
Contrast, dimensions of in flowcharts, 136–37, 138–42
Control system, 236
Conversion experience, 46–47 n.20, 151, 153, 154, 155
Conversion into the Moravian Church, 69–71
Corrupt nature, 152–53. *See also* Sinful nature
Cover terms, 252–53
Crown Inn, 89, 91, 97, 99
Cultural change. *See* Change, cultural
Cultural values and architecture, 95, 121 n.19
Cunow, John Gebhard, 42–43, 44

Daily routine, 14–15
David, Christian, 6
de Schweinitz, Lewis David, 44–45
de Watteville, Johannes, 29, 34
Death, 135; age at, 137; ambivalence about, in Period V, 191; attitudes about, Period I, 135, 170–80; attitudes about, Period V, 187–94; final illness, 135, 137, 138, 173–74, 188–89, 248; moment of, 176; relation with Heiland and, 178; religious ceremonies concerning, 135, 176–77; secularization of, 233; support of surrounding community, 134, 174; the unconverted and, 178; trombone choir and, 179. *See also* Dying; Funeral; Grief; Infant mortality; Mortality
Deaths, number of in Bethlehem, 126
Debt. *See* Finances
Decision boxes in flowcharts, 132–33, 136–37, 142, 143–44 n.6
Demographic periods, 51–52
Demographic trauma during the transition period from 1762 to 1818, 83
Development in Bethlehem, 86, 87, 89, 109
Deviance control, 18, 22–23
Discourse analysis. *See* Reformulation of texts
Divorce, 161, 196 n.31
Dober, Carl, 183, 185, 189–90, 191–92
Domesticity, 182
Dreydoppel, Otto, 50 n.79
Dryness as impediment to religous stability, 153
Duke of Weimar, 113
Dyeworks and clothiers, 91
Dying, the: active participation in own

death, 177; fantasies, a hindrance to connection with, 193; relation with Heiland and, 175–76, 179; visitors to, 175–76, 192

(Eagle) Hotel, 44, 109
Easton, 113
Eberman, Mary Ann, 180, 181, 248
Economy, The. *See* General Economy
Economy. *See* Regional economy
Einfalt. *See* Simplicity
Elderly people, 53, 84 n.5
Emmaus, 53
Equal share coefficient, 119
Erbe, Helmut, 33, 34, 49 nn.54, 56, 101, 241
Ethnic groups in Bethlehem, 126
Ethnographic Interview, The, 252
Ettwein, Johanna, 147, 148, 172
Ettwein, Johannes, 38, 39, 41, 109
Extended family. *See* Family, extended

Family: affection for, 233; as authors of biographies, 130–31; Choirs' effect on, 11; extended, 116–17, 119, 121–22 n.44; importance of during Period V, 208; nuclear, 107, 116, 119, 184; relationship with, 202, 203, 208–09, 231–36, 243; secularization of relationship with, 224–31; service to, 233
Family houses, 107
Family types and house types, 117–19
Farm, 107, 109
Fathers, 147, 184–85. *See also* Parents
Females. *See* Gender; Older Girls; Single Sisters; Widows; Women
Fertility, 75, 85 n.15
Fetter, Marcus, 183, 185, 191, 192
Final illness. *See* Death, final illness
Finances, 36, 42, 120, 242
First House, 87
Flax Breaking House, 91
Flood, 45
Flowcharts, 132–42, 143 n.3
42 Statutes, 7
French and Indian War, 38, 49 n.56
Freudigkeit. *See* Joy in one's heart
Friedenshütten, 99
Friedensthal, 53, 86
Friedrichstown, 53, 93
Fritsch, Juliana, 150, 171, 172, 173, 177
Fulling mill, 91
Funeral Biographies. *See* Biographies
Funerals, 179–80

Gemeine: acquaintance with, 135; admission into, 135, 137, 151, 152, 156, 230; as support system, 151; expulsion from, 157, 158–59; officials of, as authors of biographies, 130–31; readmittance to, 157–58; relation with, 154, 155; taxonomy of, 25
Gemeine Council, 17
Gemeinhaus, 87, 94, 103, 120n.6
Gemeinnachrichten, 16, 126
Gemeintag. *See* Gemeine Council
Gender: church membership and, 69–71; dimension of contrast, 136–37, 137–38, 138–42; marital status and, 57–59, 184; migration and, 66–71; Period I–Period V comparisons of, 142; profession and, 138, 185; sex ratios, 54–55, 83. *See also* Gender comparisons; Gender roles; Population, composition by gender
Gender comparisons, 167–70, 203, 206–208, 218–24
Gender roles, 13, 181–82; in government, 37, 43; symmetry and asymmetry of, 13, 167–70
General Economy, 52, 71, 73, 92–93; coincides with Period I, 127; dissolution of, 30–31, 32, 33, 83, 105; ease of absorbing new residents into, 31; supported by physical arrangements of buildings, 105
General Synod. *See* Synod
Georgia, 9, 38
German settlers, 94
Germantown, 93
Girls' Seminary, 92, 109
Gnadenhütten, 31, 99
Gnadenthal, 53, 86
God's Acre, 179–80
Goepp, Phillip, 45, 122n.45
Göhring, James, 181, 216, 233
Gollin, Gillian Lindt, 48n.25
Gottschalk, Mattias, 154, 179
Government, secular, 45
Great Swamp, The, 93
Gregor, founder of Unitas Fratrum, 4
Grief, 138, 193–94
Grist mill: log, 89, 90; stone, 91

Hamilton, J. Taylor and Hamilton, Kenneth G., 33, 46n.20
Harris, Zellig, 199
Hauser, Daniel, 183
Hausgemeine, 25, 52, 94
Hayden, Delores, 121n.19
Heiland: as Chief Elder, 24, 30; authority for development of communal Beth-

lehem, 240; death and, 171, 173, 175–76, 178, 194; different images of, 194–95, 218–24, 256–57; joy in one's heart and, 160–61; the Lot and, 23–24; relationship with, analysis of, 201, 202, 208, 209, 302; relationship with, awareness of need for, 151; relationship with, in biographies, 133–35, 247, 248; relationship with, expected of everyone, Period I, 170; relationship with, among Married People, 160–64; relationship with, ritualization of, 214–18; relationship with, secularization of, 233–36, 243; relationship with, struggle to maintain, 153–59; relationship with, among Widowed People, 167; service to, 145, 164, 190, 231; model for behavior, 146
Heitz, Johann Georg, 7
Helpers, 196–97n.36
Herpel, Louise, 185
Herrnhaag, 29–30, 49n.52
Herrnhut, 6–7, 33
Herrnhuters. *See* Moravian Church
Hidden Seed, Period of, 5, 6
Hirt, Martin, 165, 178–79
Homogeneity, 133–37
Horsefield House, 89, 91, 95
Horsefield, Timothy, 95
Hotel. *See* (Eagle) Hotel
House to household ratios in Bethlehem and other communities, 113
House types and family types, 117–19
Hübener, Christina, 189, 191, 192, 192
Hüffel, Sarah, 185, 186–87, 189, 191
Hus, Jan, 3
Husbands, role of, 168–69
Hymns, 14–15, 16, 21
Identity, personal: with family, 133; with Moravian history, 133
Illness, 138, 178–79, 189–90. *See* Death, final illness
Indian Chapel, 99
Indian Hotel, 91–92, 99
Indians, 86, 94, 97, 99–100
Indifference, impediment to religious stability, 153, 154
Industries, 35, 45, 97, 101
Inequality, 117–20
Infant mortality, 76, 79, 81, 181
Infants: biographies of, 138; premonition of death, 135; relationship with parents, 146–47; relationship with Gemeine members, 147; relationship with Heiland, 133, 148; weaning, 145, 146, 148

Institutes ("Anstalten"), 135, 137
Instrumental music, 22, 179

Jednota Bratrska. *See* Unitas Fratrum
Joy in one's heart, 160–61

Kannhaeuser, Elisabeth, 175
Kern, Johann, 183, 184–85
Kin terms, 236n.3, 255–56
Kin. *See* Family
Kitchens, 107
Kitschelt, Sophia, 184, 191
Kluge, Joseph, 180, 189
Kluge, Maria, 186, 188
Koeber, Johann Friedrich, 32, 34, 240, 241, 242, 243
Köhler, Balthasar, 152, 173, 175, 176, 178, 209, 230–31
Kralice Bible, 5
Kunwald, first seat of Unitas Fratrum, 4
Kunz, Margaretha, 173
Kunz, Maria, 230

Land ownership, 43, 44
Land sales, 42, 43, 45, 89
Landgemeine, 25, 48nn.41,42
Large buildings in Bethlehem, 107
Lease system, 36, 44, 45. *See also* Land ownership; Limitation clause
Lebensläufe. *See* Biographies
Lehigh Coal and Navigation Company, 44
Lehigh Coal Company, 44
Lehigh River, 97
Leibert, Catharina, 173
Levering, Joseph Mortimer, 33, 37, 101, 120nn.11,13
Life and Death, balanced attitude towards, 172–73
Life expectancy, 81
Limitation clause, 36, 43. *See also* Lease system, Land ownership
Linguistic analysis. *See* Refomulation of texts
Little Boys' Choir, entry into, 145
Little Boys, 149–50
Little Girls' Choir, entry into, 145
Little Girls, 149–50
Locksmith: stone, 91
Log construciton, 89–92
Lorenz curve, 119, 122n.45
Lot, 22, 23–24, 43, 94–95, 160
Luch, Maria, 191
Luckenbach, Israel, 180, 182, 192
Luckenbach, Sarah, 185, 216

Lukáš of Prague, 4–5
Lumber, 44

Maguntsche, 93
Main Street, 97, 107, 109
Males. *See* Gender; Men; Older Boys; Single Men; Widowers
Marital status: dimension of contrast, 136–37; gender and, 55–59; migration and, 71; Period I–Period V comparisons, 142; relationship partners, 203–206; remaining single, 56–59. *See also* Population, composition by marital status
Market Street, 107, 109
Marriage, 43, 135, 159–65; a religious institution, 163, 164; average age at first marriage, 73, 83, 84n.14; children and, 164; correlation of marriage rates with fertility rates, 75; counseling for, 162; entry into, 159, 160, 163–64, 186–87, 196n.33; individual consent for, 160; joy and, 160–61; rates of by gender, 73–75; relationship with Heiland and, 161, 162, 163; sexuality and, 163–64; teamwork, 13; the Lot and, 160
Married Brothers. *See* Married men
Married men, 94, 183
Married Men's House, 89, 90, 91, 92, 94
Married partners, as a team, 159
Married People, 92, 131, 135, 138, 163; relationship with Heiland of, 209, 217; relationship with spouse, 227; separate living quarters for men and women, 103, 107. *See also* Beds in married women's dormitory; Husband; Spouse; Wife
Married Peoples' Choir, entry into, 146
Married Sisters, 136–37
Marschall, Friedrich, 113
Medical treatment, 248
Memorabilia, New Year's, 20
Men's Infirmary, 90
Men: cared for by relatives, 138. *See also* Gender; Married Brothers; Married men; Single Brothers
Meurer, Philip, 171, 179
Michler, Rosina, 164–65, 175
Migration, 63–73, 257–58; accuracy of records, 63; emigration, 65, 84n.12; gender and, 66–71; immigration, 65, 84n.12; immigration and emigration, ratios, 65; marital status and, 71; to Maryland, 66; to New Jersey, 66; to New York, 66; to North Carolina, 66; to West Indies, 66

Migration, net, 257–58
Miller, Johann Heinrich, 196 n.31
Miller, Johanna Dorothea, 196 n.31
Millwork, 89, 90
Minimal majority, 119
Missionary focus, 25, 32, 35, 71, 86
Monocacy Creek, 97
Moravian Church: belief system of, 8–9; development into denomination, 27; early expansion of membership, 27; early missionary program, 9; governing boards, 36–37; renewal of, 6–8; reorganization of in Bethlehem in 1845, 45; roots of, 3
Mortality, 76–83; age-specific death rates, 77, 79–81, 85 n.19; comparison with Coale and Demeny's Life Table Models, 79–81; correlation of death rates with crude birth rates, 76; crude death rates, 74, 76; gender and, 81; among young children during Period I, 81–83; infant mortality, 76; life expectancy, 81; life tables, 77, 85 n.18; standardized death rates, 75, 76, 77, 79
Mothers, 146, 147–48, 184–85. See also Parents
Müller, Anna, 180
Müller, Johann Bernhard, 165
Müller, Johann, 155
Multiple office holding, 43–44
Murtagh, William John, 120 n.6
Music. See Hymns; Instrumental music; Musical instruments; Singstunde
Musical instruments, 21–22

Nailsmith, stone, 91
Nain, 97, 99
Native Americans. See Indians
Natural increase, 61–62
Navigation Company, 44
Nazareth, 52–53, 86, 87, 93, 113
Net migration, 61–63, 71, 73, 84 n.8
New Street, 109
Nitschmann, David ("Father Nitschmann"), 94, 180
Nitschmann, David (first bishop of renewed Moravian Church), 8
Nitschmann, Johann, 30
Nitschmann, Juliana, 30
Noailles, Cardinal, 6
Non-Moravians, 40, 41, 45, 46, 89, 97, 99
Non-violence. See Pacifism
Nuclear family. See Family, nuclear
Nursery, 115, 137, 145, 149
Nursing, 146–47. See also Weaning

Oberlin, Catharina, 162, 171, 172, 174–75, 176
Oerter, Joseph, 192
Offenherzigkeit. See Openheartedness
Oil mill, log, 89, 90
Old Chapel, 91
Older Boys' Choir, 146, 151
Older Boys, 150–53. See also Adolescence
Older Girls' Choir, 146, 151
Older Girls, 93, 150–53. See also Adolescence
Oley, 93
Openheartedness, 151, 152, 152, 154
Original sin, 151
Ortsgemeine, 25, 30–33, 48 n.41, 242
Outsiders. See Non-Moravians
Overseers, 151, 158, 196–97 n.36

Pacifism: dwindling of, 39; early Taborites, 3; in America, 38–39, 50 n.79; Unitas Fratrum, 4
Parents: psychological toll of infant mortality, 181; relationship with children, 214–17, 225–27, 233; and religious education of children, 216–17; roles of in Period V, 138, 184–85
Passive relationships. See Relationships, passive
Period I–Period V comparisons, 182–83, 184, 208–209; acceptance of death, 190; attitudes about illness and death, 188–89; gender roles, 187; grief, 193–94; relation to Heiland, 190, 194, 216–24
Period I: definition of, 126–27; life cycles and values, 145–80; relationship with Heiland, 209–214; social change, 239–41; structure of biographies, 133–37
Period V: definition of, 126–27; life cycles and values, 180–95; relationship partners during, 253–55; relationship with Heiland, 214–17; social change, 239–41; structure of biographies, 137–42
Person-year, 77, 85 n.17
Personal belongings, modesty of, 94, 95
Peysert, Samuel, 183
Pilgergemeine, 25, 48 n.41, 52, 71; created to serve religious mission, 94; desirability of in Bethlehem, 30–31, 33–34, 241–42; divided into two parts, 94; narrower sense, 94; values of, influenced town plan, 112
Planned community, as support for cultural values, 95
Poems, use of in biographies, 138, 142

Index

Population composition, 53–59, 83 n.1
Population growth, 31, 60–62, 84 nn.7, 10
Population, 46, 49 n.46, 52, 86, 89
Pottery: log, 89, 90, 92; stone, 91, 92
Predestination, 7, 9, 87, 151
Privacy and Bethlehem's early buildings, 103–05
Privatization, industrial, 34–35, 45
Procession to God's Acre in funerals, 179–80
Professions, 135, 138, 182, 183, 185–87, 217–18
Proprietor (holder of Bethlehem's land), 95, 120, 122 n.45
Prostration (Children's religious ritual), 150, 247
Psychological support system, 236
Purity of mind and body, 153

Railroad, 44, 109
Real estate, ownership of, 95, 117–20. *See also* Land ownership; Lease system; Limitation clause, land sales; Proprietor
Recovery from final illness, 248
Reform school, 148
Reformulation of texts, 131, 199–201
Refugees in Bethlehem, 31, 60–61
Regional economy, 44–45
Relationship partners, 201–202, 252–55
Relationship statements, 201
Relationships: active, 226–29; passive, 226–29
Religious experience, previous to Moravian affiliation, 135
Religious focus, 46, 135, 149–50, 242. *See also* Religious mission
Religious growth (personal), 9–10, 12, 133, 137–42
Religious mission, 94
Religious professionals, 233–36
Religious ritual, 137, 150, 214–17, 247
Religious status. *See* Religious growth
Reorganization of economy in 1771, 35
Resources, natural, 86
Revitalization movements, 230–31, 241
Ritual. *See* Religious ritual
Rothe, Johann Andreas, 6, 7

Sacred Canopy, The, 198
Salterbach, Johanette, 149, 154, 171, 176, 179, 202
Sampling design, 126–29, 143 n.2
Sawmill, 89, 90
Sawyer, Edwin Albert, 49 n.52

Schaaf, Anna, 164, 172
Schlegel, Johann, 148, 202
Schmidt, Johannes, 182, 183, 188
Schmidt, Lewis, 183, 191
Schmik, Anna, 150, 209–14, 246–48
Schnall, Michael, 175–76, 177
Schoen, Jacob, 156–59, 178
School, 92, 93, 138, 148. *See also* Institutes
Schropp, Sabine, 184
Schulz, Agnes, 150, 173
Schwarz, Ralph, 121 n.33
Sea Congregations, 53, 87, 94
Secularization, 198, 208, 224–30, 231, 233–36
Secularization of consciousness, 198
Seduction, the sin of, 156–57
Sehner, Johannes, 148, 150, 172, 174
Sehner(t), Maria, 148, 164
Sehner(t), Peter, 148
Seidel, Henrietta Sophia (14-year-old), 181–82, 192, 197 n.59, 216–17, 233
Seidel, Henrietta Sophia (4-year-old), 181, 193, 197 n.59
Seidel, Nathanael, 36, 165
Separation: of farm from residential area, 109; of marriage partners, 101; of Moravians from non-Moravians, 97–99; of parents from children, 148–49; of residence from industry, 97–98; of the sexes, 11–12, 100–105, 116, 143 n.4, 145, 149; of whites from Indians, 97–100
Sessler, Jacob, 49 nn.54, 56
Sexes, Separation of. *See* Separation, of sexes
Sexuality, 152, 163–64
Sickness. *See* Illness
Sifting Period, 28–29, 30, 32, 49 n.49
Simplicity, 151, 152
Sinful nature, acknowledgment of, 151. *See also* Corrupt nature
Singing. *See* Hymns, Singstunde
Single Brothers, 41, 42, 59, 136. *See also* Single men; Single People; Unmarried People
Single Brothers' Choir, 153, 184
Single Brothers' House, First, 89, 90, 92
Single Brothers' House, Second, 89, 90, 91, 92, 97, 100
Single life, as viable alternative to marriage, 162
Single men, 183. *See also* Single Brothers
Single people, 53. *See also* Unmarried people
Single People, 53, 103, 107, 145, 159; rela-

269

tionship partners, 203, 208. *See also* Single Brothers, Single Sisters
Single Peoples' Choirs, 59, 146, 153; "schools" of preparation for Moravian roles, 153; entry into, 146
Single Sisters, 93, 99, 136–37, 145, 186–87. *See also* Single People; Single women; Unmarried People
Single Sisters' Choir, 59, 135, 136, 138, 153, 184
Single Sisters' House, 89, 91, 92, 97, 100, 103, 120 n.6
Single women, 121–22 n.44, 184. *See also* Single Sisters
Singstunde, 21
Sisters' Lane, 97, 107
Size of community and effect on community spirit, 49 n.57
Slaves, 86
Social change, 239–42. *See also* Change, cultural
social usefulness, 181
Socialization through biographies, 126
Society of Little Fools, 29
Spangenberg, August Gottlieb, 9, 26, 29, 180, 243; Chief Elder in America, 30; developer of Bethlehem, 26, 27; leadership roles of Georgia settlement, 9, 37–38; restructuring of General Economy and, 32–33; second wife of, 27; Zinzendorf and, 30
Spangenberg, (Eva) Maria, 26–27, 29, 146, 149
Speaking ("Sprechen"). *See* Communion, preparation for
Spiritual Growth. *See* Religious growth
Spohn, Martin, 150, 171
Spouse, role of, 138
Spradley, James, 136, 252
Stability, marital, 161–62
Stability, religious 154–59
Stables, 90
Stadtgemeine, 25, 48 nn.41, 42
Statements, linguistically simplified, 201
Stone construction, 89–93
Stores, 91–92, 109
Stout, Dorsey, 188
Street grid, 109
Streiterehe, 159, 161
Sun Inn, 91–92, 97, 99, 109
Suicide, 173
Sünderhaftigkeit. *See* Sinful nature, acknowledgment of
Synods, 35, 43–44

Taborites, 3
Tannery: stone, 91–92; wood, 89, 90
Taxonomy of relationship partners, 252–55
Termination of membership as deviance control, 23, 158–59
Till, Joseph, 188
Town plan, influenced by values of the Pilgergemeine, 112
Transformation, of Pilgergemeine into Ortsgemeine, 113
Transition period. *See* Bethlehem, transition of
Transportation network, 44
Trombone Choir. *See* Instrumental music

Unconscious emphases in documents, 198–99, 201
Uniformity. *See* Homogeneity
Unitas Fratrum, 4–5, 7
Unity, 32, 35, 43, 153
Unmarried people, 100, 209. *See also* Single People
Upper Places, The, 53
Urban character, development of in Bethlehem, 107
Utraquists, 3

Values, cultural and architecture, 95, 112, 121 n.19
Verführung. *See* Seduction
Virgin Mary as model for behavior, 146

Wallace, Anthony, 230–31, 241
Watchword, 14–15
Water, uses of for industries, 97
Waterworks, 91–92
Weaning, 145, 146, 148, 195 n.2
Wechequetank, 100
Weinland, Catharina, 186
Weinland, David, 186, 188
Weis, Rebecca, 152–53, 196 n.12
West Indies, 86
Wetteravia, 29, 49 n.52
Whitefield House, 93
Whitefield, George, 9, 87
Widowed People, 131, 165–68. *See also* Widowers; Widows
Widowed Peoples' Choirs, 146
Widowers, 92
Widowers' residence, 100
Widows, 53, 84 n.5, 118–19, 138, 121–122 n.44
Widows' House, 93, 100
Withdrawal from the church, 65, 69

Wives, role of, 168

Wolle, Lucien, 194, 214–17

Women, 13, 119, 185–86. *See also* Gender; Married Sisters; Single Sisters

Work, 13–15, 138. *See also* Profession

Worship services, 14–15; brevity of, 15; Choir festival days, 20; Communion, 17–18; Easter week, 18–19; for children, 16–17; Lovefeast, 17; Memorial Days, 19–20; monthly schedule, 16–17; New Year's festival days, 20–21; Singstunde, 16; weekly schedule, 16; yearly schedule, 18–21. *See also* Communion; Prostration; Religious ritual

Young people, 53

Young People. *See* Youth

Youth, 53, 203, 209–17

Zinzendorf, Nicholas Ludwig von, 6; in Bethlehem, 32, 87, 94, 95; death of, 105, 32; on child rearing, 34; inspiration for social change, 240; in New World, 9; relations with Herrnhut, 6–7; relations with Moravian Church, 27–28, 8; Sifting Period and, 28–29; social change and, 242; Spangenberg and, 30